ZIONISM AND TERRITORY

RESEARCH SERIES
No. 51

Zionism
and
Territory

*The Socio-Territorial Dimensions
of Zionist Politics*

BARUCH KIMMERLING

INSTITUTE
OF INTERNATIONAL
STUDIES
University of California, Berkeley

Library of Congress Cataloging in Publication Data

Kimmerling, Baruch.
    Zionism and territory.

    (Research series, ISSN 0068-6093 ; no. 51)
    Bibliography: p.
    Includes index.
    1. Jews—Palestine—History—20th century.
2. Land settlement—Palestine. 3. Zionism—History.
4. Israel—History. 5. Jewish-Arab relations.
I. Title. II. Series: Research series (University of
California, Berkeley. Institute of International
Studies) ; no. 51.
DS125.K48 1983   956.94'004924   83-102
ISBN 0-87725-151-7

To my

Mother and Father

CONTENTS

LIST OF TABLES

FIGURE

MAPS

A NOTE ON THE TRANSLATIONS AND SOURCES

Many of the source materials used in this study are in Hebrew, and are so designated in the Sources and References section. Except where specific reference to another translator or translation is included, all quotations from these sources (as well as the English titles under which they are listed) are translated by the author. The spellings of Hebrew and Arabic terms and names are not always according to conventional rules of transliteration, but more for the convenience of the foreign reader. When newspapers and periodicals are cited, dates are given in the American style (month, day, year) rather than in the European and Israeli style (day, month, year).

ACKNOWLEDGMENTS

I would like to introduce this volume with a personal conclusion which I have reached on the basis of the study presented here—on the basis of its course rather than its content. The researcher grapples with his material in two separate arenas. The first struggle occurs between him and the material, and this struggle is individualistic. Creation must be individualistic, just as the responsibility for it devolves only on the individual, and is indivisible, even when more than one person participates in different stages of the research and the presentation and analysis of the ideas.

Secondly, the researcher must grapple with his environment. This work could not have been completed without fruitful debates and discussions with teachers and students, colleagues and assistants. From that standpoint this book is a collective creation, though it bears the name of only one author.

As great as were my difficulties and uncertainties in the first arena, so was I pampered in the second. For this I owe thanks to many people—too many to mention here.

I should like to mention my teachers: Moshe Lissak, my mentor for my doctoral work, part of which is presented here; S.N. Eisenstadt, who taught me that sociology is as exciting as a detective story; Dan Horowitz, who is unsurpassed as a partner for heated discussion. I would like also to express my appreciation to Carl Rosberg, the Director of Berkeley's Institute of International Studies, for the encouragement offered me in my effort of rewriting and reshaping the original manuscript according to the reviewers' demands.

Special thanks are due to all the students in classes and seminars who asked me the many questions for which I had no answer.

Above all, I must thank all the ladies who worked with me over the years on this study: Daniella Carmi, Rachel Zudkevitz, Orit Cahanov, and Gila Noam. My English required considerable editing effort, which was made with enormous devotion and talent by Paul Gilchrist, Principal Editor of the Institute of International Studies, and, in a preliminary draft, by Shmuel Himelstein.

My good friends Robert Brym and Russell Stone helped me in the redefinition of the first and last chapters.

I was fortunate to receive grants from research funds during various periods: the Peretz Naftali Fund, the Central Fund of the Hebrew University, and the Fund of Ford Foundation. To all—my thanks.

Some parts of this book were written when I spent a year as Visiting Scholar at the Center for International Studies of the Massachusetts Institute of Technology. It gives me great pleasure to acknowledge my gratitude to the Center—and especially to its Director, Eugene B. Skolnikoff, and to Amelia C. Leiss, Assistant Director of the Center—for the friendliness and warmth with which I felt myself surrounded while at the CIS.

B.K.

Jerusalem
November 1982

Chapter One

A SETTLER SOCIETY WITHOUT A FRONTIER

The purpose of this study is to describe and discuss the reciprocal relationship between a specific immigrant-settler society, its aims and ideology, and the physical, economic, and political environment in which it settled. The settler society referred to is the one established by immigrant Jews in Palestine beginning in the late nineteenth century. It became the State of Israel in the mid-twentieth century after the Jews acquired sovereignty over most of the land. The ideology of the settler movement was based on Zionism, derived from "Zion"— the name for the "promised land" in the Jewish religion. The area into which the settlers migrated was inhabited at the time by Arabs.

The relationship between immigrant settlers who wish to build a society in a target land and the territory itself is almost always a complex one. By definition, the territory chosen for colonization is seen as being "free land," and in most instances as having inexhaustible material potential. (This, for example, was the Puritan myth of the "Garden" as they saw the land in North America.) The original inhabitants of these lands might be viewed in different ways: they might be considered part of the natural wealth of the country (a cheap labor force, a potential source of women for gratifying sexual and emotional needs or maintaining the population, etc.), while at the same time providing instruments for fulfilling a religious-spiritual mission—that of spreading the "superior" culture of the homeland of the settlers. Or they might be regarded as part of the hostile environment and the wilderness which need to be overcome in order to establish a "holy realm." Sometimes there is a synthesis of the two: the original population is seen as being part of the hostile environment which, under certain conditions, can be utilized as a labor force and perhaps even "civilized."

The best-known (and most controversial) thesis about the relationship between the character of an immigrant-settler society and its

1

environment is the "frontier theory" of Frederick Jackson Turner, published in 1893, relating to the United States. Turner believed that the distinctive character of American society could be explained by the almost inexhaustible abundance of land in the "new world," when compared with the chronic lack of resources in the "old world." The appeal of this theory was its simplicity: it appeared to provide an explanation for a wide range of developments in a specific society—one perceived as being different from any preceding society—by means of a single variable—an abundance of land—which had almost no value in standard economic terms:*

> The existence of an area of free land, its continuous recession, and the advance of American settlement westward, explain American development. Behind institutions, behind constitutional forms and modifications, lie the vital forces that call these organs into life and shape them to meet changing conditions. . . . This perennial rebirth, this fluidity of American life, this expansion westward with its new opportunities, its continuous touch with the simplicity of primitive society, furnish the forces dominating American character (1920: 1-3).

In the formative period the existence of an unlimited territorial resource which was also the primary and basic productive means of the social system and the condition for its existence was perceived as an unprecedented phenomenon. It created a unique socioeconomic situation which provided not only a potential source for material gain and private prosperity, but also served to ensure institutional flexibility in American society, because the continuous possibility of the opening of new lands for settlement was a safety valve for relieving social pressures. According to Turner's theory, this condition allowed the American people unprecedented freedom—freedom which later became the foundation of a way of life and a tradition because it prevented the formation of strong central government (there was no need

*There is plenty of evidence that the land was seen by the immigrant settlers of the time as an "economic resource." It was understood that a minimal amount of investment was needed to prepare the land and to guarantee conditions necessary for settlement, and the disturbances caused by the local Indian inhabitants, which sometimes became small-scale wars, might be seen as one of the indirect costs of the land. In sum, while the land was seen as a resource whose commercial value was extremely low, it was cheap and available in abundance.

for such in the conditions of abundance that prevailed) and strengthened individualistic tendencies.

In the New World, as opposed to Europe, the concept of the frontier has come to refer to the line dividing inhabited from uninhabited territory (Prescott, 1965:34) rather than the border or boundary line dividing countries. Thus it has the connotation of a movement across a territorial expanse, always in the direction of the horizon, which moves as one moves, creating the illusion that the expanse is infinite.

This concept of the frontier can be translated into quantitative terms, and a measure of the free territory available to a society can be developed, taking into account both its market value and the importance the society places on it. This measure of free territory will, for the purposes of this study, be referred to as the *frontierity* of a given territory: the higher the frontierity the more readily available to settlers is the amount of free land. The quantity of free land available to the settlers is not always negatively correlated to its price on the market. Thus, for example, the first stratum which settled in Australia, who wished to build an agrarian, hierarchical society modelled on Britain's, artificially inflated land prices, while at the same time subsidizing immigration. By this means it hoped to make it difficult for new immigrants to acquire land, and thereby guarantee for itself cheap labor. Thus the degree of frontierity of Australian territory was low at certain times, at least from the viewpoint of the later immigrants, despite great reserves of free land available.* There was a similar process in South Africa.†

French political historians do not accept the contention that Algeria was an immigrant-settler society. They stress the unique relationship of France to the French settlers in Algeria, which they regarded as an integral part of France rather than as a colony. A detailed

*See, for example, Wakefield (1829). For other discussions of the Australian frontier, see Fitzpatrick (1947), Nadel (1957), Ward (1958), and Winks (1967). For comparison with the United States, see Allen (1959) and Alexander (1947); for Canada, see Mackind (1951); for both, see Sharp (1955).

†For the frontierity perception in South Africa, see Neumark (1957). The territorial movement of the Boers— the so-called *Voortrekker* movement—was motivated by the desire to build a new community away from territory controlled by the British Cape Company. The Boers were producing large families and felt a strong passion for independence which was later to lead them to Afrikaner nationalism (Mikesell, 1968: 69).

3

review of the literature, however, does not support this view.* There is no doubt that the French perceived their relationship with Algeria as "unique," but an analysis of the behavior of the French government and of the settlers themselves proves that Algeria was a colony of immigrant-settlers in the same way as America, Australia, and South Africa (Thompson and Lamar, 1981). The Berber tribes inhabiting the land were subdued after a great deal of effort, and their traditional land titles were disallowed. The primary aim of the settlers was to acquire this land, while utilizing the Berber/Muslims as cheap labor (Pickles, 1963: 23). Even though the territory was considered to be part of France, the Muslims had the status of colonial subjects, and only the French (and various categories of other Europeans and Jews) were citizens. By the time the process was concluded, the lion's share of fertile land was in the hands of the European settlers. In 1954, "75 percent of Moslem land was divided into less than 10 hectares, 80 percent of French *colon* land was divided into more than 100 hectares. . . . While Europeans owned 2.7 million hectares and the Moslems 7.3 million, the former included the richest and most fertile land" (Gordon, 1966: 51-52). The settlers justified this takeover of land from the original inhabitants in terms of their own "superiority," as reflected in this statement by Jules Roy, an Algerian-born Frenchman:

> One thing I knew because it was told to me so often, was that the Arabs belonged to a different race, one inferior to my own. We had come to clear their land and bring them civilization. And it was true; the swamp I heard about, some vestiges of which still existed on patches of land that belonged to neighboring tribes, my grandparents and my uncle had made into vineyards like those of Canaan, rich grain lands, or orange groves. By loafing? In my mother's family you died of work or swamp fever (1961:17).

Many of the Puritan settlers in North America and the Jewish settlers in Palestine might have expressed themselves in similar terms in describing their feelings about the territory to which their fathers had immigrated.

A high degree of frontierity is apparently essential for the construction of immigrant-settler societies. It would appear that the best measure of the degree of frontierity of a territory at any given time is

*See Esquer (1950), Julien (1952), Nora (1961), Tillion (1958).

the *cost of land*. Each rise in the cost of land will represent a decline in the degree of frontierity.* An interesting example of an imposed reduction in frontierity is the case of Canada. Confronted with the problem of maintaining an existence independent of its more powerful southern neighbor, Canada required a strong central government. In order for the government to preserve its political strength, it had to limit migration to its uninhabited regions. Thus, according to S.D. Clark, the claims to the interior of the continent were staked not by advancing frontiersmen, acting on their own, but by advancing armies and police forces, large corporate enterprises and ecclesiastical organizations supported by the state" (1962:214). Clark, who basically accepts the Turner thesis, argues that the difference in the way the uninhabited areas in Canada and the United States were populated explains the difference in the way the two societies developed, even though they resembled each other in terms of the origins of their settlers and in the values they held.

A useful differentiation between types of frontiers is the distinction between frontiers of exclusion and frontiers of inclusion. This refers to the patterns of contact between the immigrant-settlers and the original inhabitants. Here history does not provide sharp dichotomies, but instead shows a wide range of interrelationships along an exclusion/inclusion continuum. In North America, the original inhabitants were not included in any way in the plans for the future society. On the other hand, the Spanish settlers of Latin America of the sixteenth and seventeenth centuries reacted differently:

> In racial terms many Latin American frontiers were frontiers of inclusion. ... The absence of stable family migration, coupled with the shortage of white women and the lack of an inhibiting Puritan sexual ethic, encouraged widespread miscegenation which helped break down racial exclusiveness. It is possible to talk of biological adaptation to the environment as mestizos and mulattoes acquired immunity to disease, and a distinctive hybrid culture emerged in which Indian, European and African traits were fused (Hennessy, 1978:147).

*A distinction should be made between actual frontierity and potential frontierity. Potential frontierity refers to the total amount of land in a given territory, whether or not it is accessible. It may be blocked (partially or fully) by political, social, or economic forces or by the state of technology at a given time—or by a combination of these factors. Land may become accessible in the future as the factors hindering access to it change.

In the new nations of South America, the process of inclusion assumed its most radical form with the development of nationalistic ideologies in the 1920s and 1930s based on biological and social theories which claimed that improving the quality of the population required mixed marriages ("miscegenation"). Thus a "demographic imperative," arising from the fact that European migration had all but ended,[*] was transformed into a normative prescription, whose leading proponents were philosophers such as the Mexican José Vasconcelos and the Brazilian Gilberto Freyre. The missionaries of the Catholic Church also supported this general approach. In North America, on the other hand, the Puritan faith, with its heavy reliance on the Old Testament, favored an exclusivistic orientation.[†] Similarly, in South Africa the exclusivistic tendencies became even more marked when the Dutch Reformed Church spread the doctrine of the uniqueness and superiority of the white man (Gerhard, 1959:217). In other places there were intermediate situations, where the members of the local population were not accepted as partners for marriage, but were included in the labor force of the emerging system. This was the case in French North Africa[**] and, in its purest form, in the final stages of the institutionalization of *apartheid* in South African society.[††] As a general rule,

[*]In the hundred years from 1820 to 1920, voluntary migration to South America (which excludes about one-and-a-half million slaves forcibly taken from Africa) consisted of only about seven million Europeans, as compared to about thirty-four million who migrated to the United States. The proportion of women who migrated to South America was very small, in contrast to the situation in the northern continent, which tended to increase the demographic gaps between the local population and the settlers (Ramos, 1976).

[†]For a comparison of the relationships of Catholics and Protestants to the local population, see Bastide (1972) and Hartz (1964).

[**]Primarily in Algeria (Nora, 1961) but not in the sub-Saharan continent (e.g., the Ivory Coast).

[††]See Rhoodie and Venter (1960), Sachs (1965), Tatz (1962) and Adam (1971). It is interesting to note that the roots of *apartheid* are in the early struggle for land between the Afrikaners and the various Bantu tribes. The first segregation was territorial; according to the Act of Union (1910), it was illegal for an African to be on European land unless he was a hired servant. The primary purpose of the Act of Union was to reduce drastically the land under the control of the Africans, and under the terms of the Act the Africans kept only 7.3 percent of the land in the country even though they made up 67 percent of the population. The Africans were gathered in reserves, but this was not acceptable because the white settlers needed them as a cheap labor force. As a result, the territorial segregation doctrine was expanded into the white areas.

6

however, the orientations and patterns of relationships with the local population are a marginal aspect of Turner's frontier theory. In the present study, this aspect is stressed considerably more than it was by Turner (and most of those who have relied on his frontier hypothesis) because in the case of the Jews in Palestine, the relationship between the immigrant settlers and the local population was of major importance in determining the degree of frontierity of the territory.

The relationship between the Jewish immigrants and the local Arabs in Palestine resembled most closely the approach of the pioneer American settlers to the Spanish settlers who had preceded them, whom they first encountered in Texas (and thereafter in New Mexico, Arizona, and California). The struggle against the Spaniards had to be conducted according to different rules than those that had been used against the Indians. The Arabs evoked feelings of anxiety, as well as empathy and sympathy, attraction and curiosity, among the Jews, which was very similar to the relationship of the American pioneers to the Spaniards.

This study is concerned with the establishment of a society of settlers in the absence of a frontier, or, to be more precise, in a situation where the degree of frontierity of the territory was very low. Compared to other societies of immigrant-settlers, the Jews in Palestine had almost no primary frontierity.* This is evidenced in the fact that every bit of land which passed into the control of the Jews, at least until 1947, was in the possession of someone else before they acquired it, and in order to transfer the land to Jewish control, the collectivity had to pay an economic, political, and social price which was high by any criterion.

Whether or not one accepts Turner's thesis about the influence of the existence of free land on the character of American society *in toto*, no one can dispute its basic premise: that the tremendous amount of land available to the American immigrants and, to a certain extent, to the immigrants to other target lands influenced the character of these

---

*The primary settlement frontier marked the *de facto* limit of the state's political authority, and the secondary frontier normally reflected the limited range of economic activities by a population of low density (Prescott, 1956:35). After achieving sovereignty as the State of Israel, the society had secondary frontiers—the northern Galilee and the Negev Desert in the south. The Negev in general was regarded as a future reservoir of territory. However, because of the great investment that its development required, it was not developed until the Israeli withdrawal from Sinai in 1979-82.

societies, despite the differences in their development (which stemmed from other variables which refine the determinism of Turner).

This study asks the question: How did the absence of free land affect the building of a society of immigrant-settlers, and how did the society deal with this problem?

THE ZIONIST IDEOLOGY

An important difference between the colonization process of the Jews in Palestine and the other immigration and settlement movements in the Americas, Africa, Australia, etc. was in the choice of the target land. While the other colonizing movements chose their target lands on the basis of their political, geographical, and economic availability (the latter referring to the resources available to the immigrants), as well as their economic potential, "Zion" was *a priori* the territory involved. The Zionist movement arose to find a solution to what was known as "the Jewish Question"—that is, to seek a political answer to the problems arising from the existence of an ethnic-religious minority which had been dispersed throughout the world for a period of close to two thousand years (from the time the Jews lost their independence as a result of the Roman conquest of Judea and the rebellions which followed it, culminating in the destruction of Jerusalem), and which could not be absorbed or assimilated as a group within the so-called "host" societal systems.*

Zion or *Eretz Israel* (the Land of Israel) is a central pillar of the Jewish religion, and even though for many generations the Jews were entirely cut off from Zion, they continued observing rituals and customs which were directly connected to that country, such as festivals marking the changes of seasons there, ceremonies relating to the specific plants which grow there, and, most of all, in referring to specific places in the land as "sanctified." (In a sense, the entire country is considered to be sanctified or holy.)† During the course of time, the con-

---

*Theodor Herzl, the founder of Zionism as a modern political movement, reached the idea of the "Zionist solution" only as a second choice. His original idea was that all the Jews of the world would be converted to Christianity, and that Judaism would then cease to exist.

†In Jewish eschatology the final redemption is intrinsically bound up with the return of the Jews to "the Promised Land," and throughout Jewish history there have been many "false Messiahs" who have promised that the redemption of the Jews was about to take place by means of a return to "Zion."

8

cept of Zion became increasingly metaphysical and abstract. Its boundaries were unclear and undefined, except for its center—Jerusalem. The lack of a precise definition of the borders of Zion, because of the varying descriptions of these borders in the Old Testament, will be alluded to repeatedly in this work as one of the many factors involved in the dramatic events discussed herein.

But this Zion, abstract as it was (and perhaps partly because of that), became the mobilizing symbol of the Jewish national movement. It became apparent that only Eretz Israel could serve as a powerful enough symbol to recruit significant numbers of the Jewish people throughout the world for collective political, social, and economic activity, either as actual participants in immigration and the building of a new society, or as moral and/or material supporters of the movement. Other territorial alternatives were suggested (Uganda, northern Sinai, Argentina, and even a Soviet proposal to establish a Jewish republic in Birobidzhan) which aroused a great amount of controversy in the Zionist movement, but they were all eventually discarded as "non-Zionist."* These were territories that might have been easier to obtain, and their settlement did not seem to entail any serious political or economic problems, but they did not arouse any "sentiment" or attraction among the Jews, unlike the idea of Palestine. Zionism without Palestine was evidently doomed to failure as a nationalist movement, a movement which had imposed upon itself a task not imposed on any other nationalist movement—to build a membership from among people who were dispersed throughout almost all parts of the world (and who, as became apparent later, differed not only in terms of country of origin, but also culturally and even ethnically).

If the meaning of frontier is "free land," then in the early stages of the Zionist movement, Palestine was seen as being a frontier. This view was expressed succinctly by Israel Zangwill when he stated that Zionism was "a people [the Jews] without a land returning to a land [Palestine] without a people." There were a number of exceptions to this, but at the time of *Hibat Zion* (1880-1900) and even at the time of the beginning of Herzlian Zionism, the territory was sparsely populated, and even though the country was formally under the political control of the Ottoman Empire, this was seen as only a legal complication that could be easily bypassed, or a financial problem which

*See, for example, Laqueur (1972:157-58).

would not present a serious obstacle.* In addition, the country was seen as being potentially wealthy, and its desolation was believed to stem from the fact that it had not been under the control of the Jewish people (see Katz, 1982). After all, the Old Testament described it as "a land flowing with milk and honey."

The sobering up came as soon as the mass immigration to Zion began in 1882, increasing with the second immigration wave (1904-15). The reality was a far cry from what had been envisaged. There was very little free land available. There were a number of reasons why: (1) the local population was greater than had been estimated;† (2) the land was settled, or it was claimed that rights or titles had previously been assigned to almost all the arable land; (3) almost every tract of land where the immigrants could settle had economic value, and they had to pay prices that were high at the very outset, and which went up astronomically as immigration increased; (4) unlike the people in other target lands for immigration, the people in Palestine already had a developed sense of the ownership, individual and collective, of land; (5) even those tracts which were not inhabited, and might even be entirely arid, were at least *de jure* owned by some person or agency, whether this be the Ottoman Sultan or, later, the British Crown. (The use of and acquisition of ownership over such lands involved political difficulties and different constraints throughout the entire period covered by this study. In most countries of immigration, there was at least a partial overlap between the interests of those who exercised control over the territory and the immigrants, with each aiding the

---

*Herzl began negotiations with the Turkish Sultan Abdul Hamid in 1901 with the aim of receiving a charter for the land of Palestine in exchange for the payment of all the debts of the Ottoman Empire (which totalled about £85 million). Shortly thereafter, Herzl found that he could not raise an amount that would approach the sum required.

†Jeanette Abu-Lughod estimates that in the mid-nineteenth century there were close to half a million residents in Palestine, of whom about 7 percent were Jews (1971:140). In any event, the observation by Zangwill that "people without a land" were returning to "a land without people" was wishful thinking. The insightful Zionist publicist Asher Ginsberg (*Ahad Haam*) had already warned in 1891 of the delusion involved (in his essay "Truth from the Land of Israel"). Similar observations were made by A.L. Motzkin (1939). But one must not forget that, as will be seen below, part of the non-Jewish population in the country had come with the immigration wave at the beginning of the nineteenth century, as a result of the land shortage in Egypt.

other. In the case of the Jewish immigrants to Palestine, on the other hand, there was, until the sovereign State of Israel was established, no such community of interests.); (6) the country was not found to have great commercial potential. (Immigration and settlement not only did not enrich the immigrants, but the settlements needed—and need to this very day—external support and subsidization on an unparalleled scale, not only in comparison to other immigrant settlements, but in comparison to any other societal enterprise in history.)

As noted above, the best empirical measure of frontierity is the market price of land. It is extremely difficult to find any reliable data about land prices during the very early period of Zionist colonization, but various data from later periods, shown in Table 1.1, enable us to see a rapid increase in land prices in Palestine.

Table 1.1

RURAL LAND PRICES AND COST OF LIVING IN PALESTINE COMPARED WITH RURAL LAND PRICES IN THE UNITED STATES, 1910-1944
(*in U.S. dollars per acre*)

	1910	1922	1936	1940	1942	1944
Rural Land Prices in Palestine	$20[a]	$34	$128	$268	$470	$1050
Cost of Land Index (1936 = 100)	15.6	26.6	100	209.4	367.2	820.3
Cost of Living Index in Palestine (1936 = 100)	n.d.	128.2	100	123.6	221.7	274.2
Rural Land Prices in United States	$10-30	n.d.	$31	$32	$35	$45

Sources: Computed from (a) Jewish Agency, *Palestine-Figures and Facts* (Tel-Aviv: Economic Department, 1947), p. 78; (b) U.S. Department of Agriculture, *Census of Agriculture* (Washington, D.C., 1945); (c) Szereszewski (1968:56).

[a]Estimated.

In 1910, when the land reserves in the United States (in terms of "the opening up of land,"—West, South, and North) had already been used, and all land had commercial value, the cost of agricultural land in the United States was from ten to thirty dollars per acre. The cost of land in Palestine in 1910, when the period of Jewish colonization was beginning, was approximately the same: twenty dollars per acre. Thereafter, by almost any standard of reference (e.g., in comparison with the cost of living) the cost of land escalated at an alarming rate. This meant that a significant portion of the funds available to the immigrants went into the purchase of land, and in the period from 1921 to 1939 about 11 percent of all Jewish investments in Palestine (or nine million Palestinian pounds) was spent on the acquisition of land (see Table 1.2). To this figure should be added an estimated 5 percent invested by Jews for improving the quality of the land, draining swamps, and irrigation.

Table 1.2

ESTIMATES OF JEWISH INVESTMENTS IN PALESTINE, 1921-1939
(In 000 Palestinian pounds)

Years	Land Purchases (net)	Agriculture (including citriculture)	Building and Public Works	Industry and Handicrafts	Transport and Sundry	Total
1921-25	£2,500	£3,000	£5,000	£2,000	£2,000	£14,500
1926-29	700	3,300	1,500	700	1,000	7,200
1930-31	3,475	2,340	1,250	610	575	5,050
1932	150	1,400	1,000	1,100	200	3,850
1933	850	2,150	2,750	500	300	6,500
1934	1,650	1,750	4,000	1,300	700	9,400
1935	1,700	1,000	5,750	1,600	650	10,700
1936	150	1,000	4,000	1,100	550	6,800
1937	400	1,000	3,000	1,000	600	6,000
1938	175	800	2,100	900	725	4,700
1939	380	900	2,000	900	620	4,800
TOTALS	8,930	18,640	32,350	11,710	7,920	79,550
Percent	11.22%	23.43%	40.66%	14.72%	9.95%	99.98%

Sources: Compiled and computed from (a) Horowitz and Hinden (1938); (b) Olitzur (1939); (c) *Statistical Abstract of Palestine, 1932-1939*, various issues (Jerusalem: Office of Statistics); (d) Gurevich, Gertz, and Zenker (1947).

Perhaps the most significant difference between the Jewish immigration to Palestine and other immigrant-settler movements was that in Palestine there was no frontier whatsoever, and, as a result, this immigration not only did not become a profitable enterprise, but, on the contrary, it has consistently needed huge investments of additional material and human resources in order to ensure the acquisition of its most basic requirement—land. This has had widespread implications for the formation of its institutions and its patterns of economic, political, and social activity.

This continuing need for outside support has forced the movement to enter into certain defined patterns of interaction with the original inhabitants and to be dependent to a considerable extent upon this interaction, as will be seen below. Thus, though its basic relationship to the local population was exclusivistic, it could not be rigidly exclusive. Jewish immigration to Palestine, initiated at a time when the first glimmerings of political awareness had begun among the local population (see Porath, 1974 and 1977) and when the other colonizing movements were in decline, placed the Jews against the Arabs in a real conflict of interests over the same territorial expanse (see Coser, 1956:48-55).

THE ZIONIST TACTICS AND ARAB REACTIONS

The struggle between the Jewish and Arab communities over land in Palestine includes most of the components of the Jewish-Arab conflict. Land was perceived as the central resource in the conflict. The struggle for land ownership was the dimension of the conflict which demanded the greatest amount of interaction between the two sides. It increased the dependence of the Jewish side on the Arabs and British (or Ottomans) as go-betweens, and limited the scope of the Jewish community's independent activity, but within the Jewish community institutional arrangements, norms, and symbols were created which made it possible to deal with problems stemming from this sphere of the struggle.

From the very beginnings of the Zionist movement, its leaders were aware (a) that the acquisition of substantial areas of land in Palestine was an essential basis for the development of a future Jewish society or state, (b) that the desired land was then in someone else's hands, and (c) that it would be necessary to raise and allocate economic and political resources to obtain the land. But the acquisition of land was not only dependent on the allocation of resources, but also required the transfer of the land from one national ownership to another. This necessitated, as much as possible, neutralizing the conflictual implications of the land transfers and placing them exclusively on a basis of economic exchange—i.e., with the land price being determined exclusively by laws of supply and demand. However, as soon as the land was in Jewish hands, it would no longer have a purely economic meaning, but would acquire a national significance.

The Zionist strategy of assigning only an economic value to every resource controlled by others (as much as this was possible), while according national significance to the very same resource when it was in Jewish hands, was formulated with reference to land from almost the very beginning of settlement in Palestine. Already in 1904, Ussishkin described the possible strategies:

> In order to establish Jewish autonomy—or to be more exact, a Jewish state in Palestine—it is first of all essential that all the land of Palestine, or at least most of it, be the property of the Jewish people. Without the right of land ownership, Palestine will never be Jewish regardless of the number of Jews in it, both in the city and country. . . . But how is land ownership customarily achieved? Only in one of the following three ways: by force—that is, through conquest in war (or, in other words, by stealing land from its owners); by compulsion—that is, through government expropriation of land; and by voluntary sale on the part of the owners. Which of these three ways is appropriate in our case? The first way is out of the question, for *we are too weak for this method*. Thus, we can speak only of the second and third ways (1933:105; emphasis added).

At the First Zionist Congress in 1897, Zvi Shapiro set forth a plan to establish a national fund for the purchase of land in Palestine. The plan provided that "The land purchased can never be expropriated from the ownership of the fund and can never be sold to individual Jews. It can be rented for a period of forty-nine years" (*Die Welt*, August 1897). The plan was adopted.* Nahum Sokolov calculated

---

*Much before that the members of the Hibat Zion (Lovers of Zion) movement stressed the need for "the redemption of the land"; Rabbi Kalischer suggested

how much money would have to be collected in order to purchase all the lands in Palestine on both sides of the Jordan (*Haolam*, 6/17/1908).

Six years before the First Zionist Congress, several Arab notables in Jerusalem sent a petition to the central Ottoman government in Istanbul in which they demanded an end to Jewish immigration and land purchase (Porath, 1974:18), and about five hundred Arabs in Jaffa and Jerusalem signed a petition charging that "the Jews are taking away all the land from the Moslems" (*Hagana*, 1954:66). The extensive purchase of land by Jews in the years 1899-1902 in the Tiberias district aroused the bitter opposition of the district officer (Kamiakam Amir Amin Arsalan) because of the "change of the national form [*denationalization*] of the district" (Kalvariski, 1931:54). In July and August 1913, the Arabic newspaper *Palestine* called for the establishment of a "patriotic Palestinian organization" to be made up of wealthy persons from Nablus, Jerusalem, Jaffa, Haifa, and Gaza to purchase lands in government possession before the Zionists could do so (Porath, 1974:7).*

These were only the first signs of the political and national resistance of the Arabs to Jewish land purchases in Palestine; they were effective in the prevention of such purchases and added to them a political dimension and value. The major obstacles to Jewish land purchase were based primarily on the Arab social structure — on the patterns of land ownership and maintenance. Other obstacles were the agrarian problems inherited from centuries of Ottoman rule, a relative scarcity of resources, and the varying degrees of importance assigned

the establishment of a land-purchasing organization; Yehuda Chai Alkali stated that "We must purchase all the land"; Moses Hess demanded that funds be solicited from every Jew for the purpose of land redemption; Pinsker wrote: "This land must be national property and never fall into the hands of others"; Rabbi Mohliver stated that "We are obliged to make haste and buy all possible lands in the Holy Land" (see Avineri, 1981).

*The use of the term "Palestinian" suggests a common national outlook, but the fact that people were asked to take part in this activity on the basis of their place of residence indicates that on a practical level they could be recruited only by utilizing the *Landsmannschaft* reference group. The idea did not take shape until the early 1930s. It was renewed in 1943 when the Arab National Fund was established and succeeded in purchasing more than 15,000 dunams of lands which were supposed to have been sold to Jews (*Hagana*, 1972:112). This was one of the rate instances of Arab attempts to act on the level at which Zionism was operating.

to the land problem within the Jewish sector and the Zionist movement. While some of the arrangements contributed to the freezing of the land as a resource and made transfer to Jewish hands difficult, other aspects of the patterns of ownership increased the fluidity of the Arab lands.

Other orientations to the land were significant in various parts of the Jewish and Arab subsystems forced to coexist under the British Mandate. On the one hand, there were purchases of rural and urban lands in limited tracts; on the other hand, there was the viewpoint that Palestine would be redeemed by a one-time political act—a charter granted by a Great Power. The consent of the leadership of the Yishuv (the Jewish community in Palestine as a social polity—see Glossary) to the Partition Plan (1939) was a political act identical in its substance to this approach, since the strategy of "a dunam here and a dunam there" (see Chapter 2) laid the base for the unification of all the dunams into a national territorial continuum.*

What were the boundaries of the land area which was the object of the struggle? As previously noted, early Zionism did not specify the exact boundaries of its territorial aspirations, but in very general terms, the area seemed to include the land between the Mediterranean Sea on the west up to a point in the desert on the east (the Higazi railroad was often cited as a boundary—see p. 237), with the Jordan River dividing the area in the middle. In the north and south, the boundaries were even less defined, but the idea seems to have been generally accepted that the southwest boundary should coincide with the boundary between the Ottoman Empire and the Anglo-Egyptian dominion— that is, the boundary between Rafah and Akaba, or alternatively "from [the river] Dan to Beersheba." In two articles which appeared in 1918 and 1920, Ben Gurion (1931: 34-54) proposed the Litani River and the El-Ug stream (an area which includes Horan and Gilead), as the northern boundary, arguing that "the sometimes-heard opinion, even among Zionists, that Trans-Jordan is not Israel rests on total ignorance of the history of Palestine. As is known, the Jewish settlement of Trans-Jordan preceded their conquest of the western side of the Jordan" (41). A decision made by the Twelfth Zionist Congress (Carlsbad, September 1921) that the Jewish people viewed Trans-Jordan as an integral part of Palestine held until, in September 1922—with the consent of

*A dunam is a Turkish measure of land, commonly used in the Middle East. An acre is equal to about 4.5 dunams.

16

the League of Nations—the area was designated as outside the boundaries of Mandatory Palestine. About a fifth of all the lands purchased by Baron de Rothschild in Palestine (about 100,000 dunams out of half a million) were deep in the Trans-Jordan area,* while the first purchases of the Jewish National Fund were also undertaken on the east bank of the Jordan River, where the first settlement of workers who cultivated the land themselves was also established (Degania).

The exclusion of Trans-Jordan, as far as Zionist aspirations were concerned, reduced the land area available for possible purchase to 26,319,000 dunams. The impact of the reduction was heightened because the area that was excluded was less populous than the area west of the Jordan River. The acuteness of the conflict was intensified as a consequence of the increased scarcity of the land.

Within the boundaries of Mandatory Palestine, "purchasing agents" appeared. The need for them seems to have arisen both because of the Arab land tenure system and the Jewish purchasing customs and land politics which had developed over the years. Most of the Jewish purchases were concentrated in the valley areas, the Dead Sea coast, and in part of the Lower Galilee, while almost no land was bought (or sold!) in the mountain areas. If we do not include the southern part of the country (the Beersheba district), we find that by 1937 the Jews had purchased approximately 5 percent of the total land area of Palestine and about 10 percent of the area regarded as cultivable (Granovsky, 1940:5), and by 1947 no more than 2-3 percent additional area. Thus we have very low rates of land purchase which attracted a great deal of attention. One of the reasons for this salience was the intensive patterns of cultivation on these lands, in contrast to the extensive patterns of cultivation in the Arab sector. It is not surprising that one of the central complaints of the Arabs was that "the Jews had already received too much land" (Peel Commission, 1937:238).

Political struggles over estimates and definitions of "cultivable" land tracts were central to the conflict. The Jews claimed larger tracts of cultivable land than those specified by the British estimates (the Hope-Simpson Commission estimate in 1930 or the government estimate in the Peel Commission Report of 1937)—not only to challenge the basis upon which the British justified their limitations on land

*For Rothschild's method of operation, see Schama (1978).

purchase and Jewish immigration, but also because increasing the land area available would make its transfer easier and lower its price. While focusing the conflict on cultivable lands or the "absorption capacity of Palestine" provided the Arabs and British with arguments for slowing down the rate of development and of change in the status quo, the reduction of a central component of the conflict to an economic problem was in accordance with Jewish interests because it made it easier to defreeze the resources which were in Arab hands.

Thus the Jewish land purchases were not large, but their salience added a political value to the land, whose price was on the rise almost constantly. On the one hand, these high prices succeeded in unfreezing the lands which were in Arab hands and bringing them into the economic market; on the other hand, because of the scarcity of means at the disposal of the Zionist movement, these high prices limited the ability to take advantage of the opportunities offered by the unfreezing of the lands.

The need for the purchase and maintenance of lands brought about the development of institutions and roles which became integrated in the Yishuv's social structure. Various types of land purchasing organizations were created, and professional land buyers emerged. Later, quasi-military settlements appeared to preserve the settlement rights on the lands which had been purchased. These led to the creation of the role of the *chalutz* (pioneer), who also fulfilled a central role in granting legitimacy to a collectivity in a situation of permanent conflict which threatened its very existence.

From the end of the first decade of the century, the settlement activity, one of the central collective tasks, was undertaken by the left wing of the Zionist organization, which in exchange received the lion's share of the land and capital for the development of settlements which flowed from outside the system. As a result, the left succeeded in creating power foci which enabled it to achieve the predominant position within the Yishuv's structure—as the bearer of the power controlling the allocation of resources (national capital, immigration certificates, etc.) and political decisions and, as a result, recognition as the symbolic bearer of the central collective goals.

Until the establishment of the State of Israel, other sites of settlement were added according to the established patterns, and by 1948 there were 291 sites of agricultural settlement. At the end of World War II, the settlement process was accelerated, so that between 1948 and 1964 another 432 agricultural settlements were established. Of these, 108 were *kibbutzim* (settlements with collective ownership of means of production—see Glossary), 282 were *moshavim* (settlements with means of production equally distributed among individual small-holders—see Glossary), especially immigrant moshavim, and the rest were towns and regional centers. The main role of these settlements was to absorb the mass immigration of the period (see Shapiro, 1971; Weintraub et al.,1971), but they also fulfilled national defense roles.

The first immigrant moshavim were established on the lands of abandoned Arab villages (see Chapter 5), and sometimes within their abandoned structures in order to prevent the Arabs' return (Willner, 1969:121). In this period, the kibbutzim were perceived as more effective for security tasks, for they not only demonstrated presence on the land but were also barriers to border infiltrations, which reached their peak in the mid-1950s. Many of the immigrant moshavim were established at some distance from the borders, but most of their male populations were trained in the use of arms and helped to maintain local security. In addition, these moshavim were part of a policy of population dispersal which was partially divorced from considerations of security and defense.

Between 1967 and October 1973, however, a situation existed whereby settlement policy was totally subject to defense policy, conflict management, and efforts toward territorial expansion. (This is dealt with in detail in Chapter 6). Only much later, after the formative period ended, did Zionist tactics change. With the acquisition of sovereignty over part of the territory of Palestine, and after fighting two wars (1947/8 and 1967), Jewish control over land was obtained by power and conquest—historically the most acceptable way of acquiring territory throughout the world.

As seen previously, the pre-sovereignty period of Zionist settlement involved the creation of artificial frontiers by unfreezing some of the land under Arab ownership and converting capital into land. Once sovereignty was acquired, the frontiers were also opened by use of military force and the other means available to a sovereign state.

PRESENCE, OWNERSHIP, AND SOVEREIGNTY

Up to this point, frontierity has been defined operationally in terms of the cost of land in a given territory. This is a useful definition which permits comparisons to be drawn over a period of time in a specific territory and between territories. But it does not supply enough information for a comprehensive analysis of the settlement processes of immigrant societies. For this purpose it is worth examining the reciprocal relationships between three types of control over territorial regions: presence, ownership, and sovereignty (see Kimmerling, 1977 and 1979).

The concept of *presence* can include a number of phenomena, the common factor in all being existence within a given territory. Presence here represents either (a) a basis for claims of possession without regard to ownership, or (b) demonstration of ownership upon land or the putting into effect of that ownership—especially if one's claim is contested. Presence can sometimes be very limited or temporary, and it varies from the appearance of religious leaders and missionaries, merchants, and adventurers—a combination which opened the Latin American frontier for the Spaniards—to the establishment of permanent settlements, as in North America. All of these "presences" eventually brought a military presence in their wake, followed later by attempts at imposing sovereignty, or a measure of control equivalent to sovereignty. On the other hand, there have been many occasions when military control has preceded any other type of presence.

In the case study presented in this work, the concept of presence has a more specific meaning: the existence of Jewish settlement on any tract of land. The establishment of village settlements (as well as urban ones) was an integral part of the process of building the Israeli nation. But in the context of Ottoman (and later Mandatory) Palestine, these settlements had an additional role—the consolidation of control over the land by the creation of *faits accomplis*. In terms of the law and customs in the Middle East, not being present on land, not living on it or working it—and even more, the presence of another on it—put one's title in peril. At a later time, presence became a political means for extending control over territory which had been conquered by military force.

The second form of control of land is *ownership*. In a situation of high frontierity, presence and ownership of land are almost identical. Thus, for example, in the first fifty years of U.S. history, "the government pardoned the squatter for his illegal settlement and in addition confirmed his title on condition that he buy at a much-reduced price" (Robbins, 1976:10).

In most scholarly literature, ownership of land refers to *private* ownership. In the Israeli case, *public* or *institutional* ownership (see Chapter 4) played a decisive role, and in the period before sovereignty was a substitute for sovereignty because it was only by public ownership that it was possible to freeze the land which had been transferred from Arab to Jewish ownership.

In the first stage of Zionist settlement, the only way open for the acquisition of land was ownership—the exchange of capital for land. When the Jewish collectivity achieved sovereignty and became militarily powerful, the conquest of land replaced buying it. But even then, as we will see below, public ownership of land did not decrease in importance.

The third method of control over territory is *sovereignty*. Sovereignty is the supreme and exclusive authority exercised by the State over its territory, and is an inseparable part of the definition of the modern state. The concept is derived from the feudal system, which granted the lord exclusive rule over the vassals who lived on his land. Sovereignty as a concept in international law is conditional on the formation of a recognized State.

> The formation of a new State is a matter of [*political*] fact, [*but*] it is through [*international*] recognition, which is a matter of law, that such new State becomes a subject of International Law. As soon as such recognition is given, the new State's territory is recognized as the territory of a subject of international law, and it matters not how this territory was acquired before recognition (Oppenheim, 1957:544).

Thus, "where a new State arises the law has looked chiefly to the emergence of the new subject rather than the incidental transfer of territory; it has looked to the sovereign, rather than the territorial, element of territorial sovereignty" (Jennings, 1963:8).

These three forms of control over territory—presence, ownership, and sovereignty—exist both independently and in interrelated patterns. In all, there are eight possible patterns of control over territory (see Table 1.3). Before analyzing these patterns, however, we must assume the existence of some type of orientation, whether this is instrumental or expressive (as used by Parsons, 1951:97), toward the territory involved. The land must be within the *cognitive map* of the collectivity of people who are concerned with it—either as a target for immigra-

Table 1.3

PATTERNS OF CONTROL OF TERRITORIAL EXPANSES

Pattern	Sovereignty	Ownership	Presence
a	−	−	−
b	−	−	+
c	−	+	−
d	−	+	+
e	+	−	−
f	+	−	+
g	+	+	−
h	+	+	+

Source: Kimmerling (1977:38).

+ = Present

− = Absent

tion, as a place to return to, for conquest, for building "the City of God," or, at the least, for the use of the resources to be found there.

Pattern *a* is the frontier in its pristine purity: a target land which is uninhabited (or believed to be so). In *The First Frontier*, David Horowitz quotes from the description of one of those who sailed on the Mayflower: "These vast and unpeopled countries of America which are fruitful and fit for habitation being devoyd of all civil inhabitants; wher ther are only savage and brutish men which range up and downe. Little otherwise then the wild beasts of the same" (1978: 18). The image that the Hovevei Zion had of Zion was not much different, except for the affinity they felt for the local Arabs, who appeared to them to be "relatives," or at least as representing the type of life their forefathers had led.

Pattern *b* is the first stage in penetrating into an uninhabited country. This consists of having some type of presence, whether it was the Pilgrims in New England (before it became a colony), the Portuguese *bandeirantes* who came to search for gold in South America (but who later were used by Portugal to justify political claims), or the Spanish missionaries in the north, in New Spain (Mexico), in Peru, or along the Amazon and Orinoco rivers.* In such a pattern there is a high degree of frontierity, but a complete absence of law and order. In Palestine, until 1947, the Jews never used this pattern of control, but after the 1967 War it became central to Zionist territorial policy in accompaniment with military conquest of the areas involved.

For the emergence of control pattern c—ownership—the existence of law and order is an essential condition. Where there is the concept of ownership of land in a territory, there is a distinct drop in the degree of frontierity. Often there is an artificial decline in frontierity, using political, military, or economic means, in order to ensure large estates and haciendas, as was the case in both North and South America (see Gates, 1957; Wolf and Mintz, 1957). We shall see that not only was the "speculator," as opposed to the pioneering settler, one of the heroes of the North American frontier, but he was also important in the transfer of land from (national) Arab ownership to the Jews (see Chapter 2). Companies for acquiring land for sale and development, speculators, and private entrepreneurs whose major objective is the acquisition of land are institutions and social roles which play a significant role in frontier histories. In conditions of low frontierity, to acquire land and guarantee that the land is permanently transferred, it is not enough simply to have sufficient capital to buy the land: there must be a group of speculators and mediators, on the one hand, and economic and political institutions, on the other, to guarantee the transfer. These institutions—in the case of Palestine, the Jewish National Fund (hereafter JNF)—acted to a large extent as the functional equivalent of a sovereign state. The JNF bought land for the same reason that the United States, for example, bought Louisiana from France in 1803 and Alaska from Russia in 1867.

Pattern d, a combination of ownership and presence, can appear in some of the earliest stages of the colonializing settlement process, but in the Jewish-Palestine case, it had special significance. Until the Jews acquired sovereignty in 1948, it served the Jewish collectivity as the functional equivalent of sovereignty. Territories were acquired and

---

*Even more than that in Texas, where French threats stimulated the Spanish establishment of *presidios* (frontier garrisons) and founding of missions whose Indian converts could act as defensive auxiliaries in case of armed conflict. For discussion of the "mission frontier," see Hennessy (1978:54-60) and Bolton (1917).

settled, and a territorial continuum was formed between them (see Chapter 4). By means of these two types of control, a method of building the nation was developed, based primarily on the acquisition of adjacent tracts of land and creating settlement points on them. This method even became ideologized and was crystallized into a political movement known as "Practical Zionism" (Laqueur, 1972: 145-55). Its motto was "A dunam here, a dunam of land there," with the intention of combining all the dunams "here" and "there" into a single territorial tract.

Pattern *e* contains a new component: sovereignty. When sovereignty is not accompanied by the two other components (and especially when it does not include presence), this pattern closely resembles the "secondary settlement frontier." It is

> found in nearly all countries today where attempts are being made to extend the habitable area. . . . Any state, such as Australia or the Republic of Sudan, which includes sections of desert, provides examples of this situation. Special services are supplied for operation in the uninhabited areas if necessary (Prescott, 1965:35).

Siberia was a secondary settlement frontier for Russia, and the great drift of immigrants into Siberia in many ways resembled the westward movement in the United States (see Treadgold, 1957). In regard to Israel, the Negev Desert served as a secondary frontier and a territorial reservoir from the time it was conquered in 1949. Its importance as a secondary frontier increased when Israel agreed to vacate the Sinai peninsula as a result of the peace treaty with Egypt. Another secondary frontier is Galilee, which is sparsely populated by Jews.

The combination of presence and sovereignty creates pattern *f*. If a territory under the sovereignty of a collectivity is not a source of contention, it makes no difference if there is or is not presence on the land. But if the territory *is* a source of contention, then presence is seen as offering political support for sovereignty, and strengthens the claim to control over the land. This pattern to some extent resembles the Spanish settlement points in California which were a bone of contention with the United States. For example, San Francisco was a combination of a *presidio* (a frontier garrison), a mission, and a *pueblo* (town or village) (Bannon, 1974:233) which was meant to serve as a point which established presence both against the Indians and against the Americans who were encroaching upon it.

Pattern g—the combination of sovereignty and ownership—is very similar to pattern e, and it would appear that only in the case being analyzed here is there any significant difference between the two. The perception that sovereignty does not guarantee control over territory, and that the territory must also be under the ownership (preferably public) of the collectivity, appears to have evolved from the Jewish-Arab conflict in Palestine. While the absence of presence does not necessarily mean the presence of the opposing party in a conflict over territory, the absence of ownership in the modern system always means ownership by another. In a case where sovereignty is of one party and ownership of another, there is a highly unstable situation.

Pattern h is where the frontier actually ends. The land is under the sovereignty of the collectivity, owned by it, and settled by it. All the other patterns of control have different forms of frontiers and various degrees of frontierity, though the order in which they appear in Table 1.3 is not an ordinal scale of frontierity.*

THE STRIVING TO END FRONTIERITY

Any condition of frontierity contains an internal contradiction. On the one hand, the immigrant society needs the frontier. It is essential for the building and development of the society. On the other hand, the existence of a frontier means that there is a "territorial vacuum," and a sociopolitical system abhors a vacuum. This is especially true when (a) the vacuum involves territory over which there is a struggle between two sides, and (b) the system which regards the territory as a frontier does not have supremacy over the other side.

When a system acquires any type of control over a territory, whether it be ownership, presence, sovereignty, or any combination of these, it will attempt to gain the other types of control as well. Only pattern h means the passing of the frontier, and any territory which is a frontier is not yet fully a part of the collectivity. In the context of immigrant societies, it still does not have "law and order"—

---

*Except for the two extreme situations—when there is no control over territory but that to be found in the mind of the collectivity, or when all three components of control are present. The position of the other control patterns along the scale is likely to change over time and from culture to culture.

either in terms of the self-control of the immigrants themselves, or in terms of the local inhabitants, who need "pacification."*

With regard to Palestine, a conflict between Jews and Arabs over the land has accompanied the Jewish settlements in Zion almost from the outset to this very day, and since every type of control except h appears incomplete, there has been a constant striving to impose the remaining kind(s) of control over any territory which has only one or two of the three types of control. For example, as soon as any tract of land was transferred from Arab to Jewish ownership, the Jews would demonstrate a Jewish presence there, and eventually would extend Jewish sovereignty over the land. Alternatively, if sovereignty was acquired over territory, it was deemed necessary to demonstrate Jewish presence on the land by settlement, especially if the land remained under Arab ownership or the Arabs had any claim to that land. Such areas were seen as being in danger, and the patterns of control over them as reversible.

An example of the striving for full control in the present-day United States can be seen in what *Time* (8 January 1979) described as a "xenophobic overreaction" to the sale of land to foreigners in the U.S. farm belt. Iowa Congressman Tom Harkin, for example, warned that "the oil-producing nations . . . could buy the whole state of Iowa, every acre of farm-producing land, with just 394 days of oil production." However, *Time* quoted data from the Department of Agriculture which showed that of a billion acres of U.S. agricultural land under private ownership, only 3-5 million acres were owned by foreigners, and noted further that "most of the [*foreign*] buyers . . . lease the land back to Americans." Thus, despite American sovereignty, foreign ownership is perceived as an infringement on the control over the land, but the infringement seems less severe because in most cases American presence remains on the land.

With the transfer of land from Arab (or other)[†] to Jewish ownership, the fear always remained that the land might revert to Arab

---

*In the nineteenth century, the frontier usually ended when the railroad reached the area (see, for example, Morison and Commager, 1955:79-104), bringing with it "law and order."

[†]A few of the British crown lands were granted to the Jews, and a few to the Arabs. Most of the crown lands, though, were not arable under the available technology, or it was not worthwhile to invest the money needed to make them arable.

control. This concern led to the formulation of the "domino theory of Zionist settlement," an aspect of the striving to freeze institutionally all land in Jewish hands, and to freeze it thereafter by means of legislation. This "domino theory" is based on the Zionists' fear of "decolonization":

> That is, the fear of the recession of Zionist settlement and the "dispossession" of Jewish agriculturalists. If the first stitch is opened, the whole cloth will come apart.... Do not bother us with the argument that in the past we purchased the Arabs' lands. Indeed, we bought lands from the effendis [*landlords*] and we chased away the tenants who lived on them.... God forbid that we should stop this tradition. If we deviate from it we will only be admitting that we were not right in the past. In such a case, our whole basis will be shaken and the entire Zionist structure will tumble down (Schieff, *Haaretz*, 7/28/72).

The assumption underlying the "domino theory" is that agreeing to the justice of Arab claims over any land held by the Jews would inspire other claims and create a precedent. It is interesting to note that this same sensitivity exists in the United States in regard to the land claims of Indians. For example, in a legal struggle between the Omaha tribe and the State of Iowa over some 2,900 acres of land along the Missouri River (*Wilson* v. *Omaha Tribe*:78-160), the State of Iowa eventually won the case in the Supreme Court. Because of the possibility of what was seen to be a dangerous precedent, all the other forty-nine states joined with the State of Iowa. The danger was expressed by one of the participants involved as follows: "If they [*the Indians*] win this one, there's nothing to keep them from just going" (*New York Times*, 2/18/79). If in our times the problem of land claims by the remnants of American Indian tribes is seen as a dangerous one, and the control over the land seen as being reversible, the reader may well imagine how deep this fear must be for the Zionist colonizers, whose ability to survive in the midst of an Arab environment has always been seen as very problematic. As will be seen later, this fear of reversibility, when accompanied by a crisis of existential legitimation (see Chapter 7), had widespread implications for a number of the structures and the values of Israeli society. The potential for reversibility of part, most, or all of the land under Jewish control stems primarily from the low level of frontierity of the target territories of Zionist colonization. However, it was also rooted in the difficulty of establishing the internal and external legitimacy of the system.

THE LEGITIMACY OF THE JEWISH POLITICAL COLLECTIVITY AS A SOCIOPOLITICAL PROBLEM

We must distinguish between two dimensions of the legitimacy problem: (a) the granting of legitimacy to the Zionist settlement enterprise externally—i.e., external recognition of the Jews' right to return and settle in their ancient homeland and to build a full political life there—and (b) the self-legitimation of the Jewish system in the context of continuing conflict. The two dimensions are not independent of one another, and self-legitimation is especially likely to be affected by external legitimation.

The problem of achieving external legitimation stemmed from the fact that Zionist immigration and settlement created a condition of interminable conflict between the Jewish settlers and the immediate Arab environment (and later the broader one as well) which revolved about the striving of the two sides for sole control of the land of Palestine. The more the Zionist settlement succeeded, gaining territorial possessions and economic and political strength, the greater the opposition it created within an ever-widening radius in the Arab world. The local Arabs, as a political entity, never recognized the right of the Jews to settle in Palestine. This refusal to recognize the Jews as settlers spilled over into the entire Arab and Muslim worlds and thereafter into the Communist bloc and the Third World. Zionism was perceived as being part of the colonialist world, as the expansion of the white man into the "non-white" parts of the world for purposes of exploitation. The claim by Zionism that the Jewish immigration to Palestine had different reasons and motivations than the colonialist immigration movements was rejected. The Zionists focused on the reasons for the Jewish immigration, while the Arabs focused on its results. The Arab refusal to recognize the legitimacy of the building of a sovereign Jewish society perceived as existing in a zero-sum situation with an Arab political entity was a mixture of an ethical-ideological judgment with a tactic of political struggle. It became a powerful political weapon for those who opposed Zionism and helped to recruit political support for the Arab cause. Arab success in this regard reached its peak when the General Assembly of the United Nations defined Zionism as a "racist movement." Success on this issue appeared to be important to the opponents of Israel because the political force which made possible the founding of the State of Israel was ultimately based on the ethical claim of the Zionist Jews after the Holocaust.

The problem of external legitimation contributed in large measure to the intensification of the problem of internal legitimation. The problem of self-legitimation—i.e., questions about the right of the Jewish collectivity to exist as a political entity in Palestine, and doubts about the way the basic components of Zionism are implemented—has accompanied the Zionist settlement movement from its very early stages (see Chapter 7). It stems primarily from contradictions between the universalistic components of the Zionist movement* and the need for certain particularistic practices due to the fact that in the first stages of Jewish settlement, the Arabs in Palestine were a clear majority and most of the land was under their control. In all societies there are discrepancies between beliefs and the way institutions operate, but rarely are these discrepancies so great that they raise questions as to the right of the collectivity to exist. In 1937, E. Golomb, one of the leading figures in the Hagana organization (see Glossary) stated:

> Among some of the youth doubts are arising as to the justness of our coming here, as to the justness of Zionism. . . . This is one of the most dangerous things. We are about to undertake enterprises that will require numerous and heavy sacrifices, and if we do not have the sense of justice in coming to a barren country where there is sufficient place for the development of one more nation, we shall be powerless to achieve this enterprise (1953).

This study does not attempt to answer the question of the right of Jewish settlers to settle in Palestine and to transform the territory into an exclusivistic national territory. Questions such as these are in the realm of philosophy, international law, ideology, theology, or

---

*Except for the religious stream in the Zionist movement (and to some extent the revisionists), the two main currents—socialists and liberals—had universalistic pretensions. The socialists worked with concepts of a common class struggle which applied to the oppressed of all countries (including the Arab societies), while the liberals carried a message that was humanitarian-universalistic. See, for example, Avineri (1981) or Rubinstein (1980).

political science. The question raised here is a *sociological* one, and is divided into three parts: (a) Did the system have a problem of internal legitimation? (b) If it did, did the social system create any mechanism to deal with the problem? (c) How did the existence of this problem and the mechanism for dealing with it affect the formulation of the structure of Israeli society? In any event, if it is possible to identify any crises of legitimation which stemmed from the territorial confrontation with the Arabs, then it will be possible to identify the institutional arrangements designed to deal with such crises. Huntington (1981) contends that the gaps between its ideals and the activities of its institutions create a cognitive dissonance in American society and that Americans try to resolve this dissonance in four different ways, including (a) moralism—i.e., eliminating the gaps, (b) hypocrisy—denying that the gaps exist, (c) cynicism—tolerating the gaps, and (d) complacency—ignoring the gaps. We will see below (Chapter 7) that in Israeli society there are similar reactions to those mentioned by Huntington, but they go beyond the plane of day-to-day political stands and behavior, and are expressed in institutional arrangements which affect a wide range of cultural, social, and political activities. These arrangements exist side-by-side with those meant to ensure the maximum amount of control over territory gained and to prevent any loss of control which might be seen as the beginning of the reversal of the Zionist enterprise.

Throughout this first chapter, whose aim was to introduce the subject matter of this study and offer some insights generated by comparisons with other societies, a number of assumptions have been made about the building of an immigrant-settler society in a low frontierity situation—that is, where there is a scarcity of territorial resources, which is expressed empirically by the high price of land. The discussion which follows is divided into two parts: one relates to the social, economic, and political behavior of an immigrant-settler society which seeks to acquire territory in a low frontierity situation; the second relates to the influence of the situation of low frontierity on the structure and content of the immigrant-settler society. If one wishes, this is the Turnerian hypothesis in reverse: an analysis of what happens in a situation where there is no frontier.

Chapter Two

THE MAKING OF A FRONTIER AND A NATION

The prices for land in Palestine were high for the Jewish immigrant-settlers both because the land was already settled and because the wide range of traditional ownership patterns, all based on Ottoman law, made transfers of ownership difficult. In this chapter, the conditions of the land and the agrarian relations the Jewish settlers found, along with their first attempts to grapple with the situation, are described and analyzed.

PATTERNS OF ARAB LAND TENURE IN PALESTINE

The two main patterns of land tenure in Palestine had very different degrees of fluidity. The most common form was collective-village ownership—*Mushaa*. Shimoni offers this appraisal of the Mushaa system:

> The Mushaa lands are divided up among the various village families biennially or annually. At the time of their distribution, the lands are classified according to their nature and type (the quality of the land, the proximity to water, plain or mountain land, distance from the village, etc.), and each family receives several tracts of all types, which are split up and far from each other. The distribution is determined according to various principles: mostly by the number of work animals each family owns, but sometimes also by the number of males in the family. . . . The Mushaa system damages Arab agriculture since it necessarily maintains the backwardness: a fellah who knows that the land he is cultivating will, in a year or two, be transferred to someone else, will not bother with land improvement, tree planting, appropriate fertilization, the erection of buildings, water supply, and other means of improvement and intensification of agricultural production. The Mushaa also sometimes limits the right of the tract's owners to sell or mortgage it

and thus forces them to continue living with feudalistic and exploitative credit systems (1947:164).

For the purposes of this study, the primary significance of the Mushaa land tenure and maintenance pattern is that it removed a large part of the land in Palestine from the market. The Palestine Royal Commission (the so-called Peel Commission) report noted that "in certain areas, the Arabs regard this system [*the mushaa*] of tenancy, destructive as it is of all development, as a safeguard against alienation (or lands to Jewish hands), and that the Administration have been reluctant for political reasons to abolish it by legislation" (1937:219). Similarly, Shimoni observes that

> Arab leaders, in their war against Jewish settlement, often thought that the preservation of common property . . . in the Arab village would prevent the sale of lands to Jews, and thus there was a time when they conducted considerable propaganda against the Ifriz* and presented the Mushaa as an important national possession which must not be damaged (1947:804).

The amount of land under the Mushaa system steadily declined. At the end of the nineteenth century, most of the lands in Palestine were under collective-village ownership, and as late as 1923, a commission appointed by the High Commissioner to examine the system found that 56 percent of the 753 villages studied still maintained the collective form of ownership. The Mushaa system was most prevalent in the Jaffa, Ramle, Gaza, and Hebron districts, where 80 percent of the land was under such ownership (Abramowitz and Gelfat, 1944:46). Seven years later, however, Johnson and Crosby (see Palestine, 1930a) estimated the amount of land under the Mushaa system as only about 44 percent of the total land in Palestine, while Abramowitz and Gelfat (1944) estimated that, in 1932/33, 25 percent of the Arab-controlled agricultural lands were under collective tenure, with 35 to 40 percent of the fellaheen (in 1934/35) cultivating Mushaa lands. Thus we can see a process of the "defreezing" of land in Palestine.

---

*The conversion of the Mushaa lands to private property and their registration in the Land Register, something which was encouraged by the Mandatory Government.

The second major form of land tenure in Palestine was private ownership of large estates.* These lands, where cultivated, were cultivated by sharecroppers, tenants, or secondary tenants. Johnson and Crosby (see Palestine, 1930a) estimated that, in 1930, 29.7 percent of the lands were not cultivated by their owners. Abramowitz and Gelfat (1944:16) point out wide variations in the percentages of land in private estates in the various districts. In the Jaffa district, for example, 66 percent of the total cultivated area was in private estates; in Nazareth, 24 percent; in Acre, 22 percent. This contrasts sharply with 7.5 percent in estates in Hebron and one percent in Nablus. This type of land was among the most fluid, and the owners' willingness to sell it was dependent on its price on the market (a price which included the additional political value). The readiness of the estate owners to convert their property into capital stemmed from several factors, mainly its lack of profitability compared with the opportunity to earn large sums of money by its exchange. Other factors were the lack of emotional ties to the land of the effendis, most of whom were urban dwellers, and the fact that land property was not an important status symbol in this part of the East (Baer, 1971). Most of these estate owners had obtained de jure land tenure only one generation before the lands were offered for sale; the sharecroppers and tenants (or their fathers) who lived on the land had been the previous owners. In fact, these sharecroppers and tenants continued to believe that they owned the land even after the lands had been registered in the effendis' names in some remote city. Land registers were meaningless to them.

There were three historical reasons for the creation of the estate pattern in Palestine. The first was related to the fact that the fellaheen were forced to take out loans at a very high interest rate because of increased taxation by the central government. "This extortion forced the fellaheen into a vicious circle of debt from which they could never escape, and they were eventually obliged to hand their land over to their 'patrons' and to lease it from them as tenants

*It is rather difficult to define "large estate." The Mandatory Government tended (for political needs) to include any land not cultivated by its owners in this category, without taking size into consideration. Thus two categories of estates are cited in the official statistics: (a) estates of wealthy fellaheen who cultivated large tracts (sometimes as much as 300 dunams) by themselves and with hired laborers, and (b) estates whose owners did not cultivate the land but rented it to others.

in return for a fixed payment or a share of the crop" (A. Cohen, 1970: 56).

The second reason stemmed from a law enacted in 1858 which required all landowners to register their lands with the government. The fellaheen, who feared further taxation as a result of the registration, asked urban dwellers to register the lands in their names. Epstein describes this process:

> The Bedouin from around Safed, who feared the government and did not wish to tangle with it, came to ask the powerful city dwellers if they would lend the village lands their name, in exchange for payment. The city dwellers agreed and held the land as actual owners and then left them for their sons who rented the stolen fields to the sons of the oppressed (1908:194).

The third reason stemmed from a law enacted in the 1860s whereby leased government lands which had not been cultivated for three years were returned to the government (*miri* lands—see below). Extensive tracts which had been cultivated by fellaheen were expropriated by the Ottoman government and sold. Thus, for example, in 1872 the lands of the Jezreel Valley (including about twenty villages) were sold to a wealthy Beirut family. This pattern of estate ownership, which transformed part of the lands of Palestine into fluid lands de jure for a considerable period of time, bore with it one of the main seeds of the Jewish-Arab conflict. When these lands were purchased by Jews, they often practiced a "Jewish labor only" policy, which served to amplify the Arab agrarian problem and make it part of the national conflict.

The most frozen form of land was the *wakf*—consecrated Moslem property (see Baer, 1971:72-81). These were lands "belonging to God" and were almost completely non-transferable.* Among the various types of wakf were the *wakf Hairi*, in which both the land and its fruits were sacred (and which served functions such as maintaining mosques, Quranic schools, the Moslem bureaucracy, charity, etc.) and which was generally managed by the Supreme Moslem Council, and

---

*Wakf property could not be sold, but could, under certain conditions, be exchanged for other property (*istabdal*). It could not be rented for long periods unless it required capital investment. In such a case, a special contract (*ijartine*) was drawn up in exchange for a one-time large payment—almost equivalent to the value of the property—and subsequent symbolic payments.

the *wakf Ahali,* whose income belonged to the family and descendants of the consecrator. The latter classification was used to prevent the sale of family property and to thwart the conquest of private land by a governor or other oppressor.

From the standpoint of the fluidity of lands, it seems that there was no difference between the different types of the wakf. In the wake of the economic depression in the beginning of the 1930s, the Mandatory Government abolished the obligation of the tithes of the fellaheen to the sacred lands—an obligation which applied to about a tenth of the 800 Arab villages within the boundaries of Palestine—and in exchange gave a fixed sum to the management of the sacred lands. At any rate, the amount of land under wakf ownership was fairly small and seems generally to have been limited to small tracts. Hope-Simpson (1930:30) estimated the various wakf lands at 100,000 dunams, which may have been an exaggerated estimate. But the existence of a frozen system of land tenure, along with the disorder which prevailed in the land registers which the Mandatory Government could not overcome, had ramifications for the struggles between Jews and Arabs. Thus, for example, in the midst of the Arab struggle against the purchase of Wadi Havarat (the Hefer Valley), the claim was made that some of the valley's lands were sacred (*Hagana,* 1964:454-55).

Another form of land tenure or maintenance was the *miri,* which was land that was de facto owned by its settler and cultivator (*mulk*) but de jure by the government. The settler had the right to use the land and its fruits, to transmit this right by inheritance and to mortgage it. There were only two limitations on the use of the miri land. First, there was an obligation to constantly cultivate it. As noted earlier, a law was passed whereby all miri land which had been uncultivated for three years returned to government ownership, but during the Mandatory period this law was not enforced. The non-enforcement of the law reduced the fluidity of the land. On the other hand, the second limitation on the use of miri land—the impossibility of consecrating it—helped to defreeze the land.

There were also lands, whose extent is subject to dispute, under direct government control. Some were *jiftlik* lands which had been owned by the Ottoman regime and were transferrred to the Mandatory Government, while others were lands which could be seized by the government because they were deserted or because they were miri lands without inheritors or uncultivated for more than three years (*mahlul*).

There was fierce competition over these lands between the Jews and Arabs. The Jews demanded that the Mandatory Government exercise its right to take possession of the deserted lands, and then allocate these lands to Jewish settlements. The Arabs were, of course, opposed. First, they viewed any government seizure of deserted lands as a violation of the status quo and an opening for the transfer of the lands to Jewish ownership. Second, they claimed rights over these lands — or at least the right to prevent their sale to Jews.* In practice, from 1921 many government land tracts were allotted to Arabs and only a minority (about 20 percent) to Jewish settlement and industry.†

The Mandatory Government, aware of the economic weakness of the fellaheen and their inability to maintain the lands they were granted, declared that the fellaheen would not be permitted to sell their lands until they had paid their full value. The discharging of the debt was to be accomplished in small payments over a period of thirty years, with no possibility of discharging it earlier. Even before that, in 1920, a Land Transfer Ordinance was issued which required government approval for any transfer of land and prohibited the transfer to anyone who was not a resident of Palestine. Thus the Mandatory Government attempted, at a fairly early stage, to freeze the lands that were in Arab hands. The Jews saw this as a denial of the government's obligations in Article 6 of the Mandate, which specified that "the Administration of Palestine, while ensuring that the rights and position of other sections of the population are not prejudiced . . . shall encourage, in cooperation with the Jewish Agency . . . close settlement by Jews on the land, including State lands and waste lands not required

---

*In April 1921, the High Commissioner (Herbert Samuel) toured the Galilee and was met by a "wild demonstration" of thousands of Bedouin because a rumor had spread that his tour was connected with the distribution of jiftlik lands to Jews. The demonstrators waved black flags on which was written "Palestine is our land" (*Haaretz*, 4/18/21).

†Samuel's decision to give the Arabs large tracts of land in the Beisan and Jordan Valleys seems to have stemmed both from his desire to compensate the fellaheen who had suffered from the Zionist undertaking and from the conviction that such land transfers would calm the Arabs. Samuel also played a part in the election of Haj Amin El-Husseini, known as an Arab extremist, to the post of Mufti of Jerusalem (see Glossary), while assigning national significance to this office (Sykes, 1965:51; Porath, 1971:149-68). Granovsky (1943:11) claims that most of the 530,000 dunams of land given to the Arabs was given to owners of large estates, and he cites a series of examples to prove his point.

for public purposes" (quoted in the Peel Commission Report, 1937: 221). As we shall see later (Chapter 5), the government's most extreme effort to prevent land transfer from Arabs to Jews was expressed in legislation in 1940.

At the beginning of the Mandatory period, it seemed that the amount of land over which the government would exercise control would be great. According to the estimate of the First Report on Administration (Great Britain, 1922:15), there were between 2-3 million dunams of wasteland, most of which could be improved. In addition, there were about one million dunams of government lands, most of which were inherited from the Ottoman government. But several things soon occurred which both revealed that these estimates were exaggerated and also very much limited the scope of the land over which the Mandatory Government had ownership or title. First, more accurate measurements and extensive listings of real estate began to be undertaken. Second, Trans-Jordan was detached from the territory of Palestine ("Churchill's White Paper," June 1922), which limited not only the land resources in government hands but also the size of the resource that was part of the conflict.* Third, from about 1920 on, the land became a scarce economic good (Granovsky, 1940:27), so that landowners and those with a right to land—people who previously had not bothered to register or demonstrate ownership of their land—began to come forward. It is very likely that many of these owners were charlatans (see the Peel Commission Report). At any rate,

> If there were those in the Zionist camp who thought that the Government lands could serve as a sufficient basis for the Jewish undertaking in Palestine, this opinion was based on a lack of knowledge of the facts. . . . The area of the Government lands was too small for the establishment of an extensive Jewish undertaking (Granovsky, 1943:8).

The lands which were under the mediating government's ownership and over which the two sides competed were quite fluid, and some of them came to be owned by Jews, either by means of direct allocation (such as the coastal lands near Rishon LeZion or the lands which were given to the potash company and—much earlier—the

*These processes also seem to have intensified the perception of the limited nature of the land resource, and possibly also the belief—on both sides—of the impossibility of its satisfactory division between the two.

lands of Mikve Israel) or—in the second stage—after they had been purchased from Arabs who had been granted them by the government. In addition, some of the lands which the government could have expropriated, but which it generally did not during the Mandate period, came to be owned by Jews by means of purchases from Arabs who took advantage of this policy.

In sum, it seems that the allocation of government lands (regardless of to whom), along with the government's refraining from controlling extensive tracts of land (mawat, mahlul, etc.), contributed to the weakening of the perception of the land as a scarce resource. The weakening of such a perception was a necessary condition for the intensification of the rates of fluidity of the lands for the side which owned most of them, and thus allowed for a continuing process of land transference from Arabs to Jews.

In addition to the land tenure systems, there existed (as remnants of the nomadic-tribal society) public rights of land use (*matruka*), whether or not the lands were owned privately, including rights of pasture, irrigation, use of water, and passage. The Jewish settlers, who were unfamiliar with such rights in their countries of origin, disapproved of Arab attempts to exercise these rights on Jewish lands, while the Arabs could not comprehend the Jewish denial of rights which were (from their standpoint) self-evident and elementary. Beyond the many local quarrels which resulted, this friction helped to crystallize stereotypes on both sides.

CHANGING LAND POLICIES

The Jewish land purchases were, both in their scope and location, determined by a number of factors: (a) the immediate need for land, which was at least partially correlated with the rate and composition of the waves of immigration; (b) the financial resources at the disposal of various types of Jewish land buyers; (c) the existence of private and group initiatives and the pressures they exerted for various kinds of land purchases; (d) the scope and nature of the land supply, which was to a large extent dependent on (e) the political situation, which could intensify (f) the land problems and increase (g) the political price added to the land's value—all of these contributing to a certain extent to (h) the degree to which lands in the Arab sector were unfrozen. The efforts of the Yishuv to formulate a land policy had to be integrated with this complex of factors.

The first evidence of a land policy appeared when the process of purchasing a large tract in Marj Ibn Aamar (the Jezreel Valley) from the Sursuk family from Beirut, which included about 225,000 dunams, began. The first attempt to purchase lands in the Jezreel Valley was made in 1891, but the first purchases were made only in 1910, in the name of the Palestine Land Development Company (PLDC). These were the lands of Poolia (Merhavia) (Doukhan-Landau, 1979:109). But until the end of World War I and even later—with the transition from military to civilian rule—purchasing activities in the Valley were not renewed.

While there was no overall Jewish land policy, there was the land purchase policy of the Baron de Rothschild, which the Zionist Executive Committee attempted to pursue (by means of the JNF and PLDC). The inability to formulate a land policy was due to the fact that the land was a resource in which the economic component was dominant, and the JNF (see Chapter 3) did not have sufficient power, either economic or political, in the framework of the Mandatory system, to control land transfers alone.

Just as the Arab political elite was unsuccessful in blocking land transfer to the Jewish sector by means of its system of internal control, and was forced to enlist the support of the British,* so too was the regulation of land purchase from Arabs not included in the system (as described by Horowitz and Lissak, 1978) which allowed the Jewish market to be organized, and the Jewish political organizations' control over the "speculators" was generally inefficient (see Granovsky, 1940:170-72). On the other hand, the land which had already been transferred to the ownership of the national institutions represented a central resource, and its allocation among the various sectors was a subject for conflict within the Yishuv.

The formulators of Jewish land policy faced several basic decisions. They had to decide whether lands should be purchased anywhere they were offered, or should be purchased selectively, taking into account (1) the type and quality of land,[†] (2) the location

---

*For example, there were periods in which wealthy Arabs would buy Arab lands, consolidate them into large tracts, and wait for prices to rise in order to offer them for sale to Jews (Granovsky, 1952:79).

[†]Evaluations of the quality of land changed as new technologies allowed for transition to intensive cultivation, land improvement, swamp draining, etc. From the mid-1920s, with the spread of citrus groves, there was a rising demand among

of the land on the political map of Palestine, (3) the extent to which the land was populated by fellaheen or Bedouins, etc. Nonselective land purchase would not necessarily be a sign of a lack of policy or of rising demand, but could be a result of political considerations. For example, in the beginning of the 1940s, the prevalent opinion was that "even when the Jewish State is established, it will not be able to acquire [*by political or administrative means*] many lands" (Granovsky, 1940:21), and thus it was felt that as many lands as possible should be purchased before that time.

The location of the land purchased was a matter of special concern. The prevailing tendency was to purchase a large tract in a certain area, such as in the valleys or the coastal plain, and then expand the boundaries of ownership as much as possible. As a result, in several areas a Jewish *territorial continuum* was created which contributed both to the external image of a powerful, homogeneous political unit—which went hand in hand with the process of divergence between the Jewish and Arab economies (Kimmerling, 1979)—and to the self-image and sense of security of the Yishuv. When necessary, such territorial continuity made possible effective mutual protection of the settlements, which could quickly come to each other's aid when attacked or threatened, before the national or even local paramilitary organizations acted. In addition, the dynamics of private capital contributed to this pattern of land purchase, inasmuch as such capital was attracted by the larger purchases previously made by the national institutions. The owners of such capital generally did not wish to purchase lands far from those already owned by Jews. But as it became clearer, primarily from 1937 onwards, that the physical boundaries of the collectivity would be determined by the "facts of the field"—that is, that the territory of the Jewish state would include all the places owned and settled by Jews—the need was felt to purchase lands, especially in the Galilee and the Negev, which were scattered and far from the traditional area of settlement. Ussishkin, in speaking to the Zionist Executive Commitee (1937), summarized this point as follows:

> We must make an effort to acquire places that are far from the centers of our settlement in order to secure, as much as possible, the boundaries of our country. And indeed when the land purchase

both Arabs and Jews for lands which had until then been considered unfit for intensive cultivation—in the coastal lowlands, for example (Horowitz, 1948).

programs were established, this goal was always in our minds: to settle the distant areas. Along with the matter of the land's quality, we also always took into account our aspiration to expand the boundaries in order to guard against any trouble that might arise. We must remember that a certain part of Degania is located on the other side of the Jordan, and it nevertheless stays in our hands. This is the real conquest of boundaries, from a political standpoint. In this sense, during the last year the JNF decided to expand its activities in order to secure as quickly as possible, the northern and eastern boundaries. . . . After all, we are not dealing only with an agricultural matter, for above all we are striving to ensure the broadest possible boundaries for our nation (1939:15).

There was also a question about the pace of land purchases. Should the pace be matched to the immediate needs and possibilities for settlement, or should land reserves be created? As mentioned, there was a risk involved in the creation of reserves of uncultivated lands—first, because of the Ottoman laws which transferred unculti-vated lands to government ownership, and later, because of the Arab custom of claiming ownership of such lands. When land was purchased and not immediately settled, it was often necessary to place "conquest groups" on it. These groups performed the initial tasks of cultivation and also demonstrated Jewish presence on the land. As a solution to this problem, Ussishkin (1939:16) suggested that extensive cultivation methods be employed. Such methods not only were less profitable economically, but also negated one of the basic Zionist claims—that the Jewish-Arab conflict should not be viewed as a "zero-sum" strug-gle, because as soon as a transition was made to modern methods of cultivation, there would be room for both Jews and Arabs in Palestine.

If today we face the question: a lot of land and few people, or little land and many people, then I explicitly state: my opinion is a lot of land and few people. We will always find candidates for settlement, while only for a limited time will we be able to acquire lands for Jews (16).

An opposite pattern also stemmed from this same logic, with Jews settling in places where the land in Jewish hands was too small to be economically profitable, but where it was necessary to "establish facts" (Granovsky, 1943:49).

The land purchases of the Baron de Rothschild and his settlement organizations were well integrated into the general trends and patterns of land transfer, although at first glance they seem to have lacked the political dimension and the element of national considerations. These were purchases of large tracts which in certain areas created Jewish territorial continuity, especially after they became integrated with the other Jewish land purchases. They also indicated a trend toward the creation of land reserves. Thus an emphasis was placed on the fact that the lands would not be populated by an Arab population which might make demands. The relatively abundant capital on the one hand, and the lack of any doctrine with reference to Arab workers (some of whom continued to be employed on these lands) on the other, gave considerable flexibility to the land policy of the Baron and of the organizations which continued his activities.

In Table 2.1 we can see that there were three periods in which there was a boom in land accumulation by the Jewish community in Palestine. In the period 1923-1927 (probably the second half of that period), there was an average annual land purchase of 61,400 dunams of land, with the JNF's share of the total purchases being about 42 percent. In the years 1932-1935, which include periods of large-scale immigration and the expansion of the Yishuv and its economy, the yearly average purchase was 59,500 dunams, with the share of the JNF declining to 35.2 percent of the total. In the period 1942-1947, when the White Paper restrictions (see Bauer, 1973) were in effect, the JNF alone purchased a yearly average of 61,200 dunams of land.

In the first two years of the severely restrictive White Paper laws (1940-41), there was no boom in land purchases (despite the relative boom in the economy), but neither was there a slump, with the yearly average purchase being 36,500 dunams, as compared with 31,500 dunams during the years of the Arab uprising (1936-1939). In 1920-1922 as well, there were relatively large transfers of land to Jewish ownership (46,300 dunams yearly average), but it is impossible to ascertain how much of these had been purchased in earlier periods when there was no possibility of legal registration of land. In this period, the JNF's share rose to 40 percent of the total purchases. This was the period in which the Yishuv had at its disposal the largest amount of land per person, as a result of the shrinkage in its population because of the expulsions from Palestine during World War I by the Ottoman authorities because they suspected Jews of cooperating with

Table 2.1

ESTIMATED JEWISH LAND PURCHASES IN PALESTINE, 1882-1947
(*thousands of dunams*)

	Total Area Owned by Jews	Area Owned by JNF	Total Lands Purchased	Lands Purchased by JNF	Dunams per capita
Until 1882	22	—	22	—	.94
1883-90	104	—	82	—	2.23
1891-1900	218	—	114	—	4.36
1901-14	418	16	200	16	4.92
1914-19	No data	25	—	9	—
1920-22	557	72	139	47	6.71
1923-27	864	197	307	125	5.76
1928-31	994	289	130	92[a]	5.85
1932-35	1,232	371	238	82	3.05
1936-39	1,358	478	126	107[b]	2.92
1940-41	1,431	566	73	88[b]	2.90
1942-45	1,506	813	75	247[b]	2.42
1946-47	1,734	933	226	120[b]	2.38

Sources: JNF, 1942A; *Reports*, 1924-39; *Bulletin*, 1939-1940; Gurevich, Gertz, and Zenker, 1947; Grannot, (1956:28).

[a]Of which 59,500 dunams were bought in 1929, the year of the "riots."

[b]In this period, the JNF also bought unknown quantities of land from Jewish owners. In *Hagana*, Vol. 3, p. 1965, there is a much lower estimate of land purchases for 1939-47, but no sources for these figures are cited.

the British troops. From then on, there was a continuing decline in the amount of land at the Jewish community's disposal relative to the population, with land purchases not keeping pace with immigration. But it is likely that this was also one of the effects of deemphasizing the agricultural sector in favor of an emphasis on the growth of the urban population—that is, despite an increase in Jewish immigration to Palestine, the demand for land decreased.

From the beginning of the 1920s until the mid-1940s, the Jewish National Fund played a central role in land purchase, acquiring about a third of the Jewish-owned lands, and became a dominant factor in the Yishuv both because it was the largest "landlord" in Palestine and because through it the Yishuv's land resources were allocated to the various sectors. The JNF was also one of the mechanisms regulating the distribution of resources which flowed into the system from the outside. At the meeting of the Zionist Executive Committee in Spring 1937, the representatives of the right in the organized Yishuv bitterly complained that they were being deprived. One of their leaders asked: "Is there still a need to state that there is a strong element of pioneering and great loyalty in the settlement of the middle class as well?" (JNF, 1937). Another right-wing representative demanded the allocation of additional resources for the aid of middle-class settlements on the grounds that these settlements operated "purely by means of Jewish labour."

By 1944—i.e., during a period of about sixty years of Jewish settlement in Palestine—272 settlements were established (not all of which survived). More than 70 percent of these were on JNF lands despite the fact that the JNF owned less than half the lands under Jewish ownership (see Table 2.2). It is clear that the lion's share of the Fund's lands were allocated to the sector which turned to settlement and which lacked funds of its own. But with the intensification of pressure on the part of the right-wing sector, there was readiness on the part of the JNF to allocate lands for private settlement as well. Thus, for example, with the "conquest" of the Hefer Valley, land was allocated for eleven settlements of the middle class, eight for Histadrut (labor union—see Glossary) members, and four more for other workers' organizations (Bein, 1970:359). The trend to allocate lands to the non-workers' sector as well was particularly salient from 1933-36, with the wave of immigration from Germany, of which 25 percent were absorbed in agriculture. About 30 percent of the settle-

Table 2.2

THE DISTRIBUTION OF JEWISH SETTLEMENTS FROM THE BEGINNING
OF SETTLEMENT UNTIL 1944

| | | Date of Settlement | | | | | |
Ownership	Total	Until 1919	1920-24	1925-29	1930-34	1935-39	1940-44
JNF	193	7	19	19	49	59	40
Other	79	29	10	11	14	12	3
TOTAL	272	36	29	30	63	71	43

Sources: Pollack, 1940; Gurevich, Gertz, and Bachi (1945); Bein, 1970; Vilnai, 1956.

Note: In most cases the category of "other" ownership refers to lands in the hands of Baron de Rothschild's projects (PICA and JCA). In cases in which the settlement included several types of land, the ownership of most of the land was the determining factor. The table also includes several settlements which have disappeared from the map and some urban neighborhoods which were later annexed to urban centers.

Table 2.3

SETTLEMENTS ACCORDING TO SECTORAL MEMBERSHIP AND THE
OWNERSHIP OF THE LAND ON WHICH THEY WERE ESTABLISHED
UNTIL 1944

| | Ownership | | |
Sector	JNF	Other	Total
Labor	152	13	165
Right-wing	39	66	95
TOTAL	181	79	260[a]

Sources: See Table 2.2.

[a]There are twelve settlements which belong to other factions or whose sectoral membership is unclear.

ments which did not belong to the workers sector were established on JNF lands, but only about 16 percent of the JNF lands were allocated to the private or right-wing sectors (see Table 2.3).*

The left (excluding the Hakibbutz Haartzi), particularly Hakibbutz Hameuchad (see Glossary), benefitted from the land reserves of the PICA and the Baron's settlement projects.[†] The use of these land reserves by the left was especially prevalent during the settlement campaigns which arose in the wake of the intensification of the conflict with the Arabs during 1936-39 (Bowden, 1975) and during the political struggle with the British in 1940-44 (Bauer, 1973). There is no way of knowing if this defreezing of lands and placing them at the disposal of the left stemmed only from the intensification of the conflict, or whether it was also due to the dominance of the left in the Yishuv (Horowitz and Lissak, 1978), but it is worth noting that the kibbutz Haartzi (which was not central within the labor movement) was totally dependent on the JNF for the acquisition of land for its settlement projects, as were Hapoel Hamizrahi and Poalei Agudat Israel (see Glossary). The Moshavim Movement (Tnuat Hamoshavim), which became a central factor in Jewish settlement from the 1930s, based itself almost completely on JNF lands (49 of its 51 settlements).

The land, which was purchased with funds solicited by the JNF from world Jewry, as well as other resources which flowed from the outside (capital, manpower), was a resource over which there was a

---

*It seems that the average size of the right-wing settlements was greater. This may be explained both by the different types of agriculture adopted by the public and private sectors, and by the private sector's greater emphasis on economic profit, in contrast to the political emphasis of the left-wing settlements.

[†]The following are some of the left's settlements which were established on PICA land reserves: The Moshav (Tnuat Hamoshavim) Movement: Mishmar Hashlosha (1937), Shadmot Dvora (1939); The League of Kvutzot (Hever Hakvutzot): Kfar Giladi (1916), Ayelet Hashachar (1918), Ashdot Yaakov (1933), Maayan Zvi (1938), and Alumot (1941); the United Kibbutz (Hakibbutz Hameuchad): Ashdot Yaakov Meuchad (1933), Genossar (1937), Sdot Yam (1940), Beit Keshet (1944). It should be noted that the Genossar settlers came to the PICA land on their own initiative and refused to leave despite legal claims filed against them. In 1939, PICA transferred 600 dunams to a Beitar movement moshav—Tel Zur—and in the same year Hakibbutz Hameuchad attempted to settle on the land of the potash factory with the establishment of Beit-Haarava.

struggle, not only between Jews and Arabs but also within the Jewish community. This struggle was not particularly acute because the various sectors had different emphases. The right-wing sector (such as the Revisionists—see Glossary) did not support a settlement ideology, and when it nevertheless turned to the sphere of agriculture and settlement, it was primarily an economic action for which it used its own resources. The left supported a settlement ideology and knew how to establish a direct linkage between settlement and security, and it attempted to appropriate both from the right wing. Later it tried to have the entire system participate in the two spheres of settlement and security without relinquishing its control over them (*Hagana*, 1964). Such control seems to have been an important component in the dominance of the left-wing coalition headed by Mapai (see Glossary), beginning in 1930, within the political system of the Yishuv.

We have a general idea who in the Arab social system were the beneficiaries from the Jewish land acquisition process at different periods (see Table 2.4). In the period 1879-1890, there were only two sources for land purchases: about 72 percent of the purchased land had previously been owned by the Ottoman government, and 28 percent was bought from local large estate holders. During the period 1891-1900, the picture became more complex, with about 43 percent of the lands being sold by smallholders or local fellaheen, and another 40 percent by absentee land holders of large estates (mostly families located in Beirut and Cairo). This was also the case in the period 1901-1927, with absentee landowners selling about 68 percent of the land bought. The other major source was local Arab large estate owners, who sold more than 20 percent of the land purchased by Jews. This was the period of the purchase of whole territorial regions in the great valleys and the coastal plain. In the period 1928-1936 there were almost no large estates (or large territorial expanses) sold. The Jewish land purchasers returned partially to the smallholders (9.5 percent), but the major sources remained the wealthy city-dwelling (mainly absentee) landlords—locals (44 percent) and those from outside Palestine (36 percent). In the period from 1879 to 1936, about 53 percent of the land acquired by the Jews was originally held by absentee large estate proprietors.

Table 2.4

JEWISH LAND PURCHASES IN PALESTINE BY SOURCE, 1879-1936[a]

Period of Purchases	Total Purchases in Dunams	Source							
		Absentee Large Estate Proprietors		Local Large Estate Proprietors		Government Missions and Other		Fellaheen	
		Dunams	Percent	Dunams	Percent	Dunams	Percent	Dunams	Percent
1879-1890	67,000	—	—	19,000	28.3%	48,000	71.6%	—	—
1891-1900	60,000	24,000	40.1%	3,500	6.1	7,000	11.5	26,000	42.7%
1901-1927	421,105	286,928	68.1	86,083	20.4	35,839	8.5	12,255	2.9
1928-1936	133,582	48,145	36.1	59,232	44.4	—	—	26,205	19.6
TOTALS	681,687	359,073	52.7	167,815	24.5	90,839	13.3	64,460	9.5

Source: Computed from Granovsky (1952:307). The figures for the first two periods were rounded off.

[a]Data about the source of purchase are available for only about one-half of the land purchased by the Jews in Palestine.

THE MAKING OF A FRONTIER AND A NATION

FROM ECONOMIC SEGREGATION TO TERRITORIAL DIVISION

Along with the processes of nation-building and economic growth (see Kimmerling, 1979) which were made possible by the absolute increase in the Jewish population (see Table 4.1)—i.e., the broadening of the territorial base for the population and the development of a varied economic system which in 1936 supplied about 64 percent of the goods and services it needed (Szereszewski, 1968:9)—the dependence of the Jewish community on the Arab community steadily declined.* The Jewish community was becoming more and more of a "total society" capable of sustaining itself (Horowitz and Lissak, 1978). The Arab rebellion of 1936-39, which sought to destroy the Jewish system by stopping all economic exchange with it, failed because the Jewish system was already able to maintain itself at the level of a modern economy. It was therefore not surprising that the willingness of both sides to postpone the realization of their goals (i.e., the attainment of political control over most of the country's territory) declined steadily from the beginning of the 1930s. The Arabs became aware that the Jewish sector's rate of development meant that the status quo was no longer sufficient; action had to be taken to create a new situation which could emerge only if British rule were done away with or if a drastic change were made in the conditions of the Mandate. The Jews, on the other hand, were no longer willing to settle for the pace of development which the Mandatory framework dictated. As a result of the sense of self-confidence which the Jewish population had acquired as a direct

*In 1936, before the outbreak of the Arab rebellion (see Porath, 1977 and Kimmerling, 1979), the Jewish economy bought goods and services from the Arab sector for a total of £P3,657,000—that is, about 11 percent of the Arab GDP. The Jewish economy sold goods and services to the non-Jewish sector (which included the Mandatory Government) in the amount of £P1,108,000—about 3 percent of the Jewish GDP. In the same period, the Jewish economy imported another 26 percent of its resources from the outside, and exported 8.3 percent of its goods and services (Szereszewski, 1968:9). The economic consequences of the Arab rebellion demonstrated that the Arab dependence on the Jewish economy was greater than that of the Jews on the Arabs. Most of the flow of capital into the Arab economy came from the Jewish economy. Thus in 1936 (before the rebellion) the Jews bought between 33-40 percent of Arab agricultural produce (Sussman, 1969:51), which was the main sector of the Arab economy. It is not surprising that in the wake of the rebellion the Arab economy collapsed while the Jewish one flourished.

49

function of its increasing power, a growing portion of the Jewish leadership was willing to face its Arab opponent without the protection of the Mandatory Government.* This position was expressed by a central figure in the Jewish leadership, Chaim Arlosoroff, in June 1932 in a letter to Weizmann:

> The assumption at the base of our policy is that it is both necessary and possible to realize our goal step by step. It is clear that this was the correct and only method in the past. . . . What I mean is a certain level of development of the actual power relations between the two nations struggling in Palestine. The power of the two sides can be based on the social or economic position, the technical and financial equipment, or on the military organization and the capacity for warfare of the men of each nation.

Arlosoroff argued that the Mandate had exhausted its possibilities and listed four alternatives open to the Jewish leadership. The first was to continue with the situation as it was on the assumption that the future was fraught with so many uncertainties that there was no point in trying to exert influence on it at that stage; in the meantime they should "hold their own." The second possibility was to conclude that "with world circumstances being what they [were], the Zionist vision [could] not be realized."

> The third theoretical possibility is to maintain the basic Zionist principles, but to *limit the geographical area* in which they will be realized: instead of all of Palestine—only districts or certain parts of it. The goal is to establish *national sovereignty* in a certain area of Palestine, to create in this area all the possibilities of undisturbed development which depend on the use of the means of the state in

---

*It seems that the first to take this position was David Eder, who was the chairman of the Zionist delegation and Weizmann's representative in Palestine, writing to Joseph Cowen on 9 May 1921: "I have in mind another policy. We should request of the British Government to give up the Mandate since it is totally unable to fulfill it. We should not ask any state to take the Mandate upon itself, but rather we should be left alone to face the Arabs. I estimate that we have 10,000 people capable of bearing arms—3,000 of whom have already served as soldiers. Without intervention from outside . . . we will be able to fight properly . . . and we will have a chance to establish our own government which will treat the Arabs no less fairly than does the Mandatory Government" (Weizmann Archives, 24/16151).

the areas of administration, settlement and economy, and *to make this area a strategic base for possible progress in the future.* (Emphasis added.)

Arlosoroff's fourth alternative, which seemed to be the one he preferred, was to conclude that "under today's conditions Zionism cannot be realized without a period of transition in which the Jewish minority will govern in an organized revolutionary government" (1945:333-42). About five years later, in the wake of the Arab rebellion (see Porath, 1977) and what seemed to be Britain's decision to leave Palestine, the third alternative which Arlosoroff set forth appeared to be the most realistic—that is, the partition of the territory of Palestine between Jews and Arabs.*

From that time onward, the Jewish side faced a very difficult question: whether to give preference to *sovereignty at the expense of territories.* This not only involved value judgments, but also a situation of uncertainty in reference to several problems likely to arise as a result of the departure of the British from the area and the possible partition of the country. These included:

(1) To what extent had the Jewish community acquired sufficient power to ensure its existence in the face of organized Arab resistance, on the assumption that such resistance might come (a) only from Arabs who resided in the Jewish state, (b) from all of Palestine's Arabs, or (c) with the additional aid of the neighboring Arab states?[†]

(2) Would a state within the partitioned territory of Palestine, which would (even under optimal conditions of partition) be tiny in size, be capable of developing an economic structure which would constitute

*The first of the Zionists to conclude that the solution to the Jewish-Arab conflict might lie in the partition of Palestine and the establishment of a sovereign Jewish state in part of it was Dr. A. Jacobson (the representative of the Zionist Executive Committee in the League of Nations). At the end of 1931 he formulated a partition plan in a secret memorandum and distributed it among the members of the Executive Committee. However, they rejected the plan entirely and forbade Jacobson to mention it in his diplomatic contacts. The partition plan occurred to Jacobson after he had attempted to construct several alternative models (cantonization, different forms of federation, etc.) for the solution of the conflict (G. Cohen, 1973:360-61).

[†]The question arises: "If the Jews are capable of dealing with a general resistance of Palestine Arabs, why should they agree to partitioning of the country?" (Sharett, 1971:260).

a realistic basis for its existence, and could such a state absorb all the immigration which was the purpose for its establishment? Within this very limited territory, would it be possible to develop a political, economic, and social entity which would meet the expectations for a new society as envisioned by the vast majority of the Zionist movement?*

(3) To what extent, if any, could the Zionist leadership influence the British to continue the Mandate? (In the early 1930s, the opposite question had been posed: Could the British be persuaded to abandon their rule in Palestine?) Could the British be influenced to optimalize the Mandate's conditions for the Jews—that is, could the Jewish population and the proportion of the territory owned by it be significantly increased under British auspices?

(4) If the partitioning of Palestine was undertaken, to what extent would the Jewish side be able to exert influence to obtain optimal conditions of partition, in particular (a) granting maximum territory to the Jewish side and (b) maintaining a minimum number of Arab residents (presence) and Arab-owned lands within the territory allocated to the Jews? In this context there was another factor of uncertainty which was likely to affect the decision to support or oppose the principle of territorial partition: whether a double transfer of population would be possible. This would include the transfer of Arab residents from the territories allocated to the Jewish state to Arab territories (as proposed by the Peel Commission, 1937) and the transfer of a large number of Jews, especially from Europe, to Palestine. The attainment of sovereignty was a condition for mass immigration as long as the Arabs opposed it (which they had done unequivocally during the entire Mandatory period), but mass immigration prior to sovereignty would make its attainment a less urgent need for the Jews. Indeed, mass immigration would eliminate the necessity of accepting partition and would open the door to the realization of Arlosoroff's fourth alternative—Jewish control of Palestine prior to the attainment of a Jewish majority.

*For example, in 1937 Tabenkin (1972:313) expressed his fear that the partitioning of Palestine would eliminate the agricultural and proletarian base of the Jewish community and would return them to "the Pale of Settlement" (the narrow strip in the western area of tsarist Russia where about five million Jews were concentrated) in which they would again become "missionaries of culture and commissioners of trade."

(5) To what extent would the stability and institutionalization of the partition boundaries be a hindrance to the Jewish side? Despite Arlosoroff's contention that the acceptance of the partition principle would be only a strategic step until additional Jewish power could be accumulated which would enable "progress" to be made,* it could be seen in advance that the new partition would become an established political fact which could not be changed.† The establishment of a sovereign Arab state which would be recognized by other states as part of Palestine, or the annexation of the Arab territories to a neighboring Arab state, would become an established fact which the attainment of a power advantage could not overcome.**

Empirically, it was almost impossible to formulate responses to these questions which could aid in the resolution of the issue between acquiring additional territory and attaining sovereignty in the foreseeable future. Thus the answers given to these questions in the wake of the recommendations of the Palestine Royal Commission (1937) were in accordance with the basic predispositions and ideologies of the Jewish community's various components. The Royal Commission proposed the partition of Palestine into three parts: (1) a *Jewish state*, which would include the coastal area (south of Beer-Tuvia and up to Mount Carmel), the Jezreel Valley, and the Galilee (from which some of the Arab residents would be transferred to the Arab states); (2) an *Arab state*, which would be annexed to Trans-Jordan, and which would include the Judean mountains, Samaria, and the Negev; (3) a *British enclave*, which would include Jerusalem and Bethlehem and would have a territorial corridor to Jaffa. The proposal was based on "the natural principle"—that is, to separate the areas in which Jews had bought lands and settled from the areas settled mostly or entirely by Arabs.

*It seems this was one of the main arguments which motivated Ben-Gurion to support the partition proposal. In a letter to his son, he wrote: "My assumption— which makes me an enthusiastic supporter of the State, even if partition is involved now—is that a partial Jewish state is not an end, but a beginning.... It will give us powerful momentum in our historic efforts to redeem the entire land" (Ben-Gurion, 1968:211).

†Just as by the 1930s it was evident that restoring the territory of Trans-Jordan as a part of Palestine was not a realistic possibility.

**As argued by Dr. A. Barth, the Mizrahi representative in the Zionist Executive Committee: "The creation of a Jewish state means [*giving*] a guarantee to the boundaries of the neighboring countries, and we must recognize the Arab State just as the Arabs must recognize our State" (quoted by Eilam, 1972:93).

The Royal Commission's proposal aroused bitter controversy within the Jewish leadership (and the Jewish community in general) which was rooted in the intense emotional approaches to the subject of partition. The Jewish community was split into three camps: one group unequivocally rejected the idea of partition, even at the expense of freezing Jewish immigration;* a second camp tended to accept the partition proposal in principle, but for bargaining purposes—both with the British and Arabs—demanded its rejection as a tactical move;† the third camp wished to accept the proposal while negotiating over its details. The controversy united in one camp extreme opponents such as Poalei Zion-Smol, Hashomer Hatzair (see Glossary), and the Revisionists, each opposing the proposal for different and sometimes contradictory reasons,** and threatened to split the left, whose moderate part found itself in a pact with the General Zionists, the Farmers' Union, the Hapoel Hamizrahi, and Poalei Agudat Israel.

*It is interesting that Ussishkin tried to reach an agreement with the Arabs, who also opposed partition, even at the expense of freezing immigration and far-reaching concessions to Arab demands (S. Eliash, 1973).

†In a letter to his son dated 28 July 1937, Ben-Gurion wrote: "At present our political couch is the Mandate, and we cannot shed it. A Jewish state in part of Palestine—with an appropriate area and fair borders—seems to me to be a better thing than the Mandate. . . . We cannot force England to establish a Jewish state and to grant it the necessary borders. Thus, for the time being, we must stick to our demand that the Mandate must be maintained. The partition proposal must come from the British, and if we see that it is a favorable proposal— we will accept it, and relinquish the Mandate" (1968:182). He continued that even the friends of the Zionists in the British Parliament were wrong in thinking that the Jews opposed partition, while the friends of the Arabs adopted the policy of support of the proposal as a result of the same mistake. Sharett wrote on 7 June 1937 that "The decision of the Zionist Executive Committee as to partition— which opposes any reduction of territory—was only made for the outside world and did not set the internal position of the movement" (1971:204-5).

**Poalei Zion-Smol, Hashomer Hatzair, and Brit Shalom opposed the partition plan because they supported the idea of a bi-national state (Hattis, 1970). The Communists were totally opposed to Jewish political sovereignty and supported the establishment of what would be de facto an Arab state, with a Jewish minority within it. At this stage, Agudat Israel also tended to oppose the idea of "a premature end." The Revisionists continued to declare their desire to establish a Jewish state on both sides of the Jordan, although it seems that Jabotinsky, the Revisionist leader, at first tended to accept the Commission's proposal, since such a partition might be the first stage of the establishment of a Jewish state in all of Palestine, as Ben-Gurion thought.

The Zionist Executive Committee, at the 20th Zionist Congress, arrived at vague decisions which were open to varying interpretations in order to avoid intensifying the controversy.* But the debate became largely academic with the publication of a report in October 1938 of a commission appointed to examine to what extent the partition plan could be implemented (the Woodhead Commission), and even more so with the publication of a November 1938 White Paper in which the British government announced that it was withdrawing completely from the plan.

However, the possibility of establishing a sovereign Jewish state within the foreseeable future in exchange for territorial concessions in favor of the Arab community was not eliminated. The main result of the publication of a partition plan which would grant political sovereignty over part of Palestine's territory to the Jews was to direct thinking in the Jewish community along defined territorial lines. In 1937 plans for the total domination and protection of the collectivity's entire territory were made for the first time in the Hagana center.[†] Plans were also formulated for the development of a national army to replace the local bodies active until then.** As a result of the fact that the Arab rebellion had spread over almost the entire country, and also because of the encompassing territorial conception, the Hagana center's capacity for supervision of the local branches was strengthened (Hagana, 1964:754-55). Furthermore, the growing acceptance of the territorial concept led to a search for alternative strategies which would be more suitable to the geographic conditions which the partition plan's boundaries would dictate. Thus, while at the beginning a defensive approach was emphasized, which included the construction of fences and barriers and their protection, by August 1937 the Hagana's leaders reached the conclusion that "in light of

*The Congress censured the Royal Commission's decision to the effect that the Mandate could no longer be implemented, expressed its opposition to limiting the Jews' rights (in general) and authorized the Jewish Agency to negotiate with the British Government as to the conditions for the establishment of a Jewish state.

[†]A concrete expression of thinking in territorial terms was embodied in the "fortification" element of all these plans (see Hagana, 1964:748-56). The entire border was to be surrounded by several barbed wire belts and various blockades.

**One of the plan's components was the establishment of an army of reserves or a people's militia—similar in structure to the Swiss one (Horowitz and Kimmerling, 1974).

the *geographical reality* [*of the partition plan*], the Yishuv must establish an organization which is at least partially offensive, and not a purely defensive one" (*Hagana*, 1964:756; emphasis added). This latter approach dictated the development of a policy of land purchase and settlement to defend the boundaries of the state, to strengthen areas which were "weak links" in the Jewish territorial continuum, and to establish new territorial "facts"—all on the basis of an integrative *territorial conception*.

In 1941-42 it seemed that Jewish sovereignty over most of the area of Western Palestine would be attained within a short time as a result of the international situation created by World War II and the persecution of European Jews. This belief was based on three assumptions: (1) In Europe a stratum of millions of displaced Jews had been created, constituting a huge potential for emigration to Palestine (the extent of the physical annihilation of European Jewry was as yet unknown or had not yet penetrated the consciousness of the leadership of the Jewish community); (2) the victorious Allied powers would immediately act to transport approximately two million Jews; (3) these powers would acknowledge the Jews' right to an independent state as a moral compensation for the terrible wrong done to the European Jews and as a reward for the Palestinian Jewish Brigade's active participation in the Allied war effort. The bringing of such numbers of Jews to Palestine would completely change the power relations between Jews and Arabs, with Jewish sovereignty over all or most of the country the inevitable result. Alternatively, there was a proposal for the attainment of Jewish sovereignty immediately after the war in order to make the immigration and settlement of millions of Jews possible. The man whose name was associated with this alternative, which resembles Jabotinsky's program, was Ben-Gurion.* This proposal was adopted in a convention which met at the Biltmore Hotel in New York in May 1942 and became known as the Biltmore Program.

The Biltmore Program was a plan to avoid the exchange of territory for sovereignty in the belief that the attainment of Jewish sovereignty was possible without territorial concession. An alternative

*Actually it was Weizmann who, from the end of 1939, demanded that all of Palestine—except for the Nablus-Jenin-Tul Karem triangle—be made a Jewish state (article by Weizmann in the *New York Times*; quoted by Bauer, 1973). However, Weizmann viewed this as a maximal demand so that *something* of it might be attained, while Ben-Gurion converted the demand into a "banner"— that is, a symbol and a final program.

to the Biltmore Program was formulated, which also opposed the partition of Palestine, but demanded "the establishment of a bi-national political regime . . . which would be based on the undisturbed progress of the Zionist undertaking and on parity in government without regard for the numerical ratio between the two peoples" (Hakibbutz Haartzi, 1942:4). This alternative plan was that of Hakibbutz Haartzi-Hashomer Hatzair.* It did not make Jewish immigration to Palestine conditional on Arab agreement (Bauer, 1973), but (according to its proponents) it provided a means for preventing the use of force in the conflict between the Jewish and Arab national movements (Peretz, 1967:124). Hashomer Hatzair preferred "division of rule" to territorial division because the latter would lead to limiting "the space for settlement and for the absorption of mass immigration." There were others on the periphery of the left (besides Brit Shalom) who supported the idea of the bi-national state as opposed to the Biltmore Program. Thus, for example, Solomon Kaplansky, a leader of Poalei Zion (see Glossary), did not believe the Jews could impose a solution such as the Biltmore Program on the Arabs because after the war no Western power would be willing to use force against the Arabs.[†]

The Biltmore Program, which proposed Jewish sovereignty over most or all of the territory of Palestine, was the official Zionist program until May 1947, when a special United Nations Commission on Palestine (UNSCOP), assigned to seek solutions to the problems of Palestine, began to act. Representatives of the Jewish community cooperated fully with this commission at all stages of its activity (including the phrasing of the commission's recommendations) and avoided the presentation of extreme demands. Weizmann, appearing as a private individual, but at the invitation of the Vaad Leumi (see Glossary), suggested the partition of Palestine. The majority of the commission recommended the partition of Palestine into two states,

---

*In 1939 a League for Jewish-Arab Cooperation was established in the Yishuv; among its goals was the establishment of a bi-national government in Palestine, with a temporary limitation on Jewish immigration. The League was composed of former members of Brit Shalom, and some activists of Poalei Zion-Smol, Hashomer Hatzair, and the German immigration. In June 1942 Hashomer Hatzair officially joined the League, followed in August 1942 by the Ihud (unity) organization, successor to Brit Shalom. The Ihud cooperated with the League. Hashomer Hatzair continued to support the idea of a bi-national state almost up to the establishment of the State of Israel.

[†]According to Zionist Archive, file S/25/293.

each composed of three areas. The *Jewish state*, including 62 percent of Palestine's area, would consist of the Eastern Galilee and the Jezreel Valley, the coastal plain from south of Acre to north of Ashdod, and the Beersheba Valley. The *Arab state* would include the Western Galilee, the Judean hills and Samaria, and the coastal strip from Ashdod to Raffah. Jerusalem would be under international supervision. The two states, along with the international area, would be unified economically and monetarily. The Yishuv's representatives announced that they accepted the commission's recommendation in principle, but questioned the proposals to internationalize Jerusalem and to remove Western Galilee from the area of the Jewish state.

The UN General Assembly meeting of November 29, 1947 ratified the Partition Plan after accepting several amendments offered by various committees. These amendments included the detachment of two million dunams from the lands of the northern Negev and annexing them to the Arab state as a continuation of the Gaza Strip. As a result, only about 55 percent of West Palestine's area was to be allocated to the Jews.

SOVEREIGNTY VERSUS TERRITORY

The 1947 Partition Plan was not only accepted by the leadership of the organized Jewish community and the Zionist movement, but also enjoyed their active support.* In fact, there was a fairly broad consensus among the Jewish leadership and other groups and strata of the community on the principle of territorial concessions in exchange for immediate sovereignty. Consequently, the subsequent struggles were focused on the tactical level — that is, on the attain-

---

*At the meeting of the Zionist Executive Committee in Zurich in August 1947, a majority favored the Partition Plan as presenting the leadership with a basis for negotiation for optimal conditions (Zionist Archive, file S/25/1867). The two rival right-wing parties in the Jewish community — the General Zionists and the Revisionists — explicitly opposed the Partition Plan, but a close examination of their statements indicates that there was no active opposition to the plan by the Lehi (see Glossary) and the National Military Organization (see Yelin-Moore, 1974:424-25). Begin (1951:378) indicated that if "the Jewish People" accepted the partition, his organization would not oppose it. On the left, Hashomer Hatzair, which in June 1947 had still supported the bi-national solution, on October 15 ("Decisions of Party Headquarters") accepted the majority recommendation of the UN commission.

ment of optimal territorial conditions rather than on the basic question. Thus the political struggle revolved around (1) opposition to the conversion of Jerusalem into an international regime (surrounded by Arab territory) and (2) the inclusion of the Western Galilee, and eventually the northwestern Negev, in the boundaries of the Jewish state.

However, the implementation of the Partition Plan involved not only the loss of territory perceived as an integral part of the Jewish state, but also the loss of thirty Jewish settlements outside its boundaries,* and the absorption of a relatively large Arab population (approximately 50 percent of the total population on the territory allocated to the Jewish state). If one adds to this the doubts concerning the relative capability of the Jewish collectivity to endure a general struggle, then the price of accepting the Partition Plan's "package deal" was too high. This was especially true because the Arab side did not view the implementation of partition as a concession on the part of the Jews, but only as a tactical step in a total conflict whose basic aim was "all or nothing."

Until 1937, the process of territorial accumulation (and its complementary process in power accumulation — the increase in the relative rate of the population) was perceived both as a necessary condition and a principal means of achieving sovereignty. With the appearance of partition proposals, the process of territorial accumulation was seen as in conflict with the possibility of achieving sovereignty. This confrontation between sovereignty and the continuation of the process of territorial accumulation was the result of two distinct factors, each having special significance for the act of sovereignty achievement. From the purely territorial point of view, the acceptance of the Partition Plan would terminate the process of accumulation, but, on the other hand, this termination would result in consolidation and the granting of a final seal to the "lion's share" of the accumulated territory. Between the years 1937-42, there were intense disputes within the Yishuv and the Zionist movement over whether or not the exchange of the potential for further territorial accumulation for

---

*The Arab annexation of those settlements outside the future Jewish state's borders raised serious issues for the Jewish collectivity: whether or not to abandon these settlements (and if so, when — on the assumption that they might be a bargaining card for a reciprocal transfer of population); whether or not to defend them in case of attack (and if so, whether this should be an active or passive defense). For further discussion, see Chapter 5.

sovereignty was worthwhile—or even possible. However, by 1947 the controversy was no longer acute, and the order of priorities was clearer and more widely agreed upon.*

This change in perspective was due to a number of factors. First, while the Holocaust, by destroying a large proportion of European Jewry, had removed a potential reservoir of millions of Jews who, in the course of time, might have migrated to Israel, it had at the same time left hundreds of thousands of displaced Jews wandering throughout Europe who were an immediate potential for migration. It had also created a terrible trauma and an urgent need for a suitable locale wherein the remaining refugees could be absorbed and rehabilitated. The migration of these refugees would improve the demographic power balance for the Jewish side in Palestine; it was, however, doubtful that this was possible within the framework of the Mandate, which also had to consider the interests of the Arab side. The existence of an immediately transferable refugee population produced a sense of a one-time situation for immediate improvement of power relations to the advantage of the Jews. On the other hand, the liquidation of the main European reservoir for immigration would, in the long run, considerably decrease the Jewish collectivity's chances of survival.

Second, the Jewish collectivity had accumulated political power, military strength, and greater self-confidence while its Arab opponent had weakened both relatively and absolutely. Thus time functioned more and more to the advantage of the Jewish side.[†] When the Arab

*In fact there were some who doubted the existence of other alternatives. At the 20th Zionist Congress (December 1940), Ben-Gurion claimed that there was no doubt that the British would not extend the Mandate: "England and the Arabs are attempting to find a final solution to the question of Palestine, and rejection of the solution is not in our control" (Ben-Gurion, 1950:146). In Ben-Gurion's opinion only two possibilities existed: either Arab Palestine would achieve sovereignty (comparable to the Kingdom of Trans-Jordan) within a short time span, or there would be a future division of the country's area between the Jews and the Arabs more acceptable to the Jews.

[†]The increased perception of time as functioning to the Jewish side's advantage appears to have been one of the reasons why the Arabs desired immediate military confrontation. As early as the mid-1930s, the increased rate of growth of Jewish power made the Arabs begin to perceive that it was not enough for them to maintain the status quo to protect their interests. A change in this perception was among the causes of the Arab revolt of 1936-39, which "was a racial, religious, colonial, familial and peasant struggle intermingled" (Bowden, 1975: 147).

revolt of 1936-39 was suppressed by the British Mandate government, the whole Arab structure suffered severely (though it partly recovered during the war), and its social structure underwent an accelerated process of disintegration, mainly as a result of the liquidation of part of the Arab national leadership. On the other hand, many members of the Jewish community had acquired military experience through participation in the war or having received professional military training within the country. Although the relative rate of increase of the Jewish population had slowed temporarily, an immediate Jewish migration was expected at a rate that was likely to change entirely the demographic balance between the two sides. In addition, the international political constellation which prevailed following World War II appeared to be favorable to the Jewish side—that is, the vastly increased influence of the United States and the surprising change in the Soviet Union's position on Zionism. But above all, it seemed that the "world's conscience" about the Holocaust could be exploited, and this guilty conscience could be translated into political terms of recognition of the Jewish people's right to a state of their own. Furthermore, the Hagana, which had developed during the years of Arab rebellion from a federated alliance of local competing organizations into an organization capable of effective activity on a national scale, sensed that it would be able to contend with an armed Arab attack even if the local Arabs were to receive aid from the surrounding Arab nations (*Hagana*, 1973:984).

Third, the territorial division in the partition proposal of the United Nations commission was perceived by most elements of the Jewish collectivity as "fair" (in comparison to the Peel Commission's proposal, for example) and as the best that could be achieved under the circumstances. On 13 December 1947, at an assembly at the Mapai headquarters, Ben-Gurion expressed his view of the proposed borders:

> I do not know of a greater achievement than this [*the partition*] in all the long history of the Jewish people, since it became a nation. Most of the valleys of western Palestine and most of the Mediterranean coastline have been returned to us—this possession is priceless; along with most of the southern desert, a large and important part of the water sources in the north were returned ... and this raises unique possibilities for large-scale Jewish settlement.

The Negev was seen by Ben-Gurion as a territorial reservoir (or a secondary frontier) of the future state. He commented further:

> The new State of Israel will extend from Dan to Eilat, approximately one hundred kilometers south of Beer Sheba, and will include the area between two seacoasts. . . . This nation will not require the Suez Canal so that its vessels may reach countries of the west and the east. . . . The bay of Eilat is the principal compensation for the decrease in land area, and if we will know how to maintain this great and almost limitless blessing, then its potential is vast.

He argued in advance with those "mourning over the country's 'wholeness '":

> The country was "whole" only under the rule of foreign conquerors, who ruled both this country and other neighboring countries. The country's borders under Jewish rule constantly changed—beginning with the Judges and ending with Bar-Kochba. There aren't many concepts more ambiguous and vague than the concept of "historical" borders. From the beginning, the borders of Jewish independence retreated and advanced in accordance with the ceaseless changes in policy. . . . In addition, the Jewish settlement area was neither permanent nor consistent, but rather expanded and contracted from era to era (1950).

A note of pragmatism can be detected in Ben-Gurion's acceptance (similar to his treatment of other political issues) of the territorial division proposed under the Partition Plan. This acceptance was a result, on the one hand, of the existing power relationships, and on the other, of a hint of the possibility of other borders in the future, which had prompted Ben-Gurion's support of the Partition Plan of 1937. Thus his acceptance of the proposal at the time was not to be seen as irreversible, because the power relations and historical conditions were liable to change.

Fourth, the partition proposal was supported by at least part of the Jewish collectivity in the hope that it would bring an end to the conflict between the Jews and Arabs, or at least to a marked de-escalation of the conflict (see, for example, Weizmann, 1954:440-41), not only because the Partition Plan appeared to be a fair or "moral" solution, but also because satisfying the two sides' national aspirations was likely to institutionalize relations between them and decrease the level of mutual distrust.

What would the Arab communities gain by accepting the Partition Plan? First, they would achieve sovereignty over part (approximately 45 percent) of the territory they claimed; second, they would be able to give expression to their collective identity; third, they could stop their Jewish opponents' territorial accumulation.* However, in a situation where the Arab side believed that it still had more than a fair chance to win "everything," these gains apparently did not seem sufficient, given the circumstances.

Nonetheless, the Jewish hope that partition would de-escalate the conflict was apparently not without basis. This did occur somewhat later, following the war of 1948/49, when the territory allocated to the Palestinian-Arab nation was divided between Israel and the Hashemite Kingdom of Jordan. Under these circumstances, a common Israeli-Jordanian interest developed to dissolve the Palestinian-Arab identity for the establishment and preservation of a territorial and political status quo.†

The Jewish collectivity's acceptance of a territorial division was the turning point in the Arab-Jewish conflict. If the conflict were to continue, the pattern of at least four of its components would change:

1. The sides would confront one another without a "mediator" (the Mandatory Government). The existence of a mediator had, to a great extent, limited the conflict, and without the "third side," the conflict would either de-escalate (as had been hoped for previously) or it would escalate into a total conflict—from the standpoint of the two sides' goals (both seeking to attain all the disputed territory) and/or from the standpoint of the means invested (the use by both of all the resources available to them).

2. The potential of either side to control the other would drastically decrease in the absence of a mediator.** In conjunction with this, the opportunity for foreign policy maneuvering would increase.

*This was the main focus of Arab anxiety, and even the Jews' acceptance of the Partition Plan could not alleviate it. According to the Arabs' perception, as long as the Jewish state remained Zionist— that is, as long as its goal continued to be increased Jewish immigration—it would inevitably seek territorial expansion.

†According to the evidence of John and David Kimche (1960), if King Abdallah had not been murdered "the peace treaty between Israel and the Kingdom of Jordan would have been signed."

**This assumes that the conflict between the Jewish and Arab collectivities focuses on the territory defined in the Partition Plan. The intervention of the surrounding Arab countries is not included in this discussion.

3. At least potentially, there would be an increase in the level of control (ownership and presence) over areas within the partition territory not constituting part of the collectivity, or in which its presence was weak.

4. The achievement of sovereignty should focus the conflict outward (between nations and not between internal ethnic groups), but because of the demographic composition of the Jewish state (if the plan were executed as stipulated), the conflict would remain internal, even though the power relations would have changed to the Jewish side's advantage. In accordance with the plan, Arabs would still inhabit the Jewish area, and would presumably still remain on the other side of the conflict while controlling essential areas of the Jewish sovereign territory. If the Arabs were to settle in most of these areas, then an unbalanced situation, from the point of view of the Jewish-Zionist territorial orientation, would develop. Thus the focus of an internal conflict (if we regard the remaining Arabs as citizens, or at least as residents of the Jewish state) would persist (see Zureik, 1979; Lustick, 1980; Landau, 1969; Kimmerling, 1977).

The Partition Plan was not executed, and as a result of the 1947/48 War a different reality, both from a political and territorial point of view, was created (see Chapter 5), but some of the components analyzed in this section continued to exist within this new reality.

SUMMARY

The different patterns of ownership of the Arab lands in different regions of Palestine in essence divided the country into two regions: (1) regions with low frontierity, or, in other words, areas where, for a great deal of money, it was possible to buy large tracts of land—primarily in the valleys and the coastal plain; (2) regions with zero frontierity, where the patterns of land ownership and the Arab social structure almost entirely prevented the Jews from acquiring land—primarily in the central hilly regions, where it was almost impossible to convert money to land.

The land was bought by the Jews to establish upon it rural or urban settlements which would demonstrate Jewish presence. But there were occasions when the pattern was reversed because of the special context of relationships created between the settler population and the local residents, on the one hand, and the settlers and the government, on the other; then settlements were established in order to strengthen the control over territory. During the time preceding sovereignty, the combination of ownership and presence served as the functional equivalent of sovereignty.

Until the time just before sovereignty, a considerable quantity of land was bought, which permitted the foundation of the territorial base for the establishment of a Jewish social and political entity in Zion, but these acquisitions were only a small part of the area of the original Zionist strivings. Purely by buying land, the Jews managed to acquire control over about 6 percent of the territory of Mandatory Palestine, or about 10 percent of the area suitable for cultivation based on the technology of the era (see map, p. 238).

In the second half of the 1940s, after a hiatus of ten years caused by World War II, the Jews had to choose between two alternatives: (1) to continue with territorial accumulation by buying land and demonstrating presence, or (2) to acquire sovereignty and forego any additional accumulation of land, completely closing the artificial frontier that had existed at least potentially.

Chapter Three

INSTITUTIONS AND SYMBOLS

In order to open the maximum amount of land to Jewish hands by financial and political means, or, in other words, to create an artificial frontier, it was not enough to have the means and formulate a land policy. In addition, institutional tools were needed to implement the policy and allocate the resources. The necessary roles, organizations, and institutions were developed almost at the beginning of the Jewish settlement in Palestine, and these became more sophisticated over time. More than that—these institutions began to occupy a central place in the social structure of the Jewish society in Palestine, and afterwards in Israel, and some of them became part of the symbols and values of the Zionist social system.

Here we come to an argument similar in form to Turner's thesis: the need to create an artificial frontier caused the formation of certain social structures which influenced the character of the whole society. However, as will be seen in this chapter and in Chapter 7, the results of territorial scarcity are not the same in all areas.

First, we will examine the organizations and institutions established to deal with the acquisition of land for the building of the Jewish nation. These included:

A. Entrepreneurs: Jews and Arabs who acted as go-betweens in land sales or bought lands temporarily and then sold them with economic profit their primary motivation. They were stigmatized by both sides and were referred to as "speculators."*

B. Semi-professional land purchasers and intermediaries (usually Jews) who bought land over prolonged periods, usually in the name of organizations and institutions, but who enjoyed independent status. The purchase of land was only one component of the many roles they played as go-betweens between Jewish and Arab sectors. They

---

*"A special stratum of charlatans is created who live on the money they illicitly obtain from Jews in connection with land sale" (*Haaretz*, 3/15/36).

66

were known as "experts," specializing in problems which arose in contacts between the sectors. They were familiar with the language and customs, and had personal ties with both elite groups and individuals in the Arab community. Such ties were essential for the performance of their roles as land purchasers, because land sales were censured by Arab society and were sometimes regarded as illegal. Personal contacts also made the defreezing of land easier by removing national and political components from the transactions: the land transfer was to a specific person.

C. Organizations or societies for land purchase for specific agricultural or urban settlements for the achievement of particular goals (see Doukhan-Landau, 1979).

D. The Jewish National Fund, which even in a situation without sovereignty could transfer lands, in exchange for capital, to the ownership of the Jewish people, which made the land totally frozen and assigned national significance. The lands owned by the JNF could be rented (only to Jews) but not sold. The JNF solicited capital for land purchases from the Jewish communities in the Diaspora—not only to obtain capital but also to enlist the active participation of the Jewish world community in the process of land redemption in Palestine. The Arabs tried to set up a similar institution—that is, a type of bank which would freeze lands under national Arab ownership, or at least prevent the sale of Arab land to Jews. The JNF also sought to prevent the return of lands to Arabs which had already been purchased by Jews, which was sometimes given precedence over new purchases of land from Arabs.

E. Urban settlement points, which contributed to conflict management in the Palestinian context by demonstrating Jewish presence on the land.

The "speculators" (both Jews and Arabs), the professional "land redeemers," the special organizations, and the JNF complemented each other (even when they were competing for the same land), causing a rise in land prices which brought about the defreezing of some of the lands in Arab hands and their transfer to Jewish ownership.

Arab land brokers ("profiteers") appeared because of the existence of a dual land market, which arose as a result of legal restrictions on land sales and the unwillingness of Arabs to sell lands directly to Jews. This added a political price which made the transactions more profitable, in much the same way as the "Prohibition Law" in the United States during the 1920s. Granovsky, long-time head of the financial department and later Director of the JNF, expressed this in response to the White Paper (Great Britain, 1939): "A total prohibition of land purchase seems to us to be impossible for the simple reason that this is in direct contradiction of the most basic economic laws" (1940:17).*

In the Arab sector, fairly strong actions—albeit sporadic—were taken against the profiteers. These actions became more frequent in 1935. For example, *Haaretz* notes that in Beersheba a series of meetings were held by the Bedouins, organized by the Mufti's party, at which those present "swore not to sell lands to Jews and not to speculate in land sale." At another meeting,

> it was decided to sign a memorandum to the High Commissioner to the effect that he should dismiss the sheiks who violated their oath and sold land, to send a delegation to the Bedouin in order to influence them not to sell land and to organize a delegation of 40 horsemen that would circulate in the Bedouin camps to combat speculation and Zionism and to encourage the Bedouin to boycott the speculators (5/8/35).

The Arab press attempted to join in the struggle against the "speculators." It published lists of Arabs who sold land to Jews as well as of those who had sworn never to sell their lands—"neither they nor their sons—until the end of time." It also published names of "Jewish speculators" so that the Arab public would beware of them. (Similar methods were employed against speculators in the Yishuv.)

There were four bursts of land speculation which were connected with *aliyot* (waves of immigration—see Glossary) and/or economic prosperity. Since land was such a central resource, and the Arab-Jewish conflict made it artificially scarce, it is not surprising that at the beginning of the Jewish settlement in the 1890s, Palestine had "six societies [*for land purchase*] in addition to a large camp of small speculators which included shoemakers and tailors who had left their trade for this business, and various swindlers" ("Ahad Haam," 1902:

*Some Arabs tried to sell land *within* the Arab sector. For example, a landowner in Wadi Kavni published a notice in *El-Islamia* to the effect that the Jews were trying to purchase his lands, and that his situation forced him to sell part of his lands in order to save the rest. He asked Arabs to buy his lands (*Haaretz*, 8/9/35).

33). The Fourth Aliya (see Glossary) brought with it a second boom in land trade which, according to Granovsky, had two results:

> Economically, land values became inflated and the purchase of land was made difficult by the senseless competition of Jews with one another; morally the consequences could be seen in the corrupt methods of speculators who shamelessly cut each other's throat competing with one another while they carried on their shady dealings under the name of "Geulath Haaretz" [*redeeming the soil of the Holy Land*] without the slightest care for our primary national interests (1940a:47).

The third boom was between 1933-1935, while the fourth occurred in the midst of World War II (1940-1941). Because, in certain periods, even "shoemakers and tailors" became land brokers, and because of the "senseless" and unethical competition among the Jews noted by Granovsky, the Arab feeling was strengthened that the Jews "can buy everything," and that indeed everything would be bought by Jews if the Arabs did not react appropriately. At the same time, it seems to have had an opposite effect—by raising the land prices, it brought about the defreezing of the land (see Paz, 1963).

Between the speculators and profiteers on the one hand, and the professional land redeemers onthe other, there was a volunteer group of intermediaries linking the Jewish organizations and individuals with the Arab landowners. Some were respected individuals from among the old Sephardic Yishuv, well-versed in the local customs and having strong ties with the Arabs. Examples of this type of middleman, through whom both Jewish Colonization Associations (JCA) and the Hakhsharat Hayishuv society bought lands (see below), were Albert Antebi, the principal of the vocational school of the Alliance School (Ruppin, 1971:123), the Denin brothers, and Joseph Srumza, a lawyer (for details of their activities, see Ashbel, 1970). Another was the agronomist Hayim Margalit Kalvarisky, who was in charge of extensive land purchases as the JCA representative in the Lower Galilee. He instituted damage payments for tenants forced to leave the land, attempted to establish schools in Arab villages, sent armed "land conquerors" to the Beit Gan lands (*Hagana*, 1954:110), was active in Brit Shalom, and initiated meetings between Yishuv leaders and Arab leaders, etc.

Joseph Weitz (1951:553-74) presents the biographies of thirty persons who in various periods purchased lands or settled land disputes. Most seemed to have done this in addition to their activities in other spheres (such as law), but some were permanently employed in specific areas by the JNF and made part of their living in this way. Some began as land purchasers for private companies and others for PICA, and when they proved successful, were asked by the JNF to work for it.*

The semi-professional land redeemers had a double entrepreneurial role: not only the acquisition of Arab lands for sale, but also the solicitation of Jewish capital for the purchase of the lands, both from institutions and organizations and from private investors or philanthropists. This second role was often as difficult as that of obtaining the Arabs' consent to sell land because (a) except during periods of unusual prosperity, there was no great demand for land among private investors, (b) the purchase of land was not always given top priority by Zionist organizations, (c) economic resources were often not available at the time land was offered for sale, and (d) potential buyers were dubious about the value of the purchase of specific lands because of their location. Thus Arthur Ruppin, from 1908 the director of the Palestine Office of the World Zionist Organization, had to conduct promotional campaigns in various countries in order to interest Zionist organizations or wealthy individual Jews in specific purchases (Ruppin, 1968:114-39). Similarly, when the opportunity to purchase the Hefer Valley arose, "the President of the Jewish National Fund, M. Ussishkin, packed his bags and sailed off to Canada to arouse the dispersed Jews and encourage them to contribute to the redemption of this valley" (Weitz, 1970:58).

The most important land redeemer was Yehoshua Hankin, who was responsible for almost half the lands purchased by Jews in Palestine—about 600,000 dunams (Ashbel, 1970:258). He began his activity at the age of twenty-five with the purchase of the Duran lands (Rehovot), and he continued to purchase land in the Jezreel Valley without the power of attorney of the JCA, which refused to ratify the contract. As Ruppin reports it:

---

*It is specifically noted that some of these were "well-versed in Arabic and in the customs of the neighbors," but only Srumza and Shlomo Attia originated in the old Sephardic Yishuv.

When the JCA refused to ratify the deal, it placed Hankin in a very difficult position, as he did not want to break his word to the Arab client. He then came to me as director of the PLDC and offered the land to us. The PLDC had very little capital and was not prepared for such offers. . . . But I saw the importance of gaining a foothold in the Jezreel Valley, and after tremendous difficulties I succeeded in raising the necessary sum of money. . . . It was still necessary to overcome the objections of the Turkish authorities to the agreement. . . . Hankin had to appeal to his friends in Constantinople, who finally succeeded in having the agreement registered by the competent minister. Thus the first Jewish position in the Jezreel Valley was secured. After this first purchase, Hankin continued to work for the PLDC. . . . Between 1910 and 1940, this collaboration was responsible for most of the agreements involving the purchase of large areas of land for the JNF and for private individuals (1971:114-15).

Hankin continued to operate independently in the service of the PLDC, with his land purchases often undertaken without prior approval; as Bein puts it: "He was a man with great plans for settlement, and in his purchases he forced some of these plans on the Zionist Federation, against its will" (1970:59).*

From the end of the nineteenth century, many land purchase and settlement societies were active in Palestine, with most attached to specific countries or cities in the Diaspora (see Doukhan-Landau, 1979:172-245). One example was the Manuha and Nahala Society, founded in Warsaw in 1890, which purchased half of the Duran lands from Hankin and prepared them for settlement by its members.

The people from Manuha and Nahala began coming to Rehovot when their vineyards had already passed the first stages of cultivation and had borne fruit, so that the "head of the household" and his family could be supported. Some of the Society's members who had bought lands never reached Palestine (Roey, 1970:151).

*For example, in May 1919, Hankin presented a detailed program to the Committee of Delegates for the settlement of one million persons on an area of four million dunams within ten years. Of the total amount of land, 2.6 million dunams would be bought "from the land now cultivated by Arab fellaheen, whether belonging to them or rented by them from large landowners" (King, 1941:20-22).

Another of these societies was Kehiliat Zion, founded in New York in 1914 by the American Zionist Foundation, which began to operate in Palestine at the end of World War I. Kehiliat Zion and its subsidiary, Meshek, together with the Society for the Haifa Bay Area, purchased very extensive tracts and established an urban center in the Jezreel Valley. The activities of Kehiliat Zion reached their peak in the boom years of the Fourth Aliya. At that time it purchased almost 67,000 dunams of land and served as broker for an additional 36,000 dunams, while the Meshek society purchased more than 31,000 dunams. But with the end of the wave of immigration, which stopped the flow of private capital and caused a crisis in the Palestine economy (see Carmi and Rosenfeld, 1971), Kehiliat Zion and the other societies connected with it failed. Most of their lands were transferred to the Jewish National Fund to ensure that they would not be returned to their former Arab owners.

Another pattern of land purchase was the "estate" pattern, based on the same principles as the Manuha and Nahala Society—that is, Jews in the Diaspora were given an opportunity to buy land in a predetermined location which was made economically profitable even before the owner of the estate settled on the land. This pattern was not very successful primarily because the international instability did not permit a steady flow of capital from the owners to the estates (Bein, 1970:270).

Nevertheless, most of the capital imported into Palestine over the years was private capital brought in by the new immigrants or the various investment societies. Thus, of a total of £P95 million invested in Palestine between 1918 and 1937, £P75 million (79 percent) was private capital (Olitzur, 1939:246), and in the decisive years of Jewish demographic and economic growth between 1932 and 1937, of more than £P39 million of private capital, £P2,717,000 (6.9 percent) was invested in land purchases from Arabs. During the same period, the JNF invested more than £P1.5 million in land purchases both from Arab and Jewish owners (132).

Baron de Rothschild's various settlement projects represented a "cluster" of activities, with land purchase being only one component.*

*In the period 1883-1900, Rothschild took upon himself, through a handful of subordinates, the direct administration of his colonies in Palestine, investing £1.6 million in their development. When this system failed, he transferred his colonies (plus a sum of £600,000) to the management of the Jewish Colonization

These activities did not have any declared political purposes, but since to a large degree they overlapped the activities of Hovevei Zion and later of the Zionists, and from the standpoint of the Arabs had identical results (land purchases, expulsion of Arab tenants, encouragement of Jewish immigration, etc.), they encountered the same resistance as the Zionists from the Palestinian inhabitants. On the other hand, it was possible these settlements might fit more easily in the Arab environment and create less friction with it. First, there was no predominance of the Jewish national interest in these settlements ("Jewish labor" and "the Jewish guard" were not established until later as a result of pressure from the left—see Chapter 4). Second, there was a partial overlapping of economic interests of Jews and Arabs, deriving from the partially "inclusive" frontier approach of Rothschild (see Chapter 1). Third, because of the institutional structure of Rothschild's PICA and the relatively abundant resources at its disposal, it could respond to Arab demands with greater flexibility. It is not surprising that it was Kalvarisky, in his role as the representative of the JCA, who instituted a dual price for lands when he both paid the owners and awarded damage payments to the tenants. Possibly for this reason Hope-Simpson (1930:41) notes that "excellent neighbourly relations" prevailed between the PICA colonists and the Arabs, stemming from a "policy of friendship and reconciliation" of the PICA, in contrast with the policy of the Zionist institutions.

The declared goal of the Jewish National Fund was to purchase maximum territory in Palestine in order to establish national ownership of the land which would be nontransferable. The role of the JNF was to solicit contributions from world Jewry, some of which would serve as a permanent, interest-yielding fund, with all of the income (regular income and interest) devoted to the purchase of lands in

Association (JCA)—a society established by Baron Hirsch for encouraging the settlement of persecuted Jews outside Europe. Although their management was now in JCA hands, Rothschild continued to support the colonies and encouraged land purchases for further settlement; by the end of World War I, he had transferred another £1 million to Palestine for these purposes. In 1924 there was another institutional reorganization, and all the Baron's projects in Palestine were united under the control of Palestine Jewish Colonization Association (PICA). The PICA continued to purchase lands for settlement, and in these settlements, which primarily developed citrus groves, Rothschild invested about £5.5 million—at least twice or three times as much as the settlers themselves invested.

Palestine. At the beginning the plans were very ambitious,* but in practice little was done. The plan was to collect a sum of about £250,000 (half of which would be in the interest-earning fund), and only then to begin intensively purchasing land. Despite the initial enthusiasm, by 1908 only £60,900 had been collected, and by 1917 £380,000, with the net income (after subtracting administrative expenses and losses caused by the war) about £259,300 after fifteen years.†

The original aims of the JNF were temporarily forgotten with the establishment of the "Palestinian Office"—the operational arm of the Zionist Federation in Palestine—in 1908. At that time the JNF funds were made available for the activities of the Office, including several land purchases (e.g., Beit Arif, Ben Shemen, Hulda, Chitin, Dlika, Kinneret, and Um June--Degania), but most of the resources were allocated for support of the immigrants of the Second Aliya (see Glossary) and the Yemenite Aliya, and for the construction of homes for the workers who had just arrived. Two turning points signalled the return of the JNF to its original roles: (a) some of the left-wing sector embarked upon independent settlement in the wake of the failure of the workers who came with the Second Aliya to become integrated as a "class" in the "capitalist" economy of the *moshavot* (settlements of smallholders based on private enterprise—see Glossary); (b) at a convention of the Zionist Federation in London in July 1920, a penetrating discussion of the roles of the JNF developed, and it was decided to draw a clear-cut distinction between the function of land purchase and the roles connected with aiding settlement. As a result, Keren Hayesod was established as the major instrument of Zionist settlement, while the activity of the JNF was restricted to land purchase and, to a certain extent, afforestation and land cultivation. In 1922 the central office of the JNF was transferred from The Hague to Jerusalem (and to the directorship of Ussishkin). The estab-

---

*The decision to establish the fund was made at the Fifth Zionist Congress (1901 at Basle) under Herzl's pressure. There was intense opposition from some of the delegates because of difficulties in defining the ownership of the fund to be established and debates as to its decision-making powers.

†By the time the land registry offices were reopened after the war (October 1920), the JNF had purchased only 24,940 dunams (Granovsky, 1940:90). (All other data concerning the JNF in this section are from Olitzur [1939] unless specifically stated otherwise.)

lishment of Keren Hayesod released resources of the JNF for land purchase, but in the early years damaged the JNF's ability to solicit funds because it was perceived as an underground organization. But after a three-year period of decline, there was an increase in the JNF's income and the flow of funds to Palestine for the purpose of land purchase. From its establishment until 1937, the net income of the JNF was over £P3.5 million, of which the Jews of Palestine provided 5.2 percent. (It is interesting to note that there were significant jumps in contributions to the JNF during the periods of the Arab riots; from 1928 to 1930 there was an increase of about 40 percent, and around 1939 an increase of about 30 percent.) The JNF invested about 70 percent of its resources in the purchase of agricultural lands and 7.5 percent in urban lands, while allotting only 1.4 percent to the organizational and political activities of the Zionist Federation. One of the criticisms of the JNF was that the freezing of lands under its ownership undermined efforts to expand Jewish property in Palestine. If the JNF could not resell its lands—not even to Jews—it had no return capital, but was solely dependent on contributions. (The JNF collected rents, but these were very small sums.) It was argued that an economic orientation to the land or private ownership of land

> is more conducive to rapid economic development; as to national land, there are difficulties in purchase and sale and in transference from one person to another; the national land cannot yield the same profits as can private land, and in the final analysis we must base our undertaking only on contributions (Ussishkin, 1929:9).

It is noteworthy that a large part of the JNF contributions were made up of small contributions from Jews throughout the world. In 1937 there were about 700,000 "blue boxes" scattered in private homes in Palestine and around the world.* Contributions to the JNF rapidly acquired significance as a sign of both active and symbolic participation in the Jewish-Zionist community. The blue box was more of a determinant of the community's boundaries than was the

---

*"By the middle of 1939, the income from the blue boxes amounted to about 950,000 pounds—that is, more than from any other means of soliciting funds" (Pollack, 1940:85). The boxes also proved to be the most *stable* means of collecting contributions—the income from them was not affected by economic or political crises.

"shekel"—the annual contribution to the Zionist Federation—which involved a greater commitment and was more expensive. Thus a linkage was formed between land redemption, which was a central component in the Jewish-Arab conflict, and participation in the Zionist community, both in Palestine and in the Diaspora. This linkage was not highly visible, and it is difficult to estimate its significance, but it was part of a three-part process: (a) taking the conflictual sting out of as many aspects of the Jewish-Arab conflict as possible and defining them in "positive" terms unconnected with Jewish-Arab relations; (b) raising these aspects to the symbolic level; (c) making use of the mechanisms of socialization and social control to implant these symbols. Thus Ussishkin defined the role of collecting funds for the JNF by schoolchildren as follows:

> The penny which the child contributes or solicits for the redemption of the land is not significant in and of itself. The JNF will not be built up on it, nor can we redeem all of Palestine with it. But this penny is significant as an educational element. It is not the child who contributes to the JNF, but rather the JNF which contributes to him. The JNF provides him with a lofty ideal for all of his life. . . . When he goes to bed at night, the child must not only think "what did I learn today," but also—"what have I done today for the redemption of the nation and the redemption of the land on which this nation will rise" (1929).

In addition, the existence of the entire collectivity depended on the JNF, whose role was not only to purchase land but also to freeze it and give it primordial significance:

> If we want to be 100 percent certain that the land redeemed by Jews will always remain in their hands—then only the JNF can grant this guarantee. There is no saint in Palestine on whom we can depend never, not even in times of speculation, to sell his land. This is an everyday practice. There is only one sure way [of preventing this] : As long as the nation exists—and I believe it will exist forever—the land must continue to be the nation's property. In order to ensure the preservation of this important principle, we must guard the existence of the JNF (1933:4-5).

Thus the attempt was made to endow the JNF's activities with symbolic meaning on the national level and to make contributions toward these activities forms of participation in the collectivity.* But through an institution charged with the freezing and nationalization of the land it was not possible to develop a flexible land policy. Thus it is not surprising that the Zionist Federation established a separate organization—the Palestine Land Development Company.

The PLDC was founded in 1908, simultaneously with the Palestine Office, "as an instrument for the performance of preliminary settlement activities, e.g., land purchases, both for the JNF and for *private companies and individuals*" (Ashbel, 1970:13; emphasis added). From that time on, the JNF purchased all its land through the PLDC (Bein, 1970:59), which purchased almost one-half of the land bought by Jews. It was necessary that an instrument with an economic orientation mediate the processes of land purchase for an institution with national goals such as the JNF.

While the Yishuv system allocated resources, including capital, manpower, and organizations, for dealing with land acquisition, it was not always the leading challenge for the Jewish community (and the Zionist movement). As a result of the unexpectedly slow pace of Jewish immigration to Palestine, and the urban character of most of the aliyot, land was generally available. When the British left, only about 7 percent of Palestine's lands were under Jewish ownership.

In 1934, at a meeting of the Zionist Federation Committee, Berl Katzenelson complained of the "unfortunate land situation" (Ben-Gurion, 1972:60)—a situation created not only as a result of internal struggles within the Yishuv, which impoverished the JNF, but also because, in Katzenelson's opinion:

The Zionist movement as a whole does not yet sense the essential quality of this matter [*land purchase*], and while people speak in grandiose terms of "policy," does little in terms of land;

*Several other means of soliciting funds, besides the blue box, were of a similar nature. One was the Child's Book, where "the idea which underlay its establishment was to link the children, from earliest childhood, to the land of their fathers with a symbolic bond. The Child's Book, in time must become the genealogy book of Jewish children in all countries" (Pollack, 1940:87-88). Another was the Golden Book, which sought to establish a membership of "prominent and active personalities in Zionism or Judaism." Another was JNF stamps, which symbolized the quasi-sovereignty the "organized Yishuv" aimed at—internally (as taxation) and externally (as representation)—and were used to help define the collectivity's boundaries.

within the Zionist camp, we have not developed the sensitivity to the land. Who works for the JNF? Schoolchildren. If you try and count, you won't find ten Zionists who think of the land. I am not referring to land for the sake of personal profit, but rather to the all-important question: How can the Jewish people's land be enlarged for purposes of settlement? (Ben-Gurion, 1972:60).

What was probably even more detrimental to the land purchase effort was the stigmatizing of private initiative. The resources at the disposal of the national institutions were limited, and the normative barriers raised to the private sector's participation in land investment limited the resources the system could allocate to the purchase of land even more. In the London Convention of 1920, the left attempted to block any purchase of private land in Palestine and to convert the JNF into the exclusive instrument for the allocation of land. Among other things, the "workers" demanded that

> The purchase of land in Palestine will be concentrated only in the hands of thc Jewish National Fund, so that it may remain the permanent property of the people of Israel. Urban and agricultural settlement will be undertaken only on the land of the Jewish National Fund and in complete accordance with its principles [*i.e., Jewish labor*].

> Our financial institutions must support only those urban or agricultural settlements on Jewish National Fund lands or those granted to it.*

In other words, they demanded that the land resources of the Zionist movement be allocated to the leftist components of the system.

SETTLEMENTS AS ENDS AND MEANS

In the context of the Jewish-Arab conflict, settlement and land purchase were complementary activities: in order for the Jews to establish and maintain settlements, it was necessary to acquire land, while at later stages settlement was seen as essential to maintain land. From its very beginning, Jewish settlement aroused intense hostility among Arabs—not only among the fellaheen or Bedouins who lost

---

*Proceedings of London Meeting. This was the first meaningful international Zionist meeting after World War I (also called "the little congress").

the opportunity to cultivate the land, but also throughout the general Arab community.

This study does not analyze the reasons for Arab hostility, but it may be worthwhile to list some of the possible causes: (1) the traditional xenophobia of underdeveloped areas, whereby any contact with foreigners arouses anxiety; (2) cultural differences between Jews and Arabs, one of the most prominent being the Arab perception of immoral behavior among the Jews (e.g., in the free relations between the sexes, even among traditional Jews); (3) jealousy aroused by the relative prosperity of the Jewish colonies; (4) attitudes developed under Ottoman rule which encouraged theft, violence, and patterns of revenge; (5) the emergence of Arab national consciousness.

Mandel (1965:39-41) sees two stages in the relations between the moshavot and the Arab environment during the period of the Ottoman rule: a first stage of hostility and recurrent attempts to create disturbances, and a second stage of acceptance of the Jewish neighbors and reconciliation with them, primarily because of the economic benefits the Arabs derived from the moshavot—both from work on their lands and from trade with them.

However, the first settlements, although directed at creating a nucleus for building a nation, were not guided by long-range strategic considerations concerning the existence of the Arab population within and around the boundaries desired for the collectivity. They dealt with the immediate problems aroused by clashes with the Arabs, without being aware that the process of settlement was an integral part of the management of the conflict.

In contrast to the farmers in the moshavot, the labor settlements stemmed from, among other things, a failure to cope with the problem of Arab labor (see Chapter 4). The processes of settlement and of becoming farmers were antithetical to the ideas which guided most of the members of the Second Aliya, who sought to establish a proletarian class in Palestine. At the fourth general meeting of the Hapoel Hatzair party in 1909, after an ideological polemic between Y. Vitkin, who supported the labor sector's settlement, and Y. Aaronovitz, who expressed the "party line" against such settlement, a clear-cut decision was reached opposing settlement: "Among Poalei Zion as well, during the early years there prevailed the consciousness that the workers' role was to fight the class war in the economy that private capital would create in Palestine" (Even-Shoshan, 1963:125). The debate took various forms among the labor public. In their zeal for the proletarian way of life and the triumph of labor, and because they were against the status quo in the moshavot and the cities, they viewed all public aid, support, or *halukka* (charity doled out to the old Yishuv) in a negative light, and declined to accept such assistance. Thus they opposed the JNF's efforts to build workers' housing in the moshava. A well-known case was the Petah Tikva workers' boycott of the construction of the workers' clubhouse in the moshava: "Some did not set foot on its threshold for years" (Braslavsky, 1966:103). The argument against workers' settlement was also couched in terms of Jewish-Arab relations: as a result of the scarcity of Jewish workers, self-labor settlements would leave the moshavot at the mercy of the "foreigners" (i.e., the Arabs). Jewish labor was necessary not only for particularistic class interests, but also for the national interest; Jewish laborers staying in the moshavot meant the "conquest of labor" (that is, over the Arab workers).

> The conquest of the land [*that is, settlement*] —while a necessary goal in and of itself, since without it Zionism has no value [*sic!*] —in no way solves the question of the conquest of labor, but rather sharpens it. For if we were able to begin settlement without national capital and would have to take, for this purpose, Jewish workers from the existing moshavot, we would destroy with one hand what we were building with the other. Because it is either one or the other: either the Jewish worker goes to the farm, which Vitkin dreams of, and the thousands of workers on the capitalist moshavot will be replaced by "foreigners," or else the [*Jewish*] laborer will work in these moshavot.*

Despite the ideological restraints, the left concentrated on settlement— a characteristic pattern which quickly became one of its bases of power. The processes stemmed not only from Vitkin's statement that "All agrarian proletariats everywhere aspire to settlement on the land" (1936:11), but also from the application of this statement to the Palestinian reality, where there was a basic insecurity in the labor market as a result of the competition of the "foreign" agrarian proletariat.

*Aaronovitz, "The Conquest of Labor or the Conquest of Land," *Hapoel Hatzair* 12 (1908).

The left's patterns of settlement began as a trial-and-error process, and were accompanied by many debates and much soul-searching. In 1908 the JNF began work on its first project in Palestine—the planting of a forest in Herzl's memory on the Beit-Arif (Ben Shemen) lands. Arabs from Lydda were taken to do the job. The Jewish workers viewed this as a violation of the JNF principles,* and an insult to the memory of the Zionist leader. A group of workers from Petah Tikva was immediately formed. These workers, known as the "Romani commune" (from the city of Romani in the Ukraine), along with other workers pressured the local officials and the Palestine Office to dismiss the Arabs and to hire them in their stead. The pressure bore fruit: as a symbolic act, the saplings which had already been planted by the Arabs were uprooted and replanted, and the Jewish workers then completed the planting. This nucleus of workers later went to work on a national farm established by the Palestine Office on the lands of Delika-Um-Juni (Kinneret). Here too a conflict broke out when, in October 1909, at the height of the season, the local officials attempted to bring Arab labor onto the farm. A strike broke out, and the Romani commune left. The Choresh—the Galilee Workers' Federation—demanded that the Office turn the management of the farm over to the workers. Ruppin came to Kinneret to reduce the tension; he proposed that the area east of the Jordan be made the exclusive responsibility of the workers' group. The Choresh agreed to this proposal and formed a nucleus of seven members to manage the 1,300 dunams involved. For a period of one year, the equipment and capital were to be supplied by the PLDC. The workers' group received monthly wages from the PLDC, and it was agreed that any profits would be divided between the group's members and the organization. The Romani commune returned; this was the first *kvutza*—Degania.†

---

*In the regulations of the PLDC, the Zionist Executive established the rule that on the society's lands and in its projects Jewish workers should be hired "as much as possible"—which opened the door to the employment of Arab workers.

†Degania served as a prototype for the kvutzot and kibbutzim which were founded later. The struggle over the image of the workers' collectivity and its various forms is very interesting, but is in the main not relevant to this study. An abundance of material on the subject can be found in Weintraub, Lissak, and Atzmon (1969).

Notes Braslavsky:

> The encounter between the worker of the Second Aliya and the Jewish National Fund in its first stages has historical significance in the chronicles of Zionism and the Jewish labor movement. In this encounter, the base was laid for national labor settlement. Without a human element, the JNF would have been doomed to purposelessness and deterioration.... On the other hand—the desire of the worker for self-fulfillment had no framework in which it could be anchored. Thus history brought about a meeting of these two factors at the appropriate time, and one complemented the other (1966:101).

The leftist sector's settlements—the various forms and diversifications of the kvutza and the moshav pattern—brought about several basic changes in the management of the Jewish-Arab conflict: (1) there was an increase in the pressure on the Zionist Executive to purchase more lands; (2) on these lands, there was Jewish labor only, so that the Arabs in the area could not reap secondary rewards from the economic prosperity of the settlements; (3) the settlements maintained a low level of interaction with the Arab surroundings, which accelerated the process of segregation of the two communities; (4) since the role of watchman (*shomer*) was held exclusively by Jews, and since the left's settlements were generally sparsely populated, and sometimes even more isolated than the classic moshavot, the differences between the agriculturist, the chalutz, and the watchman almost completely disappeared. Thus a link was created between the bearer of the central role in the nation-building enterprise and the defense component, which became an integral part of this role, both in terms of the self-identity of its bearers and the expectations of the Jewish public.

We have here a clear example of the dynamics of conflict: the failure to withstand competition over labor resources brought about a far-reaching process of creation of new patterns of settlement, which in turn brought about far-reaching changes in the patterns of conflict and in the organizational structures for dealing with problems raised by the conflict.

Within a decade there was a reformulation of the left's settlement ideology, its self-image, and its perceived role in the conflictual situation of the Jewish community in Palestine. The left, especially Ahdut Haavoda (see Glossary) and Hapoel Hatzair, took upon itself the task

82

of coping with most of the problems of defense which the Jewish-Arab conflict created for the Yishuv. This was later exemplified by the founding of the Hagana as a subordinate branch of the Histadrut, which was the first step in the transformation from "a class to a nation" (in Ben-Gurion's phrase)—a transformation saliently expressed in the behavior of each of the factions of the Yishuv involved in the Tel-Hai affair.*

An analysis of the activities of each sector of the Yishuv, and especially of their attitudes as reflected in the meeting of the Provisory Committee (20 February 1920)† convened to decide what steps should be taken to assist the besieged Tel-Hai and the French Galilee as a whole, leads to the following summary:

The non-labor leadership hesitated to allocate resources for the defense of a left-sector settlement whose chances of survival seemed very slim. They accused the labor leadership of presenting the Yishuv with *faits accomplis* on the basis of which they demanded support. B.Z. Mosinzon warned:

> I want to address those who complained about the Yishuv. I agree: The Yishuv and the Committee of Delegates displayed indifference, but did you ask the Yishuv for its consent when you decided to endanger it? I put the blame for the fact that we do not have a well-organized Yishuv on ourselves. But if you want the Yishuv to help you, you have to consult it. If we want the entire Yishuv to participate in defense, everything must be done by its representatives.

*The so-called "Tel-Hai affair" remained as a traumatic episode in the Yishuv's collective memory. Tel-Hai was established by a group of workers of the Poalei Zion party in an area which, according to a French-British agreement which temporarily set boundaries, was French territory. The area became a "no-man's land" subject to uprisings of Bedouin tribes which, at the beginning, were directed against the French and the Christian villages, but later included attacks on the four Jewish settlements in the area (Metulla, Kfar Giladi, Tel-Hai, and Chamara). These settlements, almost completely isolated from the rest of the Jewish community, defended themselves for quite some time, but then fell into the hands of the Arabs. The destroyed settlement became a symbol of heroism, and its leader, Joseph Trumpeldor, who was killed there, was the first national hero in Zionist history. See *Hagana* (1956:565-85).

†The protocols of the Provisory Committee's meeting (Havaad Hazmani) can be found in Rivlin (1948).

The most clear-cut opinion was voiced by Jabotinsky, who demanded the immediate abandonment of Tel-Hai for practical reasons:

> I made a simple calculation of how much defense will cost us. We cannot maintain people without arms, and the purchase of arms will be very expensive. Where will you get the necessary funds? . . . I ask you, as people of the same mind, to tell the youngsters and the defenders the bitter truth, and maybe thus we'll save the situation. . . . You must tell them: "Come back from there and strengthen what exists here."

Jabotinsky also had political arguments to support his demand to abandon the settlement:

> We always are demanding that the British government rule over the entire land. And if we ourselves will want to defend these places, nothing will come of it. What can we do? I will tell you. We have one political organization and that is the Legion. It has ceased to exist, but we must establish another Legion, and a third and fourth. There is no other way (*Hagana*, 1956:565-85).

Jabotinsky's arguments were rooted in his general political ideology, which was a continuation of Herzl's policy of political Zionism. It had its beginning in the quest for a charter of the great powers over Palestine, and it continued with the demand for the establishment of a British-sponsored, Jewish military force to dominate the country. It was based on a belief in British willingness to fulfill the political conditions needed for the establishment of a Jewish polity in Palestine, along with a scornful attitude toward practical Zionism and the "settlement orientation" (the creation of a new ghetto). Writing six years after the Tel-Hai affair, Jabotinsky said:

> Special means are needed in order to create a Jewish majority in Palestine, so that we will be able to expand the economic absorption capacity of the land for the new settlers. Our great enthusiasm, our national funds, our powerful determination, and our many sacrifices are insufficient for this purpose. The question of the absorption of a constant, large-scale flow of immigration demands the direct intervention of the Government. . . . Only small-scale settlement, which can only create a minority—that is, a new ghetto—can go on without the aid and participation of the Government (1953:285).

As opposed to this broad political ideology, the labor parties formulated a completely different strategy for coping with the presence of the Arabs in and around the area of the aspired-for Jewish national home. This strategy, summed up in the slogan "another dunam and another goat," was characterized not only by the participation of the working class in the task of nation-building and in dealing with the conflict with the Arabs, but also by the belief that the results of the conflict were dependent on the activities of the Jewish side. In other words, the left's approach was based on the view that the Jewish side had control of the conflictual situation, in contrast to Jabotinsky's sense of dependence on factors beyond the control of the Jews—the great powers (especially Britain), world opinion, the possibility of large-scale recruitment of Jewish military divisions from abroad, etc. Ben-Gurion, who participated in the meeting, phrased the left's approach thus:

> The Yishuv itself will decide if we have to defend the Galilee or not. It depends on people feeling obligated and wanting to defend it. They [*Jabotinsky*] say that this is a diplomatic question, a question of relations with the Arabs. [*Already the suspicion arose that defense of the Galilee settlements would turn into a total war with the Arabs.*] This is not a diplomatic question [*that is, a question of relations with Britain*] nor a question which is focused on the Arabs. This is exclusively a Zionist question. . . . It depends on people who feel a responsibility and desire to defend the area (see Rivlin, 1948).

The Tel-Hai affair led the left to two operational conclusions. First, Tel-Hai and the other Jewish settlements in the area were never to be abandoned since "Once we have acquired a place, we will never leave" (Ussishkin) and "If we fail there, in the North, our retreat will continue until the desert" (Y. Tabenkin, representing the defenders of Tel-Hai). The underlying assumptions were (1) that the collectivity's boundaries would be determined by the points of Jewish settlement, and (2) a domino-type doctrine that failure in one place would bring with it a general collapse of Zionist settlement. (Indeed, throughout the entire period, both Jews and Arabs attributed great symbolic importance to the abandonment of any point of Jewish settlement.)

Second, for carrying out its defense tasks, the left required unconditional political and economic support from the rest of the Yishuv. As Ben-Gurion put it:

Hundreds of people can defend our settlements in the Galilee, if they receive food, etc. and if they receive political aid. It is clear that without this, the situation will be difficult. But we [*the workers*] will take all this upon ourselves. As long as we can, we are obliged to defend these places and not leave them (see *ibid.*)

Until 1929, the settlement projects progressed slowly. The existing settlements (both right- and left-wing sectors) tended to absorb both the population increase and the immigrant population, and new settlement projects were not high on the list of priorities of either the Yishuv as a whole or the left, whose pressure for settlement declined after the adoption of some alternative solutions to their absorption into the "capitalistic" economy. These alternatives included, apart from joining collective settlements, assimilation in urban conglomerations and individual or collective emigration. The 1929 riots—the first countrywide attempts by the Arabs to use force against the Jewish community—demonstrated the importance of settlements as factors in security. The engineer Y. Ratner, appointed as adviser to the Jewish Agency (see Glossary) for choosing the sites of new settlements, who worked "in close conjunction with the center of the Hagana" (*Hagana*, 1964:881), planned new settlements during this period in the Jordan and Hefer Valleys primarily on the basis of a locally oriented conception of security. Only from 1937 on, when the possibility existed that Palestine would be divided between Jews and Arabs, with most of the division lines following the lines of settlement, were determined efforts made to establish as many settlements as possible in accordance with a general political conception. Thus the link between political-defense pressure and institution-building— i.e., the establishment of settlements—was strengthened. When Weintraub, Lissak, and Atzmon (1969:30) divided the periods of settlement into those in which there was a "normal security situation" (1878-1914, 1922-29, and 1930-35) and those in which the security conditions were defined as "serious" (1920-21, 1936-39, and 1940-45), they found that most of the kibbutzim (68 percent) were established in times when the security situation was shaky, while almost all the moshavot (92 percent) and a large part of the moshavim (62 percent) were established when the security situation was "normal."

The relationship of security needs to the development of kibbutzim is difficult to define, but it seems apparent that the kibbutz pattern crystallized as a result of the ideological struggles between the mass pattern of the Labor Legion (Gedud Haavoda—see Glossary) and the intimate kvutza, as well as the pressures of the situation, just as the settlement activity of the left was the result of interaction between necessity and ideology.

The suitability of the kibbutz pattern for dealing with the conflictual situation is analyzed in the *History of the Hagana*:

> Of all the types of settlement, the kibbutz is, in its structure, closest to a military formation. The problem of family maintenance is solved within a general organizational framework and through a common effort; the age composition of the kibbutz, and especially in a young kibbutz—a high percentage of young people and a low percentage of the aged and children—increases its power and military strength. It has an advantage over the military framework since the kibbutz member does not spend his life in the same atmosphere of boredom which makes even the best of armies deteriorate in peacetime or in times in which there is no intensive training. Also, this form of living does not cut a person off from his family life, as does the army. It is true that the kibbutz does not possess the external military discipline . . . but this disadvantage is compensated for by the inner discipline of kibbutz members and their consciousness of the national value of the role entrusted to them (*Hagana*, 1964:860).

The greatest similarity between the kibbutz and the military formation existed during the period known as "wall and tower" (Choma Umigdal).* Between 1936 and 1939, fifty-five settlements were established with the aim of creating *faits accomplis*, before the possible partition of Palestine, by *presence* in areas which were only sparsely populated by Jews (for example, in the Northwest Galilee).† Thirty-seven of these were communal settlements, with sectoral

---

*See Bein (1970:366-80) and *Hagana* (1964:851-80).

†One area in which Jewish presence was established during these years was the Beit-Shean Valley, where ten settlements were founded for the purpose of creating a territorial continuum between the settlements of the Jordan and Jezreel Valleys—from Haifa to Tiberias—while at the same time isolating the Arab rebels' bases in Samaria (Shomron) from those in the Galilee and blocking the passages to the Jordan.

membership ranging from Hashomer Hatzair to the Hapoel Hamizrahi, Betar, and Maccabi. Some of them, especially in the problematic areas, were established by the "wall and tower" technique.

The prototype of this form of settlement was the return to kibbutz Tel-Amal (later known as Nir-David) of the Hashomer Hatzair movement, which had been abandoned at the beginning of the Arab rebellion. On 10 December 1936, a "conquering group" (*kvutzat kibbush*) came to the kibbutz fields and within one day built a wall, surrounded by a barbed wire fence, which enclosed a yard (about 40 by 40 yards) that included lodging cabins, a public mess hall, and a tower with a spotlight. Thus, within a few hours, with the help of a large manpower force (only a few of whom remained), an entire settlement was established ready to defend itself against Arab attack. Indeed, many such settlements met with heavy attacks, and all withstood them. At that time, the Hagana played a very active role in the establishment of the settlements, with the settlement of Hanita (in the Northeast Galilee) an exclusive undertaking of the Hagana.

Despite the flood of new agricultural settlements, almost all were able to maintain themselves, and within a short time became economically profitable as a result of a combination of factors. First, the nucleus of settlers who populated the settlement could almost immediately engage in extensive cultivation because the area at their disposal was equivalent to that planned for the entire settlement; second, the settlements received considerable assistance from the Jewish Agency, especially in basic equipment; third, the Arab rebellion, by reducing trade between the Arab and Jewish economies, created a great demand for Jewish agricultural produce in both the Jewish and British sectors. (The British maintained a considerable army in Palestine for suppressing the Arab rebellion and in anticipation of the beginning of World War II.)

The settlement campaigns of 1936-39 showed the Yishuv's potential for recruiting its members for the achievement of collective tasks: thousands of young people (some of them new immigrants) left their home environments to man new settlements. This was something of a return to patterns of activity characteristic of the 1920s, and was part of a process of preparation for total mobilization for World War II and in anticipation of future conflict with the Arabs. The widespread participation in the settlement projects also contributed to the intensification of social solidarity in the Yishuv.

To sum up this period, we can see that with the outbreak of World War II, the total struggle between Jews and Arabs over the political control of Palestine was postponed for nine years. By 1939 the Jews had managed to acquire only about 10 percent of the territory of Palestine and about 7 percent of its cultivable area. On this territory they established more than 230 agricultural settlements. in which about 140,000 settlers lived (of a total of 570,000 Jewish settlers in Palestine).* These settlements fulfilled the tasks allocated to them in connection with the conflictual situation: they ended the dependence of the Jews on the Arab economy and set the territorial boundaries of the future State of Israel, except in the mountain areas and the Negev.

SUMMARY

The need to acquire land and to establish presence on it had a considerable impact on the shape of the institutions of the Yishuv, and to a certain extent on the social and political processes in the Jewish collectivity from its formative stages to the present day. The concentration of a sizable part of the ownership of land in the hands of a single, central institution — the Jewish National Fund, and thereafter the Israel Lands Authority (see Chapter 5) — fit well with the paternalistic regime which subsequently developed (Horowitz and Lissak, 1978; Eisenstadt, 1967). The renting of land became one of the resources the government divided differentially on the basis of its own criteria. No doubt the low frontierity level contributed to the creation of a paternalistic regime — a conclusion Turner would be likely to support.

The need to create a Jewish presence brought about a societal institution comparable to the frontier settlements in North and South America and South Africa (Thompson and Lamar, 1981). The character of this type of settlement was not determined by economic considerations or social needs, but by its geopolitical location—

---

*It is very difficult to estimate the number of participants in the settlement projects in those years because of the lack of documentation and the great mobility of the settlers, some of whom participated in several projects while others were only "temporary."

sometimes by needs which stemmed from different views of how to manage the conflict with the Arabs. But these institutions did not serve only instrumental purposes. They also absorbed elements of sanctity, and became an inseparable part of the collectivity's system of symbols. The redeemer of the land, the settler-pioneer, and even the blue box of the JNF became the heroes of Zionist mythology, like the heroes of the American Wild West (see Smith, 1970).

Chapter Four

IMMIGRANTS AND TERRITORY

At the end of World War II, Zionism was far from a success story. Of the three million Jews who had emigrated from lands of persecution in Eastern Europe since the end of the nineteenth century, only about one percent chose "Zion" as their destination. Most of them migrated to the North American continent, with some travelling to Western Europe—primarily Germany.* Others chose to stay at home, hoping that changes would take place in their societies that would solve the Jewish Problem. In addition, after the first consolidations of the Bolshevik Revolution, the Jews were barred from leaving the Soviet Union, and that tremendous potential reservoir was frozen almost entirely for about fifty years. Most of the Jews did not wish to come to Palestine because Zionism was seen as too remote a solution to their individual and collective problems, but further, the gates of Palestine were not always open, either because of the policy of the ruling power (under pressure from the Arabs) or because of the policy of selective immigration the Zionist institutions adopted—first, to control the composition of the immigration, and second, because immigration required subsidies and physical and territorial resources which were scarce.

This chapter will focus on the reciprocal relations between territorial accumulation and the growth of population through immigration. At first glance the connection seems simple: the aim of the Jewish national movement was to gather the maximum number of the dispersed Jews of the world into Palestine, and to build for them a sovereign society so that they would be "like all the other nations."

*In 1825 there were about ten thousand Jews in North America; by 1900 the number was approaching one million. By 1933 there were close to 4.5 million Jews in North America (of about 16 million in the entire world), with about 350,000 in Latin America (mostly in Argentina, where Baron Hirsch had attempted to establish a settlement project which would compete to some extent with Zionism). Australia and New Zealand then had about 33,000 Jews, and South Africa, 90,000.

In practice, the connection was reversed: in order to establish possession of territorial expanses in Palestine, there was a need for massive Jewish immigration to establish a type of *grand presence* and determine decisive demographic strengths of the Jews in relation to the local Arab population. We have already seen, in comparing North and South America, how population ratios determined many differences between immigrant-settler societies (see Chapter 1). But for massive Jewish immigration to Palestine to be possible, there was a need for much greater land reserves than were then available to the Jewish collectivity. Thus the Zionist movement was involved in a type of "Catch-22" situation: without massive immigration there was no possibility of acquiring great quantities of land, and without large reserves of open (and cheap) land, there was almost no possibility of massive immigration. (Of course a large land reserve would by no means have guaranteed large-scale immigration.)

In the early 1930s the Jewish community constituted only about 18 percent of Palestine's population, and even after the immigration boom of the middle 1930s it comprised only little more than one quarter of the total population (see Table 4.1). This was the basic weakness of the Jewish community, and it had ramifications in other spheres: (a) from a political standpoint, the Jewish community was incapable of acting effectively within a democratic framework under the Mandate;* (b) the validity of Jewish claims to the entire territory

*The elections for a legislative council in Palestine which the High Commissioner [Herbert Samuel] tried to establish failed because of the actions of the Arab Executive Committee which was established at the Third Palestinian Convention [Haifa, 1920] (see Glossary). As a result of pressures throughout the country, only about one-sixth of the Arab population participated in the elections for the council, primarily because participation was perceived as Arab ratification of the Mandate, which promised the establishment of a Jewish national home. The Jews had agreed to participate in the elections for the council on the assurance that representation on the council would be proportional to the population (of which the Jews then constituted about 13 percent), but the elections were cancelled as a result of the Arabs' refusal to participate. Proposals for elections continued to be made until the Arab rebellion of 1936, after which the Jews vigorously opposed them. They suggested as a compromise the establishment of a "parity" legislative council in which they would share political power equally with the Arabs. In 1935 a unified Arab delegation called upon the High Commissioner [Wauchope] to demand the establishment of a democratic government in Palestine. The demand was raised again by Arab representatives to the Peel Commission (1937), while the Jews again proposed a parity government.

Table 4.1

THE INCREASE IN PALESTINE'S JEWISH POPULATION, 1914-1951

Year	Jewish Population	Percentage of Jews in Total Population
1914	56,000	9.2%
1922 [census]	83,790	12.9
1926	149,500	18.4
1931 [census]	174,606	18.1
1936	355,157	29.5
1940	463,535	31.4
1944	528,702	31.6
1948	716,678	30.1[a]
1951	1,404,400	89.0

Sources: Computed from (1) Palestine (1946a, vol. I, pp. 141-43); (2) Gurevich, Gertz, and Zenker (1947:46-47); (3) State of Israel, *Israel Statistical Annual 1952* (Jerusalem: Central Bureau of Statistics).

[a]Based on assumption of no decline in Arab population during the 1947-1948 War.

of Palestine was weakened; (c) both Jews and Arabs saw this demographic gap as tipping the power balance against the Jews;* (d) there was a scarcity of manpower for social tasks, including the establishment of new settlements which would have allowed the Jewish community to strengthen and expand its territorial control. Thus, the relative portion of the Jewish population was interwoven with the land factor in the Jewish-Arab conflict because the Jews believed

*However, when this balance is examined more systematically, it is clear that the gap between Jews and Arabs was not so great in the total balance of power. The Jewish population not only had more resources at its disposal (skills, capital, technology, etc.) and a social organization which made possible a broadly based, rapid recruitment for collective tasks, but it also had an advantage from a demographic standpoint in terms of the ratio of those who could actively participate in the conflictual situation— that is, 47 percent of the total Jewish population was between 17 and 44 years of age (Gurevitch, Gertz, and Zenker, 1947:56).

that in order to accumulate maximum territory, ever-increasing rates of immigration (along with the capital for land purchase which some of the immigrants brought with them) were necessary, while extensive land purchases were perceived as essential for the absorption of both the ongoing immigration and the immigration the Zionist movement hoped for in the future (and which the Arabs feared).

The Arab attitude toward Jewish immigration to Palestine reflected their belief that the situation was "zero-sum"—i.e., that the country could maintain only a fixed or limited population, so that the arrival of any Jew was at the expense of an Arab. From its very beginnings, much of the Arab-Palestinian political activity was directed at attempts to have, first, the Ottoman Turks and then the British (see, for example, Assaf, 1967:56; Porath, 1974) limit Jewish immigration. The arrival of Jews affected all the Arabs employed within the Jewish community, but during almost the entire period the Jewish community remained dependent on Arab manpower—particularly unskilled labor (see Sussman, 1969:34-165).

Beginning in 1922, in order to conciliate the Arabs, and especially to control the Jewish community's growth rate, semi-annual immigration quotas or schedules were fixed according to the country's economic capacity to absorb such immigration. These quotas were the subject of constant negotiation between the Jewish leadership and the Mandatory Government, with both the general economic situation and the labor markets in the Jewish and Arab sectors being taken into account, but were determined primarily by the political relations within the Jewish-British-Arab triangle. Table 4.1 shows that the result of this arrangement was a fairly slow increase (with some minor reversals) in the ratio of the Jewish to the Arab population, except for two periods characterized by a rapid increase in the Jewish population percentage—one in 1922-1926 and a second, more significant one in 1931-1936.

The initiative for these quotas began in June 1921, when in the wake of Arab-instigated riots which broke out in May, the High Commissioner promised to limit Jewish immigration in consideration of the "present inhabitants" of Palestine. (These were the second wave of riots instigated by the Arabs; the first occurred in Jerusalem and the Jordan Valley in April 1920 before the San Remo Conference.) The formal seal of approval for limitations on immigration as a British policy was given in a document known as "Churchill's White Paper"

(June 1922), which was based upon the Balfour Declaration, and stated that the Jewish national home would be built *within* Palestine, but would not *be* Palestine. This announcement, made in the wake of the report of a commission appointed to study the riots (Haycroft Commission; see Palestine, 1921), stated for the first time that Jewish immigration would be dependent on Palestine's economic absorption capacity. After more riots in 1929, an additional White Paper was published in 1930 (based upon the conclusions of the Hope-Simpson Report of 1930—see Chapter 5) proposing to make Jewish immigration dependent on (a) the number of unemployed Arabs and (b) the "suspicions of the Arab community." However, after great political pressure was applied, the British Government retracted this proposal, and in a letter from the Prime Minister (Ramsay MacDonald) to Weizmann (13 February 1931), the policy established in 1922 was reinstated.

In 1933 a comprehensive new Immigration Order was issued. It classified immigrants into four categories: (1) holders of capital, subdivided into (a) those having at least £1,000, who were permitted to immigrate without any limitations, (b) professionals and craftsmen having £500 or £250 respectively, whose immigration was dependent on the demand for their professions and crafts in the labor market, and (c) those having at least £500 whom the Director of Immigration felt had reasonable chances of being absorbed in Palestine; (2) students and those employed in religious institutions whose living was secure; (3) workers, defined as "people with definite possibilities of employment in Palestine"; and (4) the dependents of those in the first three categories and "others." Between 1922-1945, of a total of 343,901 registered immigrants, 24.9 percent belonged to the first category, 6.4 percent to the second, 51.4 percent to the third, and 17.3 percent to the fourth. In 1939 the British, along with their suppression of the Arab rebellion and the local Arab leadership, decided to drastically limit Jewish immigration. "MacDonald's White Paper" (17 March 1939) limited Jewish immigration to 75,000 persons over five years. Its purpose was to maintain the existing proportions of Palestine's population (one-third Jewish), apparently looking toward the establishment of a Palestinian state after a transition period of about ten years.

The peak years of the Third, Fourth, and Fifth Aliyot (see Glossary) were accompanied by economic prosperity, but the relationship between variations in the population growth rates and economic developments was complex. Years of economic decline were characterized both by decreased immigration and by increased emigration (the "descent" of Jews from Palestine). Under such circumstances, the relatively limited Arab immigration and the high Arab birth rates (about 3.8 percent among the Moslems and 2.3 percent among the Christians) became significant factors in determining the proportions of Jews and Arabs in the population. In 1927, for example, when Jewish emigration from Palestine (about 5,000) exceeded Jewish immigration (2,178), the Arab rate of immigration (755) was about one third the Jewish rate. By contrast, the *average* rate of Arab immigration to Palestine between 1922-1945 did not exceed 9 percent of the Jewish rate (see Palestine, 1946a:185).

The concentration of the immigration struggle around the vague concept of the country's absorption capacity enabled the Jews to claim, quite accurately, that Jewish immigration in itself increased the country's economic absorption capacity, and the greater the immigration, the greater the absorption capacity. In addition, they could claim that Jewish immigration brought with it economic prosperity whose benefits were enjoyed by the Arabs as well.

According to the "rules of the game" as set by the British Mandate, the British could determine the *amount* of Jewish immigration, making it dependent on economic or political circumstances. However, the Jewish leadership was allowed to determine the *composition* of the immigration. The Jewish leadership always worked within the framework of these rules, even in the days of the bitter struggle against the 1939 White Paper, when the British had violated the rules and the Jews demanded a return to the previously existing situation. Only at the end of 1945 was there a change in attitude of the Jewish leadership.

However, there was not a total consensus within the Jewish community's leadership on the acceptance of these principles. In June 1936, at a meeting of the Zionist Executive, Y. Greenbaum said:

> The Diaspora will view the acceptance of immigration quotas as treason to the nation, because in this realm no compromises can be made. If the Government will determine the quotas, the people will view this as a catastrophe. And if this is the main point in the negotiations [*with the Arabs—negotiations initiated by Jews*],

then I would prefer the recurrence of this situation [*riots*] every five years rather than to agree to compromises on matters of immigration. Under such circumstances we may reach a situation of open warfare, but I believe in our victory (Ben-Gurion, 1973:231).

At the same meeting, Ussishkin said he would be happy indeed if the High Commissioner were to promise an immigration of 300,000 over the course of five years,* but he would not consent to such an arrangement so as not to acknowledge the quota principle. Nevertheless, the Jewish leadership continued to accept the principle that the Mandatory Government determined the amount of immigration[†] if in exchange the leadership of the Yishuv could partially determine its composition. Had immigration not been limited, the Jewish leadership could not have controlled its composition. Such control was exercised abroad through the various preparatory organizations of the parties making up the Jewish leadership. This selection of the immigrants was an important control mechanism for preserving the left's predominance in the Jewish community. The leaders of this sector were highly conscious of the connection between control of the composition of immigration and control of the Yishuv. Thus, in 1925 Ben-Gurion wrote:

All the conquests [*of the labor movement*] in labor, the economy and in settlement, are not yet self-sufficient entities and without reinforcement, continuation, and expansion of immigration and new settlements they have no chance of survival. . . . Our movement's fate both in the present and future depends on the course of immigration in the broadest sense of the term in the training of immigrants abroad, in the ability to absorb them here, in the pioneering immigrations and in national capital, and in our portion in the general immigration. . . . The present project of the labor sector

---

*According to Ruppin's calculations, immigration on such a scale would result in the Jewish community matching the Arab community in size within ten years. Indeed, the peak volume of immigration was reached in 1935, and that year represented 15.7 percent of the total immigration to Palestine between 1919-1945.

[†]However, as noted, in addition to the quotas there were some "capitalists" who could enter Palestine without any limitations until 1939. Part of the boom of Jewish immigration in 1935 (more than 61,000) was a result of a surge in the immigration of such capitalists, especially from Germany.

in Palestine in the economic, vocational, settlement and cultural spheres will expand and be fortified, or will weaken steadily, according to our weight and representation in future immigrations (*Kuntress*, 1925:206).

Thus the right the Mandatory Government granted to the Jewish Agency, and thereby to the parties within it, to distribute the certificates whose number was determined by the immigration "schedule" was an important source of strength for the Agency. This strength was exercised both in power struggles within the Jewish community and in struggles against groups which did not acknowledge the Jewish Agency's authority. The determination of each faction's share became a subject of continuing negotiation among the various parts of the Yishuv, with orientation toward the Jewish-Arab conflict often used as a weapon in the negotiations. Thus, for example, Greenbaum reports (*Haaliya* 2 [1935] :15) that four hundred certificates had to be made available to the Farmers' Union and the Industrialists' Union in response to their threats to employ Arab laborers, particularly for work in the orchards.

The Revisionists demanded that the Government grant them quotas of certificates directly, since, they claimed, the Jewish Agency "discriminates against them, ignores their immigration demands, and grants immigration permits only to members of the General Labor Federation." However, the Mandatory Government did not yield to this demand and left the monopoly in the Jewish Agency's hands. Agudat Israel (see Glossary) also was forced to become closer to the Zionists because of its desire to obtain immigration permits for its members. Its members were compelled to accept "the burden of the rules which we [*the Zionist Executive*] have established as to immigration. In this connection, preparatory kibbutzim of Agudat Israel were established under our supervision [*that is, under the Yishuv's leadership*] " (*ibid.*).

The desire to maintain political dominance within the Jewish community by controlling the allocation of immigration certificates was complemented by the desire to preserve the existing social structure. E. Dobbkin, representing the left-wing faction Hehalutz at the Nineteenth Zionist Congress, put it thus:

The general opinion among all the members of the immigration committee [*was*] that in these times unorganized and anarchic immigration was out of the question. . . . Only four years ago 25 percent of the Yishuv were agriculturalists. . . . And now after this large immigration [of 1932-36], after having taken in 200,000 Jews in four years . . . the percentage of Jews in agriculture has declined, and is today estimated as 14 percent or possibly even less. . . . The conclusion is clear: we must make efforts at conquest in order to gain control of what we lost . . . . The right to immigrate is granted to every Jew, but there are hundreds of thousands of Jews who wish to emigrate to Palestine and we want to select the most appropriate among them.*

Thus selective immigration combined the good of the collectivity with the good of the dominant sector within it, and was helpful for coping with a problem which arose as a by-product of the Jewish-Arab conflict—i.e., the demand for the exclusive employment of Jewish labor in the Jewish economic sector.

JEWISH TERRITORY AND JEWISH LABOR†

The demand for increased employment of Jewish workers in the Jewish colonies developed at the beginning of the Second Aliya (1904). At that time, groups of immigrants who lacked capital or property and identified themselves as socialists arrived in Palestine. Their socialist ideals were combined with nationalistic-Zionist views to create a demand for revolutionary change in the structure of Jewish society in the Diaspora (as well as in Palestine), for which these groups saw themselves as the vanguard.** Aharon Aharonson, a prominent right-

---

*See The Nineteenth Zionist Congress (Stenographic Report, Lucerne, 20 August-6 September 1935; Jerusalem: Executive of the Zionist Federation, 1937), pp. 401-4.

†Detailed analysis of the struggle for the employment of exclusively Jewish labor in the Jewish economy and its effect on the collectivity's social structure and on the dynamics of Jewish-Arab relations is beyond the scope of the present study. For a historical survey of the subject, see Harpaz (1940:93-104); for an economic and social analysis, see Sussman (1969:37-65) and Shapiro (1971).

**Most of the First Aliya members also supported "independent labor," and in the settlers' code of regulations we find: "This land shall be cultivated only by Bilu members without the aid of the Arabs who live here" (Braslavsky, 1961:73); they saw themselves as farmers rather than estate holders. Under the existing economic conditions, however, it seems they could not hold fast to this regulation.

wing leader who served as a spokesman for the farmers, described the work of the "revolutionaries" on the Palestine Office's farms in Ben-Shemen and Hulda with his characteristic sarcasm:

> Under the guise of nationalism, they do very unnationalistic work. Under the guise of bombastic words, tremendous waste takes place, and all this I must say, is done innocently. But that is no justification.... Barley is sown on rocky soil and cannot be harvested by machine, and our enthusiastic workers begin to pick it while screaming nationalistic songs with Cossack tunes—and in the end they've done the work done by one Arab woman for five pennies. When we let two energetic and intelligent men demean themselves and do the work of one primitive Arab woman, that is anti-nationalistic.... To do work for twenty-five pennies which can be done for five is to cast to the winds the nation's few miserable cents (Livne, 1969:163).

The agronomist Y. Vilkinsky gave a slightly more balanced analysis: "The farmers should not be blamed for employing Arab workers ... not only for economic reasons, but also for psychological ones" (173).

Upon their arrival the new immigrants found that the farmers of the moshavot refused to employ them. There were a number of reasons for the moshav population to reject the Jewish workers. For one thing, hiring Arab laborers was cheaper (for most of them the work in the moshavot was only a seasonal supplement to their subsistence economy), and at the beginning the opinion prevailed that the Arabs were better skilled and more suited to the local conditions than the young and educated revolutionaries. In addition, the hiring of Arab workers from villages in the vicinity of the moshavot constituted a sort of insurance against attack from these villages (*Hagana*, 1967:79; Assaf, 1970:18); similarly, the employment of Arab watchmen provided a sort of protection against thefts. In addition, there was a wide gap in values between the populations of the First and Second Aliyot. The former was composed mostly of people who were relatively well-established economically, with a religious orientation and intellectual and emotional ties to Western-French culture. The latter came to Palestine to "wage a class struggle" or, at the very least, to "establish a Jewish proletariat."*

*Vilkinsky explained this farmer-worker conflict in 1918 as follows: "The Jewish worker tends to criticize, he is an extremist and rebellious, demanding an

The farmers' opposition to the hiring of Jewish workers resulted in (a) the radicalization of the latter's demands to the point of demanding exclusively Jewish labor throughout the Jewish economy in the name of both nationalism and socialism, and (b) the workers' organization for intensive political activity to ensure their economic survival in Palestine and to work toward the fulfillment of their social ideals.

In reality, the demand for exclusively Jewish labor could not possibly be met at the beginning of the century because the total supply of Jewish workers, especially in agriculture, was not sufficient for the Jewish economy. The ironic query directed to Hapoel Hatzair by the mayor of Tel-Aviv, Meir Dizengoff, in 1908—"If all Petach Tikva's inhabitants would demand that you supply them with Jewish workers instead of the Arab ones who would be discharged, could you supply them with all the necessary wagon-drivers and watchmen?" (*Hatzvi*, 25:2)—was still applicable to the situation in the 1930s, as described by Harpaz:

> The years 1931-32 were, from an objective point of view, peak years for Jewish labor. The Yishuv was steeped with an awareness that it was a basic necessity. Many groups outside of the Histadrut gave their moral support to the penetration of Jewish labor in the Jewish economy, but there was a lack of workers. In 1934 we lost considerable ground after recruiting the public for the maintenance of Jewish labor. In the watches over the orchards, poets and authors, public figures and journalists participated. Public opinion was on our side, and if despite this we did not succeed in the battle, then it was only because of a lack of workers (1940:100-101).

The scarcity of Jewish agricultural workers was intensified as a result of two developments. First, the controversy between the opponents (Abronovitz) and supporters (Vitkin) of the establishment of new independent settlements was resolved in favor of the latter, and many workers joined the farms of the Zionist Federation, established kvutzot and later kibbutzim, or turned to the Gedud Haavoda pattern

8-hour workday and the right to strike. . . . The workers' ideals do not stand the test of reality. . . . [T] he conflict between the farmers and workers is basically not economic. . . . Rather the farmers fear that the workers will become powerful. . . . They are hurt by the workers' influence, by their propaganda" (Livne, 1969:173).

101

(see Glossary: "Labor Legion"). Second, with a rise in immigration and importation of private capital,* under a stabilized Mandatory Government, the non-agricultural economic spheres—especially construction—underwent considerable development. A much higher income could be obtained there than in agriculture, especially by skilled workers.[†]

The labor movement's leaders were aware of this problem, and one of the ways they attempted to solve it was by importing Jewish workers who could compete with the Arabs both in their willingness to work in agriculture and in their salary demands. For this purpose, Y. Yavniel, a leading member of the Hapoel Hatzair party, was sent to Yemen in 1911 in the service of the Palestine Office. During 1912, about 1,500 Yemenite Jews were brought to Israel, and their numbers rose to 11,000 in 1918 as a result of natural increase and continued immigration. Between 1919 and 1928 another 1,413 Yemenite Jews emigrated to Palestine (1.4 percent of the total Jewish immigration), and by 1945 another 10,000 Yemenite Jews had arrived. The willingness to import the Yemenites, who were potential competitors not only for the Arabs but also for the Jewish workers, represented a turning point for the cause of Jewish labor. From a demand which stemmed primarily from economic need, it became (a) a demand based on a conception of how the Jewish-Arab conflict should be managed and (b) a mechanism serving the central factions of the labor movement (especially in the late 1920s and early 1930s) in their struggle against the right-wing sector. The labor movement perceived itself as representing the national interest, as opposed to the class-oriented particularistic interests of the right, and the struggles within the Jewish sector (between workers and agriculturalist employers, on the one hand, and unemployed workers and the British government, on the other) were sometimes violent.

*The flow of private capital to Palestine greatly exceeded that of the public and national capital (see Olitzur, 1939:246). From 1932-37, 51.8 percent of the private capital was invested in construction, basically land and salaries.

[†]There were two types of salary differentials in the Mandatory economy: (1) Arab workers were paid substantially less than Jewish workers for the same work and the same level of skill (the differential was sometimes three-to-one), and (2) agricultural workers earned much less than workers in industry, crafts, or services, and especially in construction (the differential was sometimes two-to-one) (Gurevich et al., 1947:298-300).

The expansion and development of the citrus groves as a major branch of Palestine's economy focused the labor struggles within the orchards, most of which used primarily cheap Arab labor. The orange growers argued that (1) they had to compete with international rivals, and (2) the Jewish citrus industry employed more Jewish workers than all the workers' settlements combined. If their competitive ability were impaired, both the workers and the Jewish economy as a whole would suffer.* However, after the outbreak of the Arab rebellion in 1936, which included a boycott of the Jewish economy by the Arab workers (Bowden, 1975; Kimmerling, 1982), the Yishuv almost immediately replaced the Arab workers with Jews.

Table 4.2 deals with the decisive period in the development of the citrus industry. In the Fall of 1933 the industry began to expand, reaching its peak in 1935. At the beginning, most of the expansion was carried out by the increased use of Arab workers, and in the five colonies in our sample, employment of Jewish workers declined about 27 percent.† In 1936 the Arab rebellion stopped the stream of Arab manpower to the Jewish economy. Nevertheless, as a result of the growing demand in foreign markets, the citrus industry continued to expand, and the Jewish economy was able to supply the manpower needed, primarily because of a rise in unemployment in the urban sector.

At the end of the strike, Arab labor in the colonies was renewed, but the struggle against it was not resumed with the same intensity, despite growing unemployment in the Jewish sector. According to Bar-Haim, this stemmed from "a radical change in the relations of the Farmers' Union and the political center, a return to the National Committee and an acceptance of the ideological principle of Jewish labor, and the abandonment of the separatist ideology" (1972:22). In other words, when a more or less general consensus was arrived at on the principle of Jewish labor, its institutionalization became secondary.

---

*The farmers proposed a subsidy for Jewish labor in the orchards from national funds.

†In other colonies (moshavot), Jewish labor and independent labor were more common, and in the newest colonies there was almost no Arab labor, primarily because of the small size of the orchards, which enabled individual families to cultivate them.

Table 4.2

JEWISH AND ARAB WORKERS IN FIVE LARGE CITRUS COLONIES,[a]
1933-1936

Month/Year	Absolute Numbers			Change: [Base Year-1933 = 100]		
	Jews	Arabs	Total	Jews	Arabs	Total
September 1933	2,197	1,674	3,871	100	100	100
September 1935	1,619	2,646	4,265	73	158	110
September 1936	3,818	896	4,714	174	53	123

Source: Haaliya, 1937, D, p. 56.

[a]Petach Tikva, Rishon Le-Zion, Rehovot, Hadera, and Nes-Ziona.

In summary, Jewish labor and the relative size of the Jewish population were interdependent elements in the determination of the size of the territory over which the Yishuv obtained control. First, since the labor market was mixed, the Mandatory Government could legitimately use unemployment within the Arab labor force as an index of the country's absorption capacity—one of the criteria for determining the limits of Jewish immigration to Palestine. Second, the Pioneering Aliya not only served the political interests of the established Jewish political leaders, but also was effective in the management of the conflict with the Arabs because it made possible the enactment of a settlement policy which established territorial facts. These settlements were based on purely Jewish labor and put islands of purely Jewish settlement on the map of the country. Thus the concept of "Jewish labor" contributed not only to social and economic differentiation but also to ecological separation between the Jewish and Arab communities, and to the creation of Jewish majorities in specific areas.

SUMMARY

The absolute and relative size of the Jewish population in Palestine had a decisive influence on the amount of land which passed to the Jewish system and upon its patterns of control. (1) When the Jewish population was small and growing relatively slowly, its demands for large tracts of land, with the aid of the Mandatory power, were not regarded as legitimate. (2) Because of the demographic inferiority of the Jewish community, it had only limited ability to control large areas of land. (3) When there was little immigration, there was little pressure upon Zionist institutions to grant higher priority to the purchase of land, but such pressure was exerted periodically, especially when immigration increased or when the conflict was seen to demand the acquisition of land and the creation of presence upon it. (4) The demographic inferiority of the Jewish population limited their "grand presence"—i.e., their presence throughout the territory which was the focus of the struggle between the Jews and Arabs. (5) The fourth (1924-1929) and the fifth (1932-1939) immigration waves brought sizable amounts of private capital, only a small part of which was invested in land. The amount of land bought by the private sector might have been greater had land purchases not been stigmatized within the system (see Chapter 3). (6) The preference given to immigrants of the left brought people to the country who were mobile in terms of geography and employment, and thus could be used to create presence on territory as the requirements of the conflict demanded. In addition, the immigration of the chalutzim (pioneers) exerted a certain amount of pressure on the Zionist leadership to direct more resources into the acquisition of land.

The most pronounced interaction between the amount of land controlled by the Jews and immigration occurred in the years 1947 to 1951. As a result of the total war between the Jews and the Arabs in 1947-1948, the majority of the Arab population left the areas conquered by the Jewish forces (see Chapter 5). Once Jewish sovereignty was achieved, all the barriers to Jewish immigration were removed, and during this period the Jewish population doubled (see Table 4.1). As a result of the complementary processes of Arabs leaving and massive Jewish immigration, the Jewish population increased from 30 to 89 percent of the total population.* The Jewish grand presence in Israel was solidified, and the country was re-divided, but not to the benefit of the Palestinian Arabs. The territorial losses of the Jews were not the gains of the Palestinian Arabs, but of Jordan and Egypt.

*Presenting the data in such a form distorts the picture: the 30 percent of the Jewish population refers to the entire territory of Mandatory Palestine, while the 89 percent refers to the area of the State of Israel alone.

Chapter Five

FROM MONEY TO SWORD

As noted earlier, processes of structural change in the Arab agrarian sector brought about the defreezing of the land in Palestine and made possible its acquisition by Jews. At the same time, because of Jewish acquisitions, there were other processes occurring in the Arab sector which had an impact both on the patterns of conflict and developments in the Jewish community. As Porath describes it:

> The very purchase of lands by Jews for purposes of settlement, and their ability to pay very high prices for them, aroused fear of their seemingly unlimited economic means. The willingness of the Jewish buyers to employ any and all means in order to overcome the obstacles placed in their path strengthened this fear. This development sustained itself and created a solid base for a radical anti-Zionist position. The quarrels over land had anti-Zionist political echoes among the urban, educated elite . . . [who] began to organize the villagers to resist and sabotage Jewish land purchases. Thus seeds of hatred for Zionism were planted in fertile soil and would come to full bloom in years following [after the beginning of the Mandate] (1974:20).

The land purchases also created a stratum of fellaheen and Bedouins who had lost the lands or been transferred to other lands. Regardless of the size of this stratum (which, as we shall see later, was very much disputed), the existence of fellaheen who saw themselves as unjustifiably evicted from their lands created an awareness within the Arab agrarian sector that this was a possible fate for every fellah. This made the struggle over land concrete and relevant for every individual in the Arab community and intensified feelings of antagonism against the Jews. It seemed to provide a focus around which all Arab groups could become politically mobilized.

The salience of the problem of the evicted fellaheen was understood within the British government, which expressed the belief "that this matter was the most important with which the Administration had to deal, and that if it could be rightly resolved, then indeed Zionism in Palestine might cease to be a problem" (Sykes, 1965:98). The Mandatory Government tried to resolve the problem from the very beginning. In the Land Transfer Ordinance (1920) it required that any land transfer be approved by the government, and the Transfer of Land Ordinance (1921) [Section 8(1)] stated that consent to transfer would be granted only after the manager of the land department "was convinced that every tenant would receive, in the same district or in another, a land tract which was sufficient to support him and his family." As might be expected, these ordinances had no effect, since in every case of land transfer between the Jews and the Arabs, the transaction was undertaken directly, without recourse to the government. Furthermore, by its very nature, such interaction in a situation of conflict was likely to demand concealment and even illegal activity. The Peel Commission reported as follows: "These Ordinances [*the prohibition of land transfer without Government consent and the protection of tenants*] ... proved in fact to be unworkable. Neither vendor nor purchaser applied for the consent of the Government to the transaction. Owners and tenants took the money for purchase or compensation and departed" (1927:222).

The dislocation of fellaheen and Bedouins from the lands on which they lived dated back to the beginning of modern Jewish settlement in Palestine. The first eighteen moshavot established in Palestine (even before the First Zionist Congress) were almost all established on lands that were being cultivated or had been cultivated by Arab tenants.* The first tract of land purchased by Karl Netter (a French-born Jewish philanthropist) for the establishment of the agricultural school at Mikve Israel (1870) belonged to (or was cultivated by) the fellaheen of Yaazur village. This caused a dispute which lasted for many years with the "fellaheen who will never

---

*Under conditions of extensive agriculture, when there is no great scarcity of land, a common method of land improvement is to let it lie fallow for a few years. Thus it seems that during the first period of Zionist settlement, there were many areas of land which were not then being cultivated, but almost all of which had been cultivated at some time in the past. This complicated the land situation even more, and provided an opening for Arab ownership claims.

forget that Netter took their land" (Y.N. Pines, "Respect for the Truth," *Hamelitz*, No. 19, 1882). The Petach Tikva colony evicted the Satiria tribe, and for a long while had to defend itself from the tribe's attacks.

One of the first settlers in Zichron Yaakov, M. Pochechevsky, wrote in his memoirs of the relations with the Samrin tribe, the previous residents of that area:

> Samrin had been settled by tenants, and the land belonged to an effendi. When he sold the land, the tenants had no choice but to leave and support themselves by theft, murder, and robbery, and since they were familiar with the many paths and caves there, they would try their luck very often and never returned empty-handed. At the beginning, when we were full of enthusiasm, we didn't even undress because we were ready for battle every night. We also acquired guns, and our room looked like a police barracks (*Bustenai*, 8/14/29).

The uprooting of six hundred Bedouins from the land on which the moshava Mettula was established served as the classic example for the first article in the history of Zionism devoted entirely to the "Arab problem." Epstein, after describing the expulsion of the Bedouins, summarized the situation thus:

> The Druze in Mettula are impoverished, and when they were expelled from the village, although each received several hundred francs, were in a bad state. . . . Under these conditions they could under no circumstances reconcile themselves to the idea that they must forget Mettula. Thus they continued to ambush the moshava and threaten it, and they also shot at one of the houses. . . . Can we rely on such a method of land purchase? Will it succeed? Is it appropriate for our goal? A hundred times—the answer is no (*Hashiloach*, No. 17, 1908).

Violent clashes on a similar basis occurred in Gedera, whose land was the "soul and spirit" of the Arab village Katra. (In opposition to this purchase, Abraham Moyal, representative of the Hovevei Zion [see Glossary: "First Aliya"], wrote a biting letter to Pinsker in 1886 [Druyanov, 1919]). Large-scale land purchases in the Tiberias district also aroused violent uprisings since

Most of the land was purchased from various effendis who owned the different villages on which the fellaheen were tenants or laborers. The transfer of the effendis' land to the Jews left many of the fellaheen without means and without work. That is why they did not want to leave the land which they had cultivated for many years, and the help of soldiers had to be enlisted in order to get the Arabs off the land (Y. Luria, *Haolam*, 3/6/1909).

The Ottoman Empire did not generally serve as an agent for Jewish interests. On the contrary, while the Turks were not worried about the landless fellaheen, they were not in favor of Jewish settlement in Palestine (see Mandel, 1965). Thus in 1882 a law was passed prohibiting land transfer to Jews. The extent to which this regulation was enforced was largely dependent on the character of the Empire's local representative. When the governor in Jerusalem could not easily be bribed and saw Jewish settlement as detrimental to the Empire (e.g., Raoul Pasha, 1876-88), he strictly enforced the regulation and used fellaheen who had suffered from the land purchases to recruit Arab villagers to attack the moshavot (Druyanov, 1919:52). As a rule, however, the regulation could be eluded by means of bribery, and its only effect was a rise in land prices, since payment had to be made both to the land owners and to the officials through whom the transaction was made. Gradually damage payments to the tenants became institutionalized to obtain their agreement to leave the lands. These damage payments were made in cash, in equivalent lands, or both. The lands were often outside the boundaries of Palestine (in Syria or Trans-Jordan), and thus a type of population transfer took place whose scope is difficult to estimate. For example, according to Assaf (quoting from the *Book of the Lower Galilee*), during the purchase of lands in Galilee:

At one time an agreement had been reached [*by Kalvarisky as the representative of JCA*] with the Amir [*Ali El G'azri, the owner of the Libya lands in the Galilee*] who promised to sell the four villages and transfer their residents to Syria. The Amir was unsuccessful in his attempts to convince the residents of the villages.... Eventually, the village of Saabat came to an agreement with the officials. ... The people from Shaara recently were persuaded as well and left when they were promised two dunams in Syria for every dunam in Palestine and were paid the price of the houses and rentals (1970:41).

In the period of the First Aliya, the problem of the removal of fellaheen and Bedouins from the lands they cultivated or lived on was not very acute. The settlement was very small, and it aroused little hostility. Where there were clashes, these could be attributed mainly to local customs or perhaps—quoting Israel Belkind—to "a result of mutual misunderstanding, lack of knowledge of the language and customs of the land" (*Hagana*, 1954:73). Another reason why the removal of the fellaheen did not become a central issue in this period was the prevalence of Arab labor in the moshavot. Although at first most of the settlements were based on the principle of self-labor, in time small colonies of Arab laborers were created around the periphery of almost all the moshavot. Thus many of the fellaheen who lived on land sold to Jews lost their land but not their livelihood. (There were periods in which the demand for Arab workers in the moshavot exceeded the supply.) The Jews stressed the fact that the fellaheen's economic situation as laborers for the Jews was often an improvement over their situations as tenants of the effendis or as independent fellaheen.

The question arises: Why were lands acquired which involved problems of tenancy, the removal of fellaheen, and a dual price when there were unsettled but cultivable lands within the territory seen as suitable for Jewish settlement? It seems that a combination of factors was involved. First, there was a preference for the purchase of large tracts of land for settlement, and the large tracts offered for sale were those owned by the powerful effendis, most of which had Arab tenants. Second, the lands perceived as cultivable were those which were being cultivated at the time of purchase or had been cultivated in the past. Only later did the ideas of land improvement and development, the draining of swamps, and "making the desert bloom" develop. Third, under the circumstances of a small settlement struggling for its very existence (see Motzkin, 1939:15-52), little attention was paid by the Yishuv to the social problems of the Arabs or the development of neighborly relations with the Arab community:

> Under the influence of the JCA officials an attempt was made to buy off influential Arabs. ... Both in the labor movement—especially among Hapoel Hatzair and part of Poalei Zion, there prevailed the belief that there was no need to come in contact with the Arabs (who were not perceived as influential)—they

should neither be shunned nor an effort be made to establish ties with them (*Sefer Hashomer*, 1957:375-76).

The next wave of immigration brought about increased alienation of the tenant fellaheen from the land purchased by Jews because the Second Aliya made Jewish labor and its "conquest" a central issue in the internal struggles of the Yishuv (see Shapiro, 1977). In addition, when some of the members of this aliya decided to settle on Jewish National Fund lands (their original intent was to organize an agrarian proletariat), the Zionist movement was encouraged to allocate greater resources for land purchase and develop a policy of land purchase.* The first step was to begin the purchase of the Jezreel Valley. The Valley was not densely populated, but in it there were several villages whose residents cultivated the area by means of tenants and hired laborers. The number of fellaheen who were alienated from the Valley as a result of the purchase by the Jews is subject to dispute. Arab witnesses who testified before the Shaw Commission (Great Britain, 1929:118) claimed that 1,746 families (or 8,730 individuals) were forced to leave the Valley as a result of the purchase, while Ruppin testified before the same commission that the number of tenants alienated from the land did not exceed 700-800 and that "most found other land in the area" (1937:250). Hope-Simpson (1930:51) states that the Northern District clerk reported that, according to the 1922 census, 4,900 persons lived in the villages purchased by the Jews, to whom should be added another 20 percent who did not register in order to evade military service. Included in the Jewish Agency memorandum submitted to Hope-Simpson was a list of 688 tenants who left the Valley, only 84 of whom were no longer employed in agriculture, and 41 for which "no information could be obtained."

For our purposes, the exact number of fellaheen alienated from the Valley lands (and who did or did not receive damage payments) is not significant. What is significant is how the matter was perceived by the parties to the conflict and what meanings were attributed to

---

*When the Zionist movement's Palestine Office was opened, the JNF owned only limited areas (Chittin, Beit Arif-Ben-Shem, and Dlaika Um-Juni, later Degania and Kinneret), and had no clear plan what to do with them. It was essential to begin cultivating these lands, however, because (as noted earlier) according to Ottoman law, lands not cultivated for more than three years are *Mahlul*, and can be confiscated.

the land purchases. Assaf quotes (from *The Book of the Lower Galilee*)
Yitzchak Ben-Zvi's impressions of a trip in the Jezreel Valley in 1910:

> All along the way the Arabs we met asked us about Poolia [*Mer-havia*], and most with surprise. The subject was discussed even in villages three or four hours distance away. Some were angry at Sursuk who sold his land to the Jews. Particularly typical was the conversation at the Makaibla fountain where we met an old man who began to speak of the subject. I asked: "What is all the noise about if the Jews bought one village?" He answered: "One thing is certain, and this our fathers have told us: If the Jews bought four cubits and took one step in Marj Ibn Aamar [*the Jezreel Valley*], in the end the whole Valley will fall into their hands" (1970:62).

In 1924, the conquest of the Valley lands was still accompanied
by violent clashes. Several tenants in Poolia refused to leave the village
when Jewish workers came to cultivate the land, even though they
had received payment for damages. In the course of the struggle, an
Arab was killed, and the event was much discussed in both communities. But between the time the Jews gained control of the Jezreel
Valley and February 1929, when they turned their attention to the
Wadi Havarat (the Hefer Valley), the problem of tenants and the
alienation of fellaheen and Bedouins from the lands was not salient,
and where friction existed, it was localized and sporadic.*

The struggle over Wadi Havarat lasted for more than four years.
Again it was Hankin who, with the aid of an Arab political leader,
Awni Abdul Haadi, purchased the land—31,000 dunams—at an
auction (*Hagana*, 1964:1174). About 1,200 Bedouins and an unknown number of tenant fellaheen from the village of Cacoon lived
on the land. The Arabs carried on a fairly unified struggle on different levels. The Supreme Moslem Council claimed that some of the
lands were wakf land, while a group of residents of Tul-Karem brought
legal charges against the seller of the land on the grounds that it had
been stolen from their families. The Bedouins then refused to leave

---

*An additional area was acquired during this period—the Zebulun Valley and
Haifa Bay—but it was poor land, much of it sandy, and the Bedouin settlement
of about one hundred families was protected by the Mandatory Government
(Granovsky, 1940:162). In the first decade after its purchase, the area was only
partly settled, and its purchase aroused controversy within the Jewish community.

the Valley, interfered with the plowing and settlement, and uprooted about 24,000 eucalyptus trees planted to mark the boundaries of the area. The British army was forced to intervene. The High Commissioner stated that "he knew the legal situation was in favor of the Jewish National Fund," but he "hesitated to evict 1,200 Arabs . . . because very minor propaganda may cause a disturbance of the peace and a new outbreak of rioting" (*Hagana*, 1964:455). Finally, the Mandatory Government rented lands in another location to the Bedouins of Wadi Havarat, to which they were transferred in 1933.

After Ben-Gurion was elected Chairman of the Zionist Executive, he decided to contact Arab leaders with the hope of arriving at an agreement with them. He met with Awni Abdul Haadi in 1934. According to Ben-Gurion's memoirs, Abdul Haadi

> opened with the land question. The Jews were buying up the best lands and dispossessing the Arabs. All the valleys were in their hands: the coastal valley, the Jezreel Valley, the Huleh. Weizmann and others were always proclaiming goodwill towards the Arabs— where was this goodwill? . . . What have you done to prove your goodwill? The settlement of the Jews undermines the existence of the Arabs. It is of no benefit to us. Individuals among us have become rich, but the people are losing their positions. The Jews have introduced speculation into the country. They pay exaggerated prices for the land. . . . Who can resist any insane prices paid by the Jews? The Englishmen are helping to dispossess the Arabs from the land, contrary to the Mandate. He was planning to go to court to protest the illegality of the Jewish purchases. He knew that he would lose, for there was no justice in the land, but he wished to try. . . . The behavior of the Jewish National Fund was particularly reprehensible. It did not leave the Arabs any trace of land (1972:18).

These complaints ran through almost all the discussions with Arab leaders, until finally Ben-Gurion despaired of the possibility of reaching an agreement.

Contrary to Abdul Haadi's complaint, the Mandatory Government attributed great significance to the problem of the fellaheen who were left without land, and in 1931 Lewis French was appointed to conduct an investigation to identify all the Arabs "who can be shown to have been displaced from the land which they occupied in consequence of the lands falling into Jewish hands, and who have not obtained other holdings on which they can establish themselves or other equally satisfactory occupation" (French, 1931:5). To locate those who had been evicted from the land, claims to land could be submitted free of charge. According to the Report on Administration (1935:5), a total of 3,271 claims were submitted, of which only 664 were found to be justified—even fewer than the 688 cases listed by the Jewish Agency for Hope-Simpson! Of these 664 claims, the government decided to grant 347 heads of household immediate preference and purchased lands for them for a total of approximately £72,000 (ESCO Foundation, 1947:717).

Even taking into account the low population density of Palestine and the fact that most of the lands purchased by Jews were in the mountain area, away from the Arab population centers, considering that by 1935 more than a million dunams of land had been purchased by Jews (see Table 2.1), even 3,271 Arab claims seems a very small number. Does the fault lie in French's narrow definition of "dispossessed persons," as charged not only by Arab and pro-Arab circles, but also by the Peel Commission (1937:240), inasmuch as his definition included neither the fellaheen who sold their lands to Arabs who later sold them to Jews nor the *charats*—the hired workers—who lost their jobs? But even the use of French's politically biased definition of "dispossessed" does not explain the small number of fellaheen's land claims. Hyamson offers a better explanation: that the Jewish buyers and Arab sellers were aware of the problematic aspects of transferring lands on which tenants lived, and took preliminary steps to vacate the lands before they were transferred:

Under this legislation [*of 1920*], land could not be transferred unless the interests of the tenant were safeguarded by the retention of sufficient land for the maintenance of himself and his family. The interests of both the vendor and the purchasers were, however, opposed to this. The purchasers were ready to pay high prices, above the hitherto current value, but required vacant land for settlement. The vendors, having no local interests, were, of course, anxious to sell at the highest possible prices. They quickly found at small cost a means of circumventing the legislation. In this they had as allies the money-lenders to whom most of the peasants were heavily indebted. The course taken was to persuade and pay the tenants, before steps were taken for a transfer of the land, to vacate their holdings. When the transfer took place the land was consequently empty, without tenants for whom to provide. And all parties were satisfied—the vendors, the purchasers and presumably the money-lenders, permanently, the tenants for only a short time. . . . These proceedings continued for eight years, during which many of the larger estates passed out of the hands of the larger owners, for the most part resident abroad, into those of one or other of the subsidiaries of the Zionist Organization (1950:87).

In addition, Mussa Alami, a Palestinian-Arab politician described by Ben-Gurion (1967:89) as a highly moral leader, maintains that the Arab money-lenders were financed by the Jewish National Fund and other Jewish land-purchase organizations (Furlonge, 1969:61).*

It can be assumed, then, that during the process of Jewish land purchase and settlement in Palestine, many more tenants were alienated from the land than is reflected in the number of claims presented (French himself estimated the number of "eligible" families as between 1,000 and 2,000). Was the small number of claims a matter of strict definitions of eligibility or "deserving" families, or was it a failure of the Arab leadership to recruit the population for an anti-Zionist demonstration? The eviction of fellaheen from the land occurred simultaneously with and seemed to contribute to the process of urbanization within Arab society in Palestine. According to the Government Survey of Palestine (1946a:697-98), in 1922 the urban Arab population represented about 29 percent of the total Arab population, while by 1944 this percentage had risen to 34 percent. According to Ruppin, families of tenants who were "banished from agriculture" (whose number he estimates at almost 1,000) received an average damage payment of £40, which was "an important sum for a fellah, with which he could pay off his debts" (1937:205)—payment which according to Hope-Simpson amounted to "27 Pounds

*C.F. Strickland (Palestine, 1930b), who was appointed to study the situation of the Arab farmers' debts, recommended the establishment of cooperatives for credit and marketing to strengthen the economic position of the fellaheen. This would lessen their direct competition with Jews and thus reduce their opposition to the development of the Jewish sector (ESCO, 1947:712-13). In December 1933, the Government enacted a law which encouraged the creation of cooperatives, and by the end of 1937, 121 associations had been founded with 5,121 members. But from that point on, the cooperative movement began to decline (Abramovitz and Gelfat, 1944:115-17).

Sterling per person, or enough to start in a new occupation" (1930:68). Some of the new occupations were concentrated in the urban areas, and those who came to the cities found work in the Jewish, Arab, and government sectors. In the traditional Arab sector, they were absorbed in service jobs or joined the masses of peddlers, small merchants, and intermediaries between the Jews and Arabs. The government sector employed more than 30,000 Arabs in 1945 in a wide variety of roles and ranks (Supplement to Survey of Palestine, 1947:89), and the Jewish community continually absorbed large numbers of Arab workers, despite the struggle over Jewish labor. Thus was created a growing Arab *lumpenproletariat* no longer confined within the traditional structure of Arab society, but not yet established as an independent stratum—a familiar phenomenon in the early stages of modernization in other societies (see, for example, Eisenstadt, 1966: 2-5). The development of a new Arab urban stratum seems to have facilitated land purchase by Jews by making a steady supply of agricultural lands available, counteracting to a certain extent the very high fertility rate of the Palestine Arabs (55.5 per 1,000 persons in 1926, 49.2 per 1,000 in 1941).

The increasing urbanization of the Arab rural population, together with the migration of Arabs out of Palestine (during 1920-1931, 16,447 Arabs emigrated from Palestine [Boneh, 1938:271]), seem to provide a partial explanation for the small number of Arab land claims between 1931 and 1935. Large numbers of Arabs immigrated *into* Palestine during this period, but they tended to join the urban population and, in any case, they could not make claims to land.

Until the end of the 1930s, Jewish land purchases did not harm a large stratum of Arabs, but rather presented a potential threat and created an impression that Jews had the ability to "buy everything." Since the Arab leadership was able to exert very little control over land sale, this aspect of the struggle became more and more symbolic. An attempt was made by the Arab leadership, and especially the Supreme Moslem Council, to assign religious significance to the conflict over land and to make the sale of land grounds for denying membership in the collectivity:

> In the thirties, when the Palestinian nationalist movement began to organize a propaganda and persuasion campaign for the prevention of sale of Arab lands to Jews, the Supreme Moslem Council and its president were the main instrument for the enactment of this policy.

116

The president of the Supreme Moslem Council and the Alaama [*Moslem religious sages*] published a Patwa [*religious decree*] prohibiting the sale of lands to Jews and threatening to excommunicate, and to refuse to marry or bury anyone who helped violate the commandment of this Patwa (Porath, 1971:166).

The Jerusalem Mufti—Haj Amin El-Husseini (see Glossary: Hussainies)—attempted to make the problem of land a central issue in the Arab struggle as part of his effort to bolster his position as a national leader. The Jewish press of the period was full of reports (usually including quotations from the Arab press) of the Mufti's propaganda campaigns relating to land. Most meetings with the Mufti ended with a collective oath by those present not to sell their lands to Jews. For example, when a delegation of leaders paid their condolences to the Mufti upon the death of his brother, the Mufti reacted as follows: "Money and man can be replaced. The thing which has no replacement is the land. Watch over your lands, and this will be my consolation" (*Haaretz*, 7/10/35; quoted from *El Jaama*).

From 1932 to 1936 was a period of economic prosperity in the Jewish economy. With the initiative of land purchase transferred to private organizations and individuals, the purchases became scattered and sporadic, and while the rate of land purchase increased only slightly, many more individuals within the Arab community were directly involved in land sales. Land prices rose sharply as a combined result of the increased demand and the addition of the political component in the price of land. These changes seem to have intensified the Arab anxiety and to spread it throughout the fellaheen. The Arab rebellion of 1936-39 was the first marked by the participation of the agricultural laborers, who soon took the initiative. While the sale of land to the Jews was not the major cause of the rebellion, the British—in their efforts to pacify and compensate the Arab community—drastically limited the rights of Jews to purchase additional lands.

Of course, such restrictions were not new. The Shaw Commission (Palestine, 1929:123) had already concluded that there was no more land in Palestine on which new immigrants could be settled without evicting the resident population. What was new was the scope and severity of the prohibitions on land sales, which were perceived by the Jews (and probably the Arabs) as a cancellation of the British obligation to aid in the establishment of a Jewish national home, as this was understood by the Zionist movement (Ussishkin, 1940: "The British Government is creating a *ghetto* for the Jewish people"). According to the Land Transfer Ordinance published on 28 February 1940 as an appendix to the 1939 White Paper, the land in Palestine was to be divided into three areas:

(A) An area in which all purchase or transfer of lands from Palestine Arabs to Jews and/or any foreign citizens was prohibited. This area included about 16,000,000 dunams, of which 5,400,000 were in the Northern Negev—about 63 percent of the total area of West Palestine, but only about 2 percent of the Jewish-owned lands.

(B) An area in which the sale of land to Jews was prohibited, except in special cases which the High Commissioner could designate. This included about 32 percent of the total area of Palestine (about 8,530,000 dunams), within which were about 33 percent of the Jewish-owned lands.

(C) An area in which land sale to all was permitted without restriction. This included about 5 percent of the total land area in Palestine (about 1,300,000 dunams), of which about one-half was already Jewish-owned.

The prohibitions did not include urban lands, and Ussishkin contended that "the Government's main purpose is that the social structure of the Jewish community in Palestine should remain as it was in the Diaspora lands" (1940). But the British aim, along with ensuring an "Arab rear guard" during wartime, seems to have been to enact the partition program of the Woodhead Commission*—a narrow coastal strip for the Jews, with the rest of the area of Palestine to be a British Mandate and an Arab state. This was not the original intention of the ordinance as described by Ramsay MacDonald in Parliament (23 May 1939)—i.e., to prevent the eviction of Arabs in areas densely populated by them and where the Jews had already purchased much land" (Bauer, 1973:46).

There was controversy within the Yishuv concerning how to react to the White Paper policy and the Land Transfer Ordinances. There was pressure from a minority of the leadership of the Yishuv, headed by Ben-Gurion, for a militant policy. At the beginning, demonstrations and protest activities were organized by the Hagana, but the moderate sector of the leadership, which supported the use

*A commission headed by Sir John Woodhead assigned to work out details of the Partition Plan proposed in 1937 by the Royal [Peel] Commission.

of political means, finally won out—almost splitting the labor movement. With the intensification of the World War, the political struggle against the White Paper lost its force. It became clear that the slogan "We will fight the White Paper as if Hitler did not exist, and we will fight Hitler as if the White Paper did not exist" (coined by Ben-Gurion) was not realistic under the prevailing conditions. Or as Weizmann put it:

> Our protest against the White Paper ran parallel with our solemn declaration that in the coming world struggle we stood committed more than any other people in the world to the defence of democracy, and therefore to cooperation with England—author of the White Paper. Such was the paradox of our position (1940:509).

The Land Transfer Ordinance did not seriously limit the land transfers from the Arab to the Jewish sector, however, and even during the Arab rebellion the rate of Jewish land purchases was high. The annual report of the Jewish National Fund's central office commented:

> In 1939, 53,499 dunams were redeemed by the Jewish National Fund, an area of a size which had never been purchased in any one year, except for 1929. . . . From the outbreak of the riots until the end of 1939, despite the great handicaps of the time, the Jewish National Fund succeeded in redeeming, in these three and one-half years, no less than 108,000 dunams, and these were not just any lands—these were most important areas in almost all parts of the country (JNF, 1939).

A report of 1942 notes further:

> In the last three years [1940-42], 22.5 percent of all the lands which were purchased by the Jewish National Fund since it came into existence were acquired. . . . The lands purchased in 1942 [48,981 dunams] were not all bought from Arabs. Some were registered in the names of Jewish societies or individuals who could not pay their debts or who did not in actuality own the land (JNF, 1942).

During the first year of operation of the Land Transfer Ordinance, of a total of 33,270 dunams of land purchased by the JNF, 33.3 percent were purchased from Arab owners in the limited and prohibited areas (see Table 5.1); in fact, most of the JNF's purchases were from the limited and prohibited areas. In the areas in which land transfer was permitted, the great majority of the purchases were from Arabs. Even as during the Arab rebellion (which occurred at a time of economic recession, when the JNF was forced to buy Jewish land so that it would not fall back into Arab hands), only about 30 percent of the extensive purchases by the JNF were lands bought from Jews (JNF, 1939). Marlow (1951:169) reports that from 1940-1947 (during which time the Land Transfer Ordinance was in effect), the JNF purchased 275,000 dunams of land in the limited and prohibited areas, doubling its land holdings.

We do not know what would have happened if the British had

Table 5.1

JEWISH NATIONAL FUND LAND PURCHASE DURING FIRST YEAR OF LAND TRANSFER ORDINANCE (MARCH 1940-FEBRUARY 1941) BY AREA TYPE AND NATIONAL ORIGIN OF OWNER

Area Type	National Origin of Owner		
	Jews	Arabs	Total
	In dunams		
Permitted	—	12,300	12,300
Limited	3,000	8,770	11,770
Prohibited	6,900	2,300	9,200
TOTAL	9,900	23,370	33,270
	By percent		
Permitted	—	36.9	36.9
Limited	9.0	26.4	35.4
Prohibited	20.7	6.9	27.6
TOTAL	29.7	70.2	99.9

Source: Computed from Granovsky (1941:8).

not attempted to severely restrict land transfers, but comparison with other periods suggests that the British effort had little or no effect on the process of land transfer. On the contrary, it appears that the political intervention, by raising the price of land and creating a condition of low frontierity, provided sufficient incentive to ensure that land would be available at a rate to meet the settlement needs and capacities of the Yishuv. That is the paradox of low frontierity: as the land rises in price, its fluidity and availability increase.

The Arab rebellion of 1936-39, and the economic sanctions the Arabs enforced against the Yishuv and the British, brought about economic collapse within the Arab sector, with a great scarcity of capital. According to Granovsky, the price of land declined for a period, flooding the market:

> The prices [of land] declined so much that land could be acquired for two-thirds of the former price, and often for half the price before the riots, during the time of immigration and prosperity. . . . [The decline in land prices] enabled the Jews to take advantage of these offers on a larger scale (1940:36-37).

Thus, by providing one of the catalysts of the Arab rebellion, the Jewish purchase of land acted as a "boomerang" against the Arabs by accelerating the process of land transfer, at least on a short-term basis.

THE 1948 WAR AND ITS RESULTS

On 29 November 1947, the United Nations General Assembly decided, on the basis of a recommendation of the United Nations Special Committee on Palestine (UNSCOP), to divide Palestine into two states—one Jewish and the other Arab. The Jews accepted the General Assembly's recommendation, while the local Arabs (after consultation with neighboring Arab nations) rejected the plan to establish an Arab state in the part of Palestine allocated to them.*

*The boundaries of the Partition Plan of 1947 were such that most of the areas densely populated by Jews were included in the Jewish state, as well as most of the Central and Southeastern Negev. The southern half of the coastal area, the Jaffa region, the Judean and Samarian hills, and the western Galilee were included in the proposed Arab state. Jerusalem and Bethlehem were to be under the authority of the United Nations. Within a Jewish state of about 600,000 Jews, there would be a minority of about 500,000 Arabs, while several points of Jewish settlement would lie within sovereign Arab territory.

Hostilities broke out immediately, and gradually intensified. The first stage of the struggle resembled the Arab rebellion of 1936-39, except that this time the Jewish forces took offensive initiatives while the British avoided any significant intervention. The second stage of the struggle began on 14 May 1948, when, coincident with the declaration by the Jews of the establishment of the Jewish state, regular Arab forces began an invasion into Palestine. The military and political results of this two-stage struggle are well-known (see Hurewitz, 1950; Gabbay, 1959; Khouri, 1968), and for our purposes can be summarized thus: (a) the Jewish State of Israel attained political control over an area about 20 percent larger than that allocated to it under the 1947 Partition Plan (about 20,250 sq. km. compared to 16,000); (b) the Arab population in the State of Israel's total area was reduced by about 80 percent from that which had been in this same area prior to the war.

At the war's end, Israeli sovereignty was distributed over five types of lands: (1) lands newly under government ownership, almost all of which were uncultivated and located in the Negev Desert, (2) lands that had been under public or private Jewish ownership even before the war, (3) lands owned by Arabs who remained on those lands during the war, (4) lands owned by Arabs who remained in Israel but who were legally defined as absent from their lands (see below), and (5) lands owned by Arabs who were not in Israel when the armistice agreements were signed.

While there is controversy as to the reasons why Arab owners abandoned their lands, there is almost no controversy concerning the extent of the lands regarded as abandoned by their Arab owners, living either within Israel's boundaries (until the 1967 War) or outside them, and transferred to Israeli sovereign control and later to Jewish ownership. As reported in an official publication of the State of Israel: "The rural property which was in the hands of the Custodian [*on Arab property which was defined as abandoned*] included about 350 abandoned and partially abandoned villages whose total area was 3 1/4 million dunams" (Israel, 1949:74). According to an Arab source, 385 Arab villages within the boundaries of Israel were destroyed between the 1948 War and the 1967 War. The Israeli estimate is lower, but only by 23 villages.

If we accept the Israeli estimate (see Table 5.2), then about 86 percent of the Arab villages existing at the time of the Mandate

Table 5.2

ESTIMATE OF ARAB VILLAGES IN DISTRICTS INCLUDED IN ISRAEL BEFORE AND AFTER 1947/48 WAR

District	Number of Villages		
	In 1945	In 1950	Abandoned, 1945-1950
Haifa	48	6	42
Acre	49	27	22
Nazareth	27	22	5
Safed	73	4	69
Tiberias	21	2	19
Jenin	8	3	5
Beith Shean	24	1	23
Tul-Karem	33	28	5
Lod-Ramle	58	0	58
Jaffa	23	0	23
Jerusalem (inc. Bethlehem)	28	3	25
Hebron	15	0	15
Gaza	45	0	45
TOTALS	452	96	356

Sources: (1) Palestine, 1946b; (2) Israel, 1951a:261; (3) Palestine, 1946c; (4) State of Israel, Dept. of Public Measurements, updating of Palestine, 1946c (Tel Aviv).

Note: In Source 4, 218 destroyed Arab settlements are cited. This does not include smaller settlements which did not appear on the map but which were included in Palestine (1946c), nor does it include settlements which the Arabs left and the Jews took over, but which were not destroyed. A partial indicator of this can be found in Israel (1951a:276-77), in which 66 Arab settlements which were given Israeli names are listed. Thus the number of Arab settlements which disappeared is 284, according to official Israeli sources.

which were included within the boundaries of the State of Israel were abandoned.* This is in addition to urban areas, almost all of which were abandoned. (Jaffa, a city of 70,000 inhabitants, was almost totally abandoned, and of about 45,000 Arab residents in Haifa, only 4,000 remained—most of them Christians. Tiberias was abandoned in similar fashion.) Also, many Bedouin tribes which had wandered between the Sinai Desert and Trans-Jordan, making the Negev Desert their center, were transferred across the armistice boundaries—or their wandering was prohibited.

This de-Arabization of very large parts of the territories captured by Jewish forces was a result of two complementary factors: (a) the basic weakness of the Arabic-Palestinian social structure, and (b) military decisions made in the Hagana command which were perceived as necessary under conditions of conflict, but arrived at without taking their wider political implications into account.

When the decisive struggle for political control of Palestine began, it appeared to all sides that the Arabs possessed a clear advantage, and that if the local Palestinians, with the help of the Arab Liberation Army[†] and volunteers from neighboring countries, failed to gain a victory, the regular Arab armies were likely to intervene (including the Jordanian Legion, which had previously served in Palestine under British supervision). But by May 1948 (the date of the official declaration of the establishment of the State of Israel and the British departure from Palestine), the military defeat and political and social collapse of the Arab Palestinians had become inevitable.

The Arab flight and military defeat were very closely interrelated, and both reflected weaknesses in the structure of Arab society. From the beginning of December 1947, along with the renewal of the Arab

---

*According to the *Israel Statistical Yearbook* (1970:32), ninety-nine Arab villages remained within the armistice lines in Israel's territory. According to Dayan (*Haaretz*, 6/29/73), about 700,000 Arabs, who left about four million dunams of land, left the area. A demographer, Janet Abu-Lughod (1971:161), estimated the number of Arabs who left at about 775,000.

[†]The Arab Liberation Army was an organization of Palestinian and other Arab volunteers formed after a convention of representatives of the Arab states (Cairo, 8 December 1947) rejected the Partition Plan. For information on the Arab and Jewish forces during the war, see Gabbay (1959) and Lorch (1961).

rebellion,* population movements began within the Arab community. The first was the departure of some of the wealthy families from the country (a departure whose beginnings can already be seen in 1936-39), and the second was the movement of Arab families *within* the country's boundaries from mixed areas of Jews and Arabs to exclusively Arab areas (Assaf, 1967:180). As Mussa Alami describes it:

> At first the Arab flight from Palestine was only a trickle, consisting mostly either of the inhabitants of isolated settlements who found themselves cut off from larger Arab groupings by Jewish-controlled areas and who, rather than risk being shot by trying to cross them, made their way on foot or by sea to the Egyptian border beyond Gaza or to the Lebanon; or some of the more well-to-do families who sensing trouble ahead, followed the immemorial desert-bred custom of moving elsewhere until it should blow over (Furlonge, 1969:155).

At the same time there was movement in the opposite direction, with thousands of Arab volunteers infiltrating the boundaries of Mandatory Palestine and joining the guerilla units fighting inside the country. (The first large-scale attack by the Arab Liberation Army was in the middle of February on kibbutz Tirat-Zvi.) Even though there was a fair number of military officers among the volunteers, most of whom had received their training in the Arab Legion or the Egyptian and Iraqi armies, the caliber of this army was not high. It included many unemployed persons, adventurers, and marginal people who had not been absorbed into Arab society.†

*The rebellion began with an Arab attack on the Jews' commercial center in Jerusalem on 2 December 1947. This was followed by an attempt to attack a neighborhood in the south of Tel-Aviv (8 December) and an attempt to destroy Kfar Etzion (14 January 1948)— the center of a small cluster of Jewish settlements in a mountainous area which was almost totally Arab. The latter two attempts convinced the Arabs it would be difficult for them to attack Jewish settlements directly, so they returned to the patterns of 1936-39: sporadic bursts of guerilla warfare and actions to cut off transportation between clusters of Jewish settlement. The latter was very successful from the Arab standpoint and represented an immediate threat to the Jewish community, which faced the prospect of total destruction of its military, economic, and political potential if its various parts became detached.

†The volunteers were generally from a lower social stratum than the local Arabs, creating friction between the two groups which sometimes compelled the local residents to abandon their homes; see the Iraqi Parliament's Investigation Commission (1954:97) and Furlonge (1969:150).

The general low caliber of the local fighting forces was again reflective of the social situation. There was a common pattern in the Arab groups. Villagers or tribesmen would unite under a local leader for a large-scale ad hoc action (the Faza's pattern), and then scatter after the action. (The nucleus of a regular army would usually remain around the leader—see Arnon-Ohanna, 1981a and 1981b). In addition, two paramilitary organizations were active—the Najada in Jaffa and the Futuwa in Jerusalem. These were composed of urban nuclei, and at first glance seemed to be equivalent to the Jewish Hagana. But they suffered from faulty organization and inability to recruit, and in 1947, when the British ceased fulfilling their protector roles and left a vacuum which put the Arabs and Jews in confrontation, the Palestinian Arab organizations were not able to play any significant military role. There was often competition and hostility between the local leaders, and only Haj Amin El-Husseini had a measure of political authority on the national level.* There were two military leaders whose authority was national, but each had his own private army.†
Thus this "national" rebellion was managed at the local level.

As a result, when the Jewish forces began their well-organized counter-offensive (see below), the Arabs were no match for them. The Arab villages and cities attacked by the Jews (except for some villages on Mount Carmel) could not withstand the military assault, even when they received reinforcement from Liberation Army volunteers.

The capture of an Arab village by Jewish forces meant, in most cases, its evacuation, since the Hagana did not have the manpower to leave a holding army to prevent the return of the Arab forces. In many cases the Arab villages were found abandoned or partially abandoned by the entering Jewish forces because the inhabitants had

---

*Haj Amin El-Husseini was the most prominent Arab Palestinian leader who sought to establish an exclusively Arab state throughout the whole of Palestine. At the Arab League Convention in Cairo, he argued that the defense of Palestine could be left entirely to the local Arabs. Husseini's greatest error, apart from his unrealistic estimate of Arab power as compared to that of the Jews, was siding with the Germans at the beginning of World War II. He went to Berlin and aided in the establishment of an Arab division within the Axis armies. From the time the British suppressed the Arab rebellion in 1939, the Palestinian Arabs were without significant political leadership (Shimoni, 1962).

†These two commanders were Abdul Kader El-Husseini and Hassan Saalame, both of whom fell at the beginning of the fighting.

retreated along with the defeated Arab defense forces. In the early stages of the war, often nothing was left for the Jewish forces to do after capturing a village but to destroy the abandoned houses. The Jewish forces did not interfere with the Arabs' abandonment of entire areas, but even helped to complete their evacuation. Uri Avneri describes the dynamics of Arab abandonment as follows:

> The main flight of the Arabs was not the result of any deliberate policy, neither of the Arabs nor of the Zionists, but a natural result of the War itself. Few realize today that the Arabs never fled the country. What actually happened was that when an Arab military unit would retreat from a village to one behind it during an Israeli attack, the population of the abandoned village would also retreat, for fear of being harmed. The Israelis often say that the Arabs were frightened because they knew what they would do to the Israelis if the situation had been reversed. The truth is that it is natural for backward people to abandon their homes for several days in time of a military attack on their village. If kibbutz members and other villagers in Israel did not act thus, but rather stayed in their homes and fought until the last minute side by side with the soldiers, this stemmed from the special nature of these villages with their strong defence consciousness and with their appropriate organization. This stemmed also from the feeling, which was common to all the Israelis in that War, that "there is no choice," and nowhere to retreat (1968).

There was also a very specific reason for the Arabs' fear of remaining in captured villages. On 9 April 1948, the National Military Organization (NMO) and Lehi forces attacked the village of Deir Yassin, near Jerusalem. The attack took place despite the fact that only two weeks before the village dignitaries had arranged a truce with the Jewish forces in the area. The capture of Deir Yassin was undertaken as part of an overall campaign by the Jewish forces to gain control of the road to Jerusalem (the "Nahshon" campaign). A few days before, several other Arab villages in the area (Kastel, Hulda, and Dir-Mochsin) had been captured by the Hagana forces. The Hagana also gained control over the village of Abu Gosh, whose inhabitants did not flee—nor were they forced to flee.* The taking of

*Abu-Gosh was a large village on the route to Jerusalem known for its friendliness to the Jews. It seems to have been the only Arab village on the way to

Deir Yassin by the NMO and Lehi was approved by the commander of Jerusalem

> on the condition that you are capable of holding it. If you cannot, then I warn you not to bomb the village, because such a bombing will bring about the abandonment of the village by its inhabitants and the capture of the ruins and abandoned houses by foreign forces. Such a situation will make the general battle more difficult rather than easier (*Hagana*, 1972:1546-47).

The NMO and Lehi suffered many casualties at the beginning of the attack on the village, but in the process of gaining control over it, they killed almost all its inhabitants; in addition, a number of captured prisoners were murdered after being displayed in a victory parade in Jerusalem. All told, 245 of Deir Yassin's inhabitants were killed.

The Deir Yassin slaughter, which was performed by a marginal group apparently acting on its own, was of course not "acceptable conflictual behavior" in the Jews' eyes, as described in the official history (see *Hagana*, 1972:1547). But the incident gained wide publicity among the Arabs, who blew it up even beyond its already immense proportions. The Arab leadership was interested in demonstrating the Jews' cruelty in order to recruit as many strata of the Arab populace as possible to the struggle, but the rumors of Jewish horrors had the opposite effect and intensified the mass panic and flight.* In the words of Alami:

> Fear gripped the countryside after the Deir Yassin massacre, and the trickle of refugees became a flood. When on May 15 the last British troops left and the Arab Legion was at last able to enter

Jerusalem which did not participate in the efforts to block Jewish transportation to the city—both in 1936-39 and in 1948. In 1953 the Abu Gosh villagers complained to a *Haaretz* reporter that the government was trying to force them to abandon their lands (9/28/53). According to Geries (1969:119), on 7 July 1953 about one hundred residents of Abu Gosh were already exiled "to an unknown destination."

*Begin (1951:155) claimed that the Deir Yassin events, which he described as a routine war action in which many from both sides were injured, had immediate desirable results. The village of Kolonia, which threatened the transportation to Jerusalem and rebuffed several Hagana attacks, was abandoned without a battle; similarly, Beit-Iksa and the Kastel promptly fell into the Hagana's hands. The head of the NMO observed that "What was invented about Deir Yassin helped in fact to carve the way to Jewish victories on the battlefield."

Palestine and to occupy as much as it could of the Arab zone, there was a general rush to take refuge behind its bayonets (Furlonge, 1969:171).

Actually there was a mass flight of refugees even before word of the horrors of Deir Yassin spread.* It began with the counteroffensive of the Jewish forces, who feared the isolation of large areas of Jewish settlement, by the cutting of the transportation routes between them, and the destruction of remote villages—the same fears that Alami discusses from the Arab point of view. The period between 9 April and 15 May was decisive, both in terms of the military situation and its demographic results, with approximately 250,000 Arabs abandoning their traditional places of residence.

From the Arab side, the Arab collapse and flight can be explained as stemming from two deep-rooted causes and five immediate causes directly related to the war. The first deep-rooted cause was the semi-feudal structure of Arab society and the dependence of the masses on the traditional elite (sheikhs, mukhtars, landowners, etc.) and the more modern elite (administrative officials, lawyers, doctors, etc.):

> For the fellaheen or the bedouins, who are primitive, economically depressed and politically neglected, the landlord, the Sheikh, the teacher or the clergyman is worthy of respect and appreciation. To them, he is the symbol of knowledge and power. He is educated, intelligent and well-informed. He can understand broadcasts, read newspapers, and through his personal relations knows everything, and thus he is to be followed, especially in time of danger and general strife (Gabbay, 1959:871).†

According to Gabbay, the second deep-rooted cause was a psychological one—the tendency in Arab society to exaggerate in describing events. This tendency was intensified in a situation of

---

*Analysis of the Jewish press of the period indicates frequent reports of large-scale Arab flight even before 9 April 1948.

†This does not explain why the leadership itself abandoned the country. We can only hypothesize, following Gabbay's logic, that this semi-feudal leadership had no belief in or link to its followers. This description of Arab society is somewhat simplistic, but it resembles Lerner's (1958:20-28) description of a Turkish village before beginning the processes of modernization.

pressure and uncertainty, where a lack of channels of information was coupled with an abundance of contradictory information—an ideal situation for the creation and spreading of rumors. The effect of this under wartime conditions was (1) a psychosis of fear among the Arab population, (2) the lack of a coordinated military program between the various Arab participants, (3) the encouragement of the flight of Arab citizens, (4) the flight of the Arab leadership, both local and national, and, finally, (5) the collapse of the Arab economy. Pail (1973) shows how sovereignty was expropriated from the local Arabs by the Arab states, which acted mainly to protect their own interests—another component in the political-military impotence of the Palestinians at the time.

Until now, we have summarized briefly the causes of the Arab exodus rooted in Arab society, but—as already noted—the process of "de-Arabization" of much of the disputed territory was aided by the perception of the situation by the Jewish side.

The Jewish perception of the situation was that the very existence of the Jewish collectivity was seriously threatened—even within the area allocated to it by the Partition Plan. This perception was summarized by Ben-Gurion on 8 January 1948 in the Mapai party's center as follows:

> The political goal of this War is Arab rule over Palestine. This basic goal has three aspects: (A) This is a war for the destruction of the Yishuv. The Arabs know that there can be no Arab rule over the land as long as the Yishuv exists. . . . (B) This is a war against the establishment of a Jewish State—even in part of the land. . . . (C) If the first two goals are not achieved . . . the war is aimed at limiting the boundaries of the Jewish State in the Negev and in the Galilee, and possibly also in Haifa and other places (1950:23-24).

The threat was perceived to stem not so much from the Palestinian Arabs* as from the combined regular and irregular army forces— supported by a local "fifth column"—which would operate mostly against the transportation lines linking the clusters of Jewish settle-

---

*On 18 June 1947, Ben-Gurion had offered this evaluation: "Although the Arabs now have much more arms than in 1936, and I fear that their arms are increasing more than ours, I have no doubt that without the English and the Arabs from outside, we would overcome them without much difficulty and we would force them to surrender" (1950:30).

ment or the roads leading to remote Jewish settlements. To meet this threat, the Hagana's General Staff worked out a detailed plan of action known as Plan D. Its goals are described in the preface:

> The aim of this plan is the control of the area of the Jewish State and the defence of its borders [*as determined by the Partition Plan*] and of the clusters of settlement and population outside the boundaries, against regular and irregular enemy forces operating from bases outside and inside the State (*Hagana*, 1972:1955).

The plan proposes many types of actions, but for the purposes of this study, perhaps the most noteworthy are these:

> Actions against enemy settlements *located in or near our defense system*, with the aim of preventing their use as bases for active armed forces. These actions will be divided into the following types:

> —The destruction of villages (by fire, bombing, and mining)—*especially* of those villages over which we cannot gain control.

> —Gaining of control will be accomplished in accordance with the following instructions: The encircling of the village and the search of it. In the event of resistance—the destruction of the armed forces and the *expulsion of the population beyond the boundaries of the State* (*Hagana*, 1972:1957; emphases added).

At first glance, this seems to be only a military-operational program for providing maximum protection to the area of the Jewish state and defense of the Jewish settlements outside the state's boundaries. But the plan had far-reaching political implications—especially the decision to defend the Jewish settlements outside the boundaries designated in the Partition Plan.* As we have seen, the plan permitted the expulsion of "resistant" populations beyond the boundaries of the state if necessary to gain control of all the territories within the Jewish defense system.† In addition, city-dwelling Arabs scattered in

---

*One exception was Beit-Haarava, located north of the Dead Sea, which was deemed to be militarily indefensible (Allon, 1968:31).

†The plan did not specifically define the "defense system," which could include every place within or near the state's boundaries as well as all the areas of Jewish settlement outside the boundaries and the roads leading to them. In addition, there was no exact definition of "resistance." It seems that the commanders in the field were permitted to make their own definitions.

various urban areas could be concentrated in one place to make supervision of them easier. Thus, to ensure the success of military action, general permission was granted to move Arab inhabitants both within and outside the boundaries of the future Jewish state. The decision to defend points of settlement and settlement centers not included within the Jewish state's boundaries had the effect of expanding the Jewish territory beyond what was specified by the Partition Plan. Plan D, therefore, developed as a basis for military activity, had political effects of two types: (1) the expulsion of most of the Arab population from the Jewish state, and (2) the potential extension of Jewish control over territories outside the boundaries set by the Partition Plan.*

It is difficult to know to what extent the authors of Plan D were aware of its political implications, but it is very likely that the formulators of the plan—and especially their head, Yigael Yadin (Sukenik)—were oblivious to its political implications, and based it on purely military considerations. This hypothesis is somewhat reinforced by an interview granted by Yadin to *Maariv* (5/17/73) in which he reacts vehemently to the charge that one of the plan's aims was the expulsion of the Palestinian Arabs. Elsewhere in the interview we learn that at the time the plan was devised there was almost no connection between the political sphere, represented by Ben-Gurion, and the Hagana's General Staff, and that internal friction almost completely cut off communication between the political leadership and the heads of the armed forces. At a later stage of the war, the General Staff sought to intensify the Arabs' flight in the belief that the stream of refugees increased the economic and psychological pressures on the Arab states and hindered their military efforts.

Whether or not the political leadership was a participant in the military actions which resulted in the de-Arabization of part of the conquered territories, there is no doubt that it was aware of this result, either while it was occurring or soon after. Already on 7 December 1948—when the Arabs' flight from the country was still very limited

*This should not be seen as a decision to violate the Partition Plan. Had the Arabs accepted the partition, these military actions would have been unnecessary, since Jewish settlements could have existed within Arab Palestine just as Arab settlements could have existed within the Jewish state.

and consisted primarily of departures from mixed areas, Ben-Gurion stated in the Mapai Council:

> I am not sure that the Arab leadership's thinking, to the effect that they have nothing to lose, is correct. What happened in Jerusalem and Haifa [*Arab flight*] can happen in large parts of the land— if we succeed. . . . It is likely that in the next six or eight or ten months of the war, great changes will take place in the country— and not all of them to our disadvantage. *No doubt, there will be great changes in the composition of the country's population* (1950:59; emphasis added).*

It is difficult to determine—particularly in a matter so fraught with emotion and so politically explosive—to what extent these sections of the plan were implemented, but for the purpose of our analysis it is sufficient to note that they were part of the orders given to the Jewish commanders on the assumption that the commanders were likely to face situations to which they would be applicable. And indeed there were cases in which the populations of entire villages were expelled (see Kimmerling, 1977). It seems, therefore, that the military actions combined with the structural weaknesses of Palestinian-Arab society and the fears each side had of the other[†] to bring about the de-Arabization of the lion's share of the territories captured by the Jews in the 1947/48 War.

Thus large tracts of land of the Arab population which moved— or was transferred—outside the state's boundaries fell into the State of Israel's hands. All that was left was to determine the legal status of these lands.

---

*MacDonald writes in his memoirs: "No responsible Zionist leader had anticipated such a 'miraculous' clearing of the land. Dr. Weizmann, despite his ingrained rationalism, spoke to me emotionally of this 'miraculous simplification of Israel's task' " (1951:176).

[†]The fears on both sides stemmed from well-documented events which illustrated the other side's potential for cruelty. Just as the example of Deir Yassin was cited as a possible fate for all Arabs who were conquered by Jews, so the slaughter of the Jews of Safed, the destruction of the entire Jewish community in Hebron in the 1929 riots, and the slaughter of the caravan of students and professors who went up to the Hebrew University campus on Mount Scopus on 13 March 1948 were cited as examples of the probable fate of any members of the Jewish collectivity who fell into Arab hands.

THE ISRAELIFICATION OF THE LANDS

In the 1947/48 War, Israel attained political sovereignty over a territory of 7,819 square miles. However, this did not remove the land issue from the Jewish-Arab conflict, but merely changed its character. For the Jews the central problem now was how to translate the Israeli sovereignty over lands which remained under various forms of Arab ownership to Israeli ownership, and how to strengthen the claims to both sovereignty and ownership by establishing Israeli presence.

Already in the war's final stages, an Israeli policy had begun to be formulated whereby Arabs who had abandoned their lands would not be permitted to return to them (Ben-Gurion, 1950:130-31), though future peace settlements would require that they be appropriately compensated after all sides' "obligations" had been met (see, for example, M. Attar, "A Program for Arab Refugees," *Haaretz*, 7/28/48). Here we see a new attempt to convert lands into economic resources in order to gain ownership of them. Prior to this, the Provisional Council of the State had cancelled the 1940 land transfer regulations retroactively to give legal validity to all the Jewish land purchases made in the areas where they had been prohibited under those regulations.

In addition, the Provisional Council of the State appointed a custodian for the land to deal with the property the Arabs had abandoned. Abandoned area was defined in the Abandoned Areas Ordinance,* adopted on 24 June 1948, in which it was stated that

The government may apply to any abandoned area part or all of the existing law while preserving the religious and ritual rights of the inhabitants, as long as this does not impair public security and order, and empowers the Prime Minister or any other Minister to enact any regulation which he sees fit in reference to the defence of the State, the public's security, essential supplies and services . . . [*including*] expropriation and confiscation of any movable and

*According to the Abandoned Areas Ordinance, Section 1(A), "abandoned area" means land abandoned by all or some of its inhabitants which was declared abandoned, or any area captured by Jewish armed forces or surrendering to them. By this definition, any conquered area—whether or not it was abandoned—could be classified as an abandoned area.

immovable property within any abandoned area (*Official Paper*, No. 7, June 1948, p. 19).

This was only a temporary order. The first legislation aimed at bridging the gap between the de-Arabization of the territories (and property) and their Israelification was the Absentees' Property Law—1950, which sought to freeze the abandonment of lands by broadly defining the concept of "absentee" as follows:

A person who, at any time during the period between the 29th November, 1947 and the day on which a declaration is published . . . that the state of emergency declared by the Provisional Council of the State . . . has ceased to exist, was a legal owner of any property situated in the area of Israel or enjoyed or held it, whether by himself or through another, and who, at any time during the said period

(i) was a national or citizen of Lebanon, Egypt, Syria, Saudi-Arabia, Trans-Jordan, Iraq, or the Yemen, or

(ii) was in one of these countries or any part of Palestine outside the area of Israel, or

(iii) was a Palestinian citizen and left his ordinary place of residence in Palestine

    (a) for a place outside Palestine before the 1st September, 1948; or

    (b) for a place in Palestine held at the time by forces which sought to prevent the establishment of the State of Israel or which fought against it after its establishment (*Laws of the State of Israel*, Vol. 4, 1949/50, p. 68).

It is particularly interesting that this law made all the Arab residents found in Israel (including those who had received Israeli citizenship) into absentees if they had left their places of residence to go to a place "held at the time by forces which sought to prevent the establishment of the State of Israel or which fought against it after its establishment." As noted, during the 1947/48 War most of the Arab villagers attempted to escape to other villages in which there were "forces which sought to prevent. . . " Thus almost every Arab inhabitant of Israeli territory who had at any time left his place of residence or who had been transferred to Israel was considered an absentee. A stratum of "present absentees" was created, most of whom were the residents of the villages annexed to Israel as part of the armistice agreement with Jordan. In another section of the Absentees' Property Law, consecrated Moslem property—the wakf—was included in the category of absentees' property.*

Another legal instrument for freezing absentee property was Regulation 125 of the Defence Regulations (Emergency)—1945, which empowered military commanders to declare certain areas as closed to all persons not having written permission from the commander to enter or leave.[†] Twelve villages and their lands were declared closed.**

Legal instruments were made available for the evacuation of the Arab population even after the mass exodus of the war. Thus Regulation 8A of the Emergency Regulations (Security Areas)—1949, which was extended several times, stated that "an authorized source may command a permanent resident of a security area to leave the area." The security areas included the Upper and Eastern Galilee and a strip ten kilometers wide along the boundary with Jordan. In principle, this regulation made it possible to expel the residents of most of the villages in the Galilee and the "Little Triangle,"[††] but it seems to have been enforced only in a few cases (see Kimmerling, 1977). Similarly, the Law of Land Acquisition in Time of Emergency authorized

*The Moslem community in Israel continued to demand the release of the wakf property, which had been transferred to the Custodian, and in 1952 a committee was established to examine the problem. The committee submitted its recommendations in 1961, proposing that the government "submit the consecrated Moslem property which is allocated for charitable and ritual purposes to the self-management of the urban Moslem communities" (*Government Yearbook*, 1961:25). A law was adopted after much deliberation on 2 February 1965 (*Book of Laws*, 445, 1965:58) which stated that all property defined as consecrated "would be allocated to a custodian with no conditions or limits."

[†]Until 1966, the vast majority of the Arab population in Israel was subject to the authority of the military government. Any temporary or permanent move required the permission of a military commander, and such permits were often used to reward "appropriate" behavior. This military rule was highly controversial in the Jewish community.

**The affected villages were Paradis, Amka, Araan, Rabesia, Rovas, Tzipori, Magdal, Mear, Quikad, Birveh, Damon, and Birim.

[††]A narrow strip of land—averaging about two miles wide—along a fifty-five mile section of the eastern front where Arab-controlled territory extended so far west and northwest of Jerusalem that it nearly cut Israel into two sections. This area was ceded to Israel under the terms of the armistice with Jordan.

the government to issue "land acquisition orders" when "necessary for the defence of the State and public security," and to hold these lands for up to three years. The law expired in August 1958, but some lands held after this date were considered expropriated by the state (*Book of Laws*, 149, 1955:159).

The next legislative stage was aimed at facilitating the transfer of lands from a condition of "no ownership" to Israeli ownership—that is, for completing the Israelification of the land. This stage was begun with a law which, among other things, granted special powers to a Development Authority to acquire land, in particular:

2(a) Property in respect of which the Minister certifies by certificate under his hand:

(1) that on the 1st April, 1952 was not in the possession of its owners, and

(2) that within the period between the 14th May, 1948 and 1st April, 1952 was used or assigned for purposes essential to development, settlement, or security, and

(3) that is still required for any of these purposes—shall rest in the Development Authority and be regarded as free from any charge, and that the Development Authority may forthwith take possession thereof . . . *

3(a) The owners of acquired property are entitled to compensation thereof from the Development Authority. The compensation shall be given in money, unless otherwise agreed between the owners and the Development Authority . . . (*Laws of the State of Israel*, Vol. 122, 1953:44).

About half a year after this law was enacted, regulations were published which expropriated the lands of about 250 abandoned Arab villages and individual parcels of land belonging to absentees which amounted to about 1,250,000 dunams. This law was more stringent than the Absentees' Property Law—1950. It not only transferred abandoned lands to government ownership, but also did not establish any "authority" to release lands which had become government property. On the other hand, it allocated damage payments to the former landowners who remained in Israel and provided that:

*The Development Authority was established in 1950 for the purpose of acquiring ownership of and developing abandoned Arab territories, including the "present absentees'" property.

137

Where the acquired property was used for agriculture and was the main source of livelihood of its owner, and he has no other land sufficient for his livelihood, the Development Authority shall, on his demand, offer him other property, either for ownership or for lease, as full or partial compensation.

In the 1972 *Report of the Israel Land Authority*, it was reported that "From the time the law was enacted until . . . 1970/71, 12,244 claims over an area of about 174,000 dunams were made, and in exchange about I£25 million were paid and about 45 thousand dunams of land were given as compensation" (1972:55). However, many Arabs did not file claims for compensation for their lands for a combination of reasons: (a) in the Arab community, the relinquishing of land was still viewed as unpatriotic, as it had been during the Mandate; (b) the compensation offered was often land belonging to other Arab absentees—sometimes members of the same family—which was certainly unacceptable in a familistic society such as that of the Palestinian Arabs; (c) the rate of compensation was low. (The base for computing the value of the expropriated property was its value on 1 January 1950, when land prices were low, with an annual increment of only 3 percent, even though the value of the Israeli lira had declined at a much greater rate than 3 percent a year.) The 1973 law set much higher compensation rates, but the Knesset member from Rakah (see Glossary), Tufik Tubi, referred to these as "nominal prices . . . of robbery and theft" (*Maariv*, 6/28/73).

Another regulation which could be used for the de-Arabization of lands was the Emergency Regulation for the Cultivation of Fallow Lands, 1948 (*Official Paper*, 15 October 1945), but it does not seem to have been widely used for this purpose. This regulation empowered the Minister of Agriculture to take over fallow lands to ensure their cultivation. In combination with the Security Areas regulation or the Regulation on Closed Areas, it could be used to transfer lands forbidden to their Arab owners to Jewish hands. Here, too, the lands first underwent de-Arabization and then were later transferred to the state's ownership.

Thus the political system made use of its legislative institutions for the management of the conflict. However it is essential to distinguish between two types of legislative activity. The first type established the legal basis for the Israelification of the lands whose Arab owners were outside the boundaries of the Jewish state at the end of the 1948 War. The second type facilitated the de-Arabization of lands whose owners were inhabitants of Israel at the end of the war. The first type was clearly directed against the opponents in a conflict in accordance with the collectivity's perception of its cardinal interests. The second type was more complex and raised some basic issues:

1. As a result of the change from a community lacking political sovereignty but quite homogeneous in its composition to a sovereign state including within it a distinct minority, it became difficult to define the collectivity—to decide whether and to what extent the Arab minority should be considered part of the collectivity. This created difficulties in differentiating between sovereignty, ownership, and presence in relation to territory. Ownership or maintenance of territory by Arabs was perceived as a threat to Israeli sovereignty because it was difficult to regard the Arabs who remained within the state's boundaries as belonging to the same collectivity as the Jews as long as the potential for warfare between the Jews and Arabs had not ceased. As a result:

2. There was a conflict between the desire to build an open and democratic society patterned on the Western democracies and the collectivity's need to maximize control of the land resources, with the price being denial of democratic privileges to the Arab minority.*

The Israelification of lands was undertaken by extra-legal means as well. Between 1949 and 1959, Arabs—individuals, villages, and tribes—were compelled to leave their lands. Some were expelled to other areas within Israel and others to places beyond the armistice lines.

According to the survey submitted to the Anglo-American Committee (Palestine, 1946a:151), the population of the town of

---

*It was often asserted that not only was it not democratic to apply certain regulations and laws only to the Arab population, but that this double standard would in the end harm the Israelis themselves. It is likely that the Jewish attitude toward the Arab minority stemmed in large part from the dynamics of relations with minorities in a system with no tradition of tolerance. While tolerance toward minorities plays an important role in Zionist ideology, particularly in the light of Jewish history as victims of intolerance, most studies show that negative stereotypes of minorities are prevalent in Israel (Peres, 1971: Tamarin, 1973), and the Jewish-Arab conflict only strengthens them.

Magdal was 9,910 in 1944, while after the war only about 2,500 residents remained. In August 1950 almost all the town's residents were transferred to the Gaza Strip (the few remaining were transferred to Jaffa, Lod, and Ramle), some of whom received material compensation. The Israeli press gave this partial report:

> All during 21 August, 1950, "departure fever" prevailed in Migdal Gad [*the Hebrew name of Magdal, which was later changed to Migdal-Ashkelon*]. Hundreds of the 1,700 residents in the Arab ghetto registered for transfer to the Gaza Strip. . . . Most of those leaving have parts of their families in the refugee camps in Gaza and have given up hope of a change in their political status which would allow for the refugees' return (*Yediot Achronot*, 8/22/50).

> Seven hundred Arabs voluntarily departed from Migdal Gad for the Gaza Strip. In the first stage, their transfer was undertaken in complete secrecy and met with the Egyptian government's refusal to accept the Arabs. Another 500 Arabs are about to leave Migdal Gad for Egyptian areas. It should be noted that the transfer is being undertaken without any coercion being exerted by the Israeli government, and the Arabs are permitted to take their belongings with them (*Haaretz*, 8/22/50).

It is very difficult to estimate the extent of land which was expropriated from Arabs living within Israel's boundaries. Geries (1969:138) estimates a million dunams, while Naim Makhul, Chairman of the National Organization of Arab Farmers in Israel, estimated that 65 percent of the lands which were in the hands of Arab farmers from the end of the 1948 War until 1963 were expropriated (*Haaretz*, 3/6/65).

A complementary dimension of the Israelification of Israeli territory was the settlement of areas with a sparse Jewish population (such as the Negev and the Galilee), or as we have referred to it, the demonstration of Jewish presence. This presence was perceived not only as a narrow security need, but also as a fulfillment of sovereignty. Shimon Peres, while serving as the Vice-Minister of Defense, stated that

> Unsettled or partly settled areas within Israel represent and will represent a subject of interest beyond the sphere of settlement

policy. The Arab countries have their eyes on the area settled by Jews, so that they are obviously even more desirous of areas which are not at all settled or which are not settled by Jews (*Davar*, 1/26/69).

One of the results of the Israelification process was the establishment of the town of Carmiel. In the first years of the State of Israel's existence, the Galilee area was neglected and absorbed almost none of the waves of Jewish immigration, possibly because it lacked a base of urban Jewish settlement. As noted, the Galilee was mostly an Arab area when captured in 1948. At the end of the 1960s, the government began to feel uneasy about the lack of Jewish presence in the Galilee.* A journalist summarized this feeling as follows:

There are those who encourage the [*illegal*] spread [*capture and cultivation of absentees' lands*] of the Arab minority in the heart of the Galilee ... in writing and orally, in Hebrew and Arabic publications, in meetings in public and at home: "Your lands were stolen by the Jews. Take them back. Your forefathers held onto these stones. They are yours." ... They have forgotten the meaning of the "abandoned Arab village" whose residents fled across the border and want to blot out the memory of the conquest of the Galilee by the Israel Defence Forces and the fact that the land of the Galilee is the land of the State of Israel and its land laws apply to it.

In addition, in less public—but not less well-known—forums, again and again one hears the claim that the Galilee did not fall into Israel's hands in accordance with the partition of the country and that there is still justification for holding a public referendum in this area, which is Arab rather than Jewish.

"Our Galilee?" Maybe on the map. In reality, on the territory itself things look entirely different, and only we are to blame, for the problem of the Galilee is a Jewish problem.

In reality almost 120,000 Arabs ... live in this area, and a total

---

*See Kimmerling (1977), where the case of Ikrit and Birim is analyzed; see also Zureik (1979) and Lustick (1980).

of about 10,000 Jews, that is—only about eight percent (*Yediot Achronot*, 12/12/63).*

Plans for the establishment of a Jewish city in the Galilee began to be formulated in government offices in 1959 with great secrecy: "All publicizing of a plan for the establishment of a town or city in this area was forbidden" (*Haaretz*, 9/22/64). In his budget proposal for 1963, the Minister of the Treasury, Levi Eshkol, included a section to provide for the establishment of a new city in the Galilee. At the beginning of 1963 he announced the expropriation of an area of 5,500 dunams for this purpose, most of it belonging to the residents of the Arab villages of Nahf, Dir-El-Assad, and Anna. The village residents embarked on a legal battle against the expropriation of the lands, at the same time utilizing the "Zionist method" of attempting to create established facts in the area. For example, *Haaretz* (4/6/63) reported that

> Recently, there have been efforts at plowing the lands expropriated for the building of the new city of Carmiel. These efforts have been made by the inhabitants of Dir-El-Assad, who have been removed from the area by the police and have been charged with trespassing. . . . At the beginning it seemed as though the former owners wish to gain greater compensation for their lands by proving that they had plowed the fields. However, it now seems that the plowing of the expropriated area was planned to create a nuisance and to prove that the villages oppose the expropriation of the area, although its expropriation was certified in all the legal stages.

In addition, the villagers appealed to the High Court and to Jewish public opinion, but without success. Except for a marginal group of Communists and intellectuals, the public was not interested in the Arab "cause," despite considerable attention from the press. As in other cases of this type, the judicial and legislative branches of the state tended to adopt a particularistic orientation and act in accordance with the Jewish interest.

---

*Almost identical arguments were offered two years later as justification for the establishment of Carmiel (*Davar*, 9/24/64). It is interesting that in 1975 the low percentage of Jews was still regarded as a serious problem in the Lower Galilee, where there were 3,500 Jews and 27,000 Arabs (*Maariv*, 8/12/75).

The Israelification of state lands until the 1967 War can be seen in summary form by comparing Table 5.3 with Table 2.1. From Table 5.3 it is clear that the Israelification went hand in hand with the nationalization of lands, with about 92.6 percent of Israel's lands belonging to the state or the Jewish National Fund, and only 7.3 percent privately owned by Jews or Arabs. If we assume that by 1948 the Jewish National Fund held about a million dunams of land, then the Jewish people's portion increased about three and a half times by 1962. About half of the lands defined as privately owned were owned by Arabs—that is, about 750,000 dunams. Thus the Israelification of lands in Israel was almost total.

Table 5.3

THE DISTRIBUTION OF LANDS IN ISRAEL ACCORDING TO OWNERSHIP, 1962

	Dunams	Percent
State and Development Authority lands	15,205,000	75.07%
Jewish National Fund lands	3,570,000	17.62
Privately owned land	1,480,000	7.31
TOTAL	20,255,000	100.00

Source: Israel Land Authority, Report for 1961/62 (Jerusalem, June 1962, p. 7). [Hebrew]

The collectivity's orientation to land is expressed in the first section of the Basic Law: Israel Lands, adopted by the Knesset on 19 July 1960:

1. The ownership of Israel lands, being the lands in Israel of the State, the Development Authority or the Jewish National Fund, shall not be transferred either by sale or in any other manner.

This Basic Law (and its operational complement—Israel Lands Administration Law, 1960) along with the political center's systematic action to gain ownership of maximum amounts of land within the state (and beginning with 1967, in the occupied territories as well) expresses the aspiration to freeze most of the land owned by the collectivity or, as expressed by the Chairman of the Constitution and Law Committee, Z. Warhaftig, in the Knesset during a discussion of the law:

> The law [*Basic Law—Israel Lands*] deals with land which is the people's property and expresses a basic principle in the life of our people—that is, that ownership of the land may never be permanently transferred. . . . The reasons for the suggestion of this law . . . are: granting a legal aspect to a basic religious principle, that is— "The land shall never be sold because the land is mine" (*Leviticus* 25:23).
>
> Whether this biblical verse was mentioned in this law (according to one suggestion) or not, the law represents a legal expression of the same rule and principle found in our Bible. This law expresses our basic view as to the sacredness of Israel. . . . The second reason is a practical one: the land was captured by the entire nation. God promised it to our forefathers—Abraham, Isaac, and Jacob, and it was first conquered by the entire nation—by Joshua and all those who came out of Egypt, and by David and the entire people, and again by the Babylonian exiles, and again—in our time—by the people residing in Zion with the help of our people all over the world.
>
> The lands of the Jewish National Fund were also purchased with pennies which came from all our people in all their dispersions, and *the lands of the Development Authority were sanctified with the blood of our young soldiers.* We have no right to convert this property, which was purchased and captured by the entire people, to private property (*Divrei Haknesset*, 1960:1916; emphasis added).*

However, the basic assumptions underlying this law are both collectivist in nature—that is, that the land was promised by God's command to the entire tribe, which acquired additional right to it through three conquests—and particularistic, since the land could not be returned in any form to the Arabs. M. Sneh, a Member of the Parliament (MAKI party—see Glossary) said in a discussion of this Basic Law and in reference to lands of the Jewish National Fund:

---

*The Basic Law is not so strict, however, and permits certain forms of sale on a limited scale.

How much land is today in JNF hands in comparison with the amount before the establishment of the State? What brought about this increase? The State took over abandoned lands of Arab refugees and transferred them to the JNF. After their transfer, it was stated that Arabs may not be settled on these lands which had been taken from them (*Divrei Haknesset* 1960:1022).

Since "After the establishment of the State, the purchase of land by the JNF from non-Jewish owners declined, while ... the State became the owner of most of Israel's lands with the Government managing them and developing them,"* the JNF and the Israeli government reached an agreement in 1961 whereby "the State would be in charge of managing its lands, lands of the Development Authority, or JNF lands—whether purchased in the past or to be purchased in the future." Furthermore it was decided that a united management (the Israel Land Authority) would be established, without any changes being made in the ownership of the land. Even after the establishment of the Authority, JNF lands would be managed subject to JNF regulations which, as mentioned, had been adapted to the management of the conflict according to the views which had been crystallized in the pre-sovereign period.

SUMMARY

The processes which were reviewed in this chapter are divided into three periods. The first is the period of the original territorial accumulation, during which the Jewish immigrants converted money into land. The Arabs involved in this conversion were those who owned the land and those who worked it—two categories which seldom overlapped. The Arab landowners were the main beneficiaries, with the Palestinian Arab economy also benefitting from the influx of capital (see Kimmerling, 1979). The most adversely affected were the tenants, especially at the beginning of the period, which caused a great deal of tension between the two communities, and laid the foundation for the perception of the conflict between them as pri-

*From the "agreement" between the Israeli Government and the Jewish National Fund, World Zionist Federation, Jerusalem, 28 November 1961 (mimeographed), p. 1.

marily a territorial conflict. In later stages, the Jews tried to reduce the tension by paying compensation to the tenants, which raised the cost of land considerably and limited the frontierity even further. The accumulation of land by the Jews was very slow partly because of the low frontierity and partly because of the limited amount of capital available to the Zionist movement, but also to a large measure because of the internal disputes in the Jewish community (see Chapter 3). Nevertheless, enough land was transferred to Jewish possession in this period to provide the basis for the establishment of a small Jewish society, varied in structure, which would be able to gather enough political, social, and military strength to acquire territory in new ways.

(2) The second period was closer to the "Turnerian situation" of the existence of frontiers. As a result of its victory in armed conflict with the local Arab society and the seven Arab nations surrounding it, the Jewish community was to acquire land by military force. This was akin to the opening of the frontier to the Jewish society. It was a limited frontier, but it enabled the society to control much larger areas of land than before. When the war ended and ceasefire agreements had been signed which divided the land between Israel, on the one hand, and the Hashemite Kingdom and Egypt, on the other, the frontier was completely closed for several years.

(3) In the third period, the territory that was acquired was consolidated, or the level of control over it increased, as much as possible, while continuing attempts were made to add the component of sovereignty to those of ownership and presence (see pp. 19-25 above). The failure of Jews to own land or be present on it—or even more, Arab ownership or presence—was seen as a "dangerous" condition, and in order to establish Israeli control, the sovereign power of the state was used. Thus sovereignty became a means to achieve ownership and presence.

Chapter Six

THE REOPENING OF FRONTIERS: 1967-1982

In May 1967 Egypt violated two of the tacit agreements which had provided the basis for the *status quo* between Israel and Egypt since 1957: it concentrated forces in the Sinai Desert near the cease-fire line with Israel (at the same time expelling the UN Emergency Force stationed there as part of the 1957 settlement for Israeli withdrawal), and it closed the Straits of Tiran. From the Israeli perspective, each of these acts constituted a *casus belli*.* On 5 June Israel attacked the Egyptian forces in the Sinai and in Egypt itself. On the same day, Jordan and Syria entered the war in support of Egypt. The results of the war are well known. Israel defeated the three Arab states in what became known as the Six-Day War, and gained control of the Sinai Peninsula, the west bank of the Jordan, and the Syrian Golan Heights. As a consequence, Israel controlled additional territories totalling about 26,158 square miles, including about 23,166 square miles in the Sinai Desert—an area more than three times as large as its total territory prior to the 1967 War. Israel immediately annexed the eastern part of Jerusalem and unified the city, which had been divided since 1949. Along with the additional territories, more than a million Arabs fell under Israel's administration.†

---

*In 1964, Shimon Peres (*Bemaarachot*, 146, p. 3) listed three possible circumstances which would be cause for war: (1) the blockage of navigation to Eilat, (2) the conquest of Jordan, or (3) the concentration of forces in such proximity to Israel as to threaten its existence.

†After the waves of flight of Arabs from the captured territories died down, the Central Bureau of Statistics undertook a census (1967, 1968). In the West Bank, 598,687 inhabitants were reported (compared to about 730,000 under Jordanian rule); in the Gaza Strip and Northern Sinai there were 356,261 inhabitants (compared to a previous 450,000—an Egyptian estimate, probably inflated); in East Jerusalem there were 66,857 inhabitants (compared to 75,800

The acquisition of these extensive territories had not been anticipated, and stemmed in part from the war's outcome and in part from a constellation of international circumstances favorable to the Israelis. Israeli society adjusted very rapidly to the new situation, which significantly enhanced its self-image and had far-reaching effects on its actions in various spheres and many different directions. The purpose of this chapter is, *inter alia*, to describe the process of adjustment to the new situation and analyze some of its effects. We will discuss how the situation was perceived by various social and political groups, how it affected the struggles among them, and how these struggles influenced the Arab-Israeli conflict.

As soon as the new territories were acquired, the ambivalent attitude of the Israeli sociopolitical system toward them became apparent along four dimensions:

A. The Dimension of Collective Symbols. Until 1948, Judea and Samaria had always been an integral part of the Land of Israel (*Eretz Israel*). During the periods of the First and Second Temples, the Jews lived in the mountain area rather than in the coastal plain where most of modern Israel is located. Many Jewish symbols were linked to this area. Almost every place which was captured was the site of graves of the forefathers of ancient Israel and stirred recollections of biblical places about which every Israeli child had learned. This depth of feeling was expressed by Moshe Dayan immediately after the war when he declared that "We have returned to our people's holy places, to Shiloh and Anatot,* and we will never leave them." Religious sentiments were heightened by the interaction between the feelings aroused by the war and the encounter with places which were the cradle of Jewish mythology. This encounter also had negative effects: it challenged the consensus which had been arrived at through the first nineteen years of the Jewish state's existence. Ideological debates on basic questions of the Zionist

under Jordanian rule); and in the Golan Heights, there were 6,396 inhabitants (previous number unknown). Today this Arab population is estimated to be more than 20 percent larger because of the high rate of natural increase (close to 3 percent annually) and because Israel has permitted many residents who fled during the 1967 War to reunite with their families.

*Shiloh was a political-religious center at one period at the beginning of the Jewish nation, while Anatot was a village of priests near Jerusalem and the birthplace of the prophet Jeremiah.

movement were renewed, such as the demographic composition of the Jewish state, the extent of land needed for its existence, and especially the right of the Jewish people to settle in Israel.* The resolution of this issue would help to determine the attitude to be adopted toward the Palestinians. Did a Palestinian nation exist? (Did the Israelis want it to exist?) If it did exist, was a new explanation required for the persistence of the Jewish-Arab conflict?

B. *The Demographic Dimension.* The issue of the demographic composition of Israeli society arose because this time—in contrast to 1948/49—the vast majority of the Arab population did not abandon the occupied territories and did not aid in their "de-Arabization."† Had Israel claimed sovereignty over the West Bank territories, it would have had to accept—along with the territories—an Arab population which would constitute a very large minority. The inclusion of this minority in the collectivity, while preserving its democratic character, would have transformed it into a de facto bi-national state, which would severely threaten its basic self-image as a primarily Jewish society. Thus was created an internal conflict between demands to "open up the fatherland" by absorbing some of the new territories and the fear of threatening the collective identity and its societal boundaries if these demands were met.

In order to compute the "demographic threat" to the collectivity, estimates were published which showed the composition of Israel's population between 1990 and 2010 depending upon, variously, (1) how many and which territories were annexed to Israel, (2) three different growth rates of the Jewish population (level of fertility), and (3) three different rates of Jewish immigration to Israel (see Table 6.1).

From these estimates it is clear that if Israel annexed all the occupied territories and the average annual rates of Jewish immigration were low (the pessimistic view), then in thirty years the country's Arab population would be almost half of the total population, while if Israel did not annex any of the territories (excluding East

---

*For a comprehensive discussion of this issue, see Chapter 7.

†In fact it seems that, as a complement to the guerilla actions of the Palestinian organizations, which were undertaken mostly outside the boundaries of Israel and the occupied territories, the patriotic Arabs remained in the territories to prevent the type of de-Arabization which occurred in 1947.

Table 6.1

ESTIMATED PERCENTAGE JEWISH POPULATION
OF ISRAEL IN 1990, 2000, AND 2010
BASED ON VARIOUS TERRITORIAL,
IMMIGRATION, AND FERTILITY ASSUMPTIONS

Territorial and Immigration Assumptions	Level of Jewish Fertility[a]		
	Low Fertility	Medium Fertility	High Fertility

Israel returns to pre-1967 boundaries,
  annexing only East Jerusalem

		Year 2000	
	77.3%	78.0%	78.8%

Israel annexes West Bank, Gaza Strip,
  and Golan Heights

		Year 1990	
Zero immigration	54.0	54.7	55.0
20,000 annual immigration	57.2	57.9	58.5
40,000 annual immigration	59.9	60.6	61.2
		Year 2010	
Zero immigration	45.0	48.4	50.2
20,000 annual immigration	50.6	53.9	55.6
40,000 annual immigration	55.0	58.0	59.6

Sources: Central Bureau of Statistics (1981); Friedlander and Goldscheider (1979: 197).

[a]Medium fertility level assumed for the Arab population throughout.

Jerusalem, which is already annexed), the Arab population would only be about 21 percent of the total if Jewish fertility rates were high and 23 percent if Jewish fertility rates were low. The demographers Friedlander and Goldscheider (1979) calculated that if Israel annexed all the conquered territories and the rates of Jewish immigration were low or nil, the Jews would constitute 45-55 percent of the state's population in 2010, whereas if Jewish immigration were above average (40,000 immigrants annually) and Jewish fertility high, the Jewish population would constitute 60 percent of the total population. On the other hand, if Israel annexed only East Jerusalem, and Jewish immigration and fertility were both high, in 2010 the Jews would constitute 79 percent of the population of Israel (Central Bureau of Statistics, 1981).

C. The Dimension of Central Interests. The perceptions of interests involved in Jewish control of the territories were also widely varied. (1) All the territories captured in the 1967 War were perceived as drastically improving Israel's strategic position. The Suez Canal and the Sinai Desert gave the country a sense of security by creating a buffer zone between it and its most powerful enemy—Egypt. The Jordan River and the Jordan Valley provided a much more defensible boundary than the tortuous armistice line of 1947, while control of the Golan Heights also meant control of the lion's share of water sources essential to Israel.* (2) Some of the lands—especially the unsettled areas—were perceived by political leaders as valuable frontier essential to Israel's continued development and the absorption of new immigrants. This perception was a carryover of the agrarian views of the traditional Zionists. (3) The territories brought control of such additional resources as minerals in Sinai (e.g., manganese, uranium), relatively cheap manpower from Judea and Samaria,[†] and, as noted, water in the Golan Heights.

---

*The main border clashes with Syria from the beginning of the 1960s until the 1967 War grew out of Syria's attempts to divert the path of the Jordan River and its flow to the Negev through the Israeli pipeline. For several years the United States attempted to help the two sides reach an agreement on a just division of the Jordan's waters (the Johnston Plan).

†Within a short period, tens of thousands of workers from the occupied territories streamed to Israel in the wake of a postwar economic boom. These unskilled or semiskilled workers were concentrated mainly in the service and construction industries.

Later, oil fields were found in Sinai that, until 1977, supplied about one-fourth of Israeli oil consumption. (4) The control of the occupied territories brought to Israel a sense of change of status from a *tiny* state to one comparable in size to other *small* states—more in keeping with its social development, its international political role, and its level of technological and scientific advancement. (5) However, all these other interests were perceived as only of secondary importance when compared with the hope aroused in the Jewish community that the Israeli-Arab conflict might be resolved through negotiations over these territories. In the immediate postwar period it was widely felt both inside and outside Israel that the Arabs would be willing to acknowledge Israel's right to exist in exchange for the return of some or all of the conquered territories. However, it is important to emphasize that from the beginning there were many who were opposed to any such return, either because they saw symbolic gains or other interests as more important than peace, or because resolution of the Israeli-Arab conflict did not seem to them to be possible. (6) The interests involved in Israel's orientation to the occupied territories extended to its ties with other countries, especially the United States, whose policy of political and economic support is perceived as a cardinal Israeli interest.

D. The Perception of the Direction of the Action of Time. During the Mandatory Period, the Arabs sought to preserve the existing power relations—the status quo—while the Jewish community was interested in changing them in order to gain strength for a future showdown. From this perspective, time was perceived as favoring the Jewish side, so long as it undermined the status quo. To a certain extent, the situation was reversed between 1949 and 1967. The Arabs perceived of Israel as destined to continue its territorial expansion at their expense, so that they sought to gather strength to achieve their goal of destroying Israel (see Harkabi, 1972). Israel simultaneously strove to achieve two goals: first, in the long run, to gain Arab recognition of Israel's right to exist; second, in the short run, to prevent the Arabs from achieving their goal. Dan Horowitz (1971), in analyzing the Jewish-Arab conflict, concluded that

> The Israeli approach (which granted priority to the attainment of short-range goals even at the expense of the long-range goal)

stemmed from the assumption that existence *per se* takes precedence over peaceful existence. According to this assumption, the chances for peace are always doubtful, while the destruction of Israel in the event of military defeat is certain. From this stemmed the Israeli tendency to grant priority to short and middle-range security considerations over long-range political considerations, including those long-range goals linked with the chance of realizing Israel's declared ultimate goal. From the standpoint of Israel's long-range goal, it should have acted *to promote peace [i.e. the recognition of its legitimate existence]* whether the prognosis for this was optimistic or pessimistic. In reality, though, whenever a conflict emerged between the promotion of peace and Israeli-Arab power balance considerations ... Israel gave priority to doing away with the immediate danger (1971:7).

After 1948, Israel sought to preserve the status quo and the Arabs to undermine it. The effect of the time element was clear: time was perceived as working in the Arab's favor as long as the power relations—military, political, and social—were changing but as working in Israel's interest to the extent that her legitimated existence within the 1949 boundaries became institutionalized.

Between 1967 and 1973—with Israel administering the extensive captured territories—the view was strengthened on both sides that time was clearly operating in favor of the Israeli strategy of preserving the new territorial status quo.* Actually, Israel was pursuing the strategy of preservation of the status quo while creating *faits accomplis* in the territories to strengthen its position (1) inasmuch as it felt it would be unable to translate its war gains into Arab recognition of its existence and (2) inasmuch as chauvinistic trends were nurtured by the Arab refusal to recognize Israel. Nevertheless, the Israeli political system still had to decide whether to grant priority to the long-range goal—that is, to leave the territories available for possible exchange for Arab recognition—or to favor secondary goals, such as preserving maximum territory to ensure immediate security.

Israel's control of the territories created a much more complex conflict with the Arabs than before and confronted the system with

*It seems that the Egyptian belief that time was working in favor of Israel was a major factor in the initiation of war against Israel by the Egyptians (and the Syrians) in October 1973.

additional cross-pressures and internal cleavages.* The high degree of consensus which had prevailed in Israeli society between 1949 and 1967 on matters of national defense declined.[†] Some of the divisions led to the creation of political factions and parties as the conflicts concerning the captured territories cut across the political and ideological orientations which had been dominant in Israeli society.

In most of the controversies over defense policy, the future of the conquered territories and their inhabitants, and relations with the Arab states, the antagonists were divided into two camps, referred to colloquially as "hawks" and "doves." In broad outlines, the "doves" (a) were willing to relinquish all or most of the territories captured in 1967 in exchange for "some sort of peace,"** (b) wanted more active peace initiatives by the Israeli government toward the Arab states, (c) opposed the establishment of *faits accomplis* in the territories because they limited future options for peace, and (d) acknowledged the Palestinians' rights to parts of Palestine.

The elements common to the "hawks" view are less easily summarized: (a) they demanded annexation of all the territory acquired in the 1967 War to achieve strategic depth and easily defensible boundaries; (b) they sought to resolve the problem of the existence of large Arab populations in some of the territories by

---

*The situation after June 1967 was similar in complexity and type of problems to that before the "simplification" which had come about in 1948/49 with the de-Arabization of the country (see p. 133n above).

[†]During this period, security was a central concern in Israeli society. Any action linked to it became a sort of sacred rite (see Eisenstadt et al., 1972:205). Not only was it perceived as a vital need, but it was linked to the "prophetic" leadership of Ben-Gurion (see, for example, Brecher, 1972). The emphasis on security had far-reaching institutional effects: (a) the military became highly autonomous, since it lay beyond the political system's control; (b) there were attempts to convert military power and prestige to economic and political power, such as the attempt of the ruling party—Mapai—to gain votes in the 1955 elections by claiming credit for a technological-military achievement or the attempt to stifle criticism of the government on the grounds that it was damaging to the state's security. This abuse of the concept of national security was referred to as "defensism."

**The nature of the settlement for which the doves were willing to surrender territories is a subject of controversy. Some demanded nothing less than "real peace" as a condition, while others were willing to accept less on the grounds that one could not demand a total and immediate revolution in Arab attitudes.

granting Israeli citizenship, with all its rights and obligations, to all residents of the territories "who would so desire"; (c) they wanted to make it possible for agents of the government and private entrepreneurs to acquire Arab lands in the occupied territories to facilitate the de-freezing of ownership of these lands and permit the establishment of Jewish settlements in the territories—the first step toward establishment of sovereignty over the area.

There were only marginal attempts at building political groups and parties based on these opposing views. While an integral part of the nationalist right-wing program of the Gahal party (see Glossary)— and later the Likud (see Glossary), which succeeded it—was the idea of "no re-division of the land," this was only one of a series of opposing positions whose radicalism varied according to the times. After the 1967 War there were new parties which opposed Gahal, their very existence based on their opposition to retreat from the territories. One such party was that of Dr. Israel Eldad (right-wing leader and one-time major ideologue of the Lehi) in the 1969 Knesset elections. (It failed to win even one seat.) In addition, a Movement for a Whole Israel was established, lasting until September 1973, when it joined the Likud. The Thiya party (see Glossary) split from the Likud after the Camp David agreement. But the most salient hawkish sociopolitical movement in this period was the Gush Emunim (see below).

There were also several groupings of doves on the fringes of Israeli politics. One was Uri Avneri's party—Haolam Hazeh—which favored withdrawal from all the territories and Israeli peace initiatives "in exchange for territories." There were two other small parties in the Israeli parliament which favored withdrawal from all the territories. These were the Communist parties—one of which would have made withdrawal conditional on the achievement of a settlement, while the other favored unconditional withdrawal.* (The first of these merged with Avneri's party in 1977 to form the Zionist Sheli party.) Prior to the 1969 elections, a Peace List was organized by several professors (mostly from the Hebrew University) and intellectuals, who sought to pressure the government to adopt

*In 1965 the Israeli Communist Party split into two factions—an Arab faction and a Jewish faction. The Arab faction adopted a pro-Soviet policy, while the Jewish faction supported Israeli national interests (as perceived by them). Before the 1973 elections the Jewish faction united with leftist Zionist groups.

a more flexible position on territorial questions. Two other extra-parliamentary groups—Siah (the Israeli New Left) and Matzpen (see Glossary)—adopted extreme leftist positions on Israel-Arab relations and demanded unconditional withdrawal from the territories. (Siah defined itself as Zionist, while Matzpen was known for its anti-Zionist position.) Two parties in the government coalition—the National Religious Party and the Independent Liberal Party—generally adopted opposing positions, the first being hawkish and the second moderately dovish. After the Sadat visit to Jerusalem, a movement known as Shalom Akhshav [Peace Now] was formed, which tried to accelerate the peace negotiations with Egypt by encouraging the Israeli leadership to offer more concessions and be more flexible, mainly in regard to the Palestinian problem.

PRESSURES FROM THE PUBLIC

From the standpoint of this study, the most interesting early postwar grouping was that of the Hebron/Kiryat Arba settlers, which succeeded in forcing the government to include a large area in the map of Israeli presence in the territories.

As a densely populated Arab center, the city of Hebron had been outside the initial Israeli "settlement map." On the other hand, Hebron is part of the Jewish mythological past: it is the location of the graves of some of the Jewish forefathers and until 1929 the site of an ancient Jewish community, some of whose members were killed in the riots of that year, which completely destroyed the community. The destruction of Hebron was a traumatic event for the Jews of Palestine, which provides the background for the initiative of the Hebron settlers and the government's reaction to it.

Prior to Passover of 1968, a religious group led by a young and unknown rabbi (M. Levinger) came to Hebron claiming that it wished to celebrate the holiday there. The group rented a hotel near the center of town and prolonged its stay. For the time being, the military government was ordered "neither to help nor to hinder them" (*Maariv*, 6/5/73), but three months later the military agreed to ensure the group's safety on condition it would leave the hotel and move to a nearby area under military supervision. In effect, the government had recognized the group in order to control it. Later the group members were promised a place to live, and under pressure of the right-wing opposition (principally the National Religious Party in the coalition), the government was forced to acknowledge the "fact" of a Jewish quarter near Hebron/Kiryat Arba.

There were several reasons for the government's change of policy in response to the group's pressure. First, the group based its struggle on two principles of great potency in Israeli society: personal fulfillment through pioneering and the return to a place perceived as belonging to the collectivity in terms of both the recent past and Jewish mythology. Second, the group was seeking very diligently the fulfillment of the collectivity's central task of continuing direct conflict with the Arabs without threatening the government's power to control the conflict in other spheres. Third, the collectivity's goals were not clearly defined, and the action of the Hebron settlers had the political and material support of some of the hawkish components of the government and public. Finally, the group's militant action was perceived as in accordance with legitimate norms and values, and it is very difficult for a political establishment to counter radical groups claiming to be more effectively pursuing legitimate goals. (Later on, the patterns of activities and symbols employed by this group would provide a model for another militant movement—Gush Emunim.)

THE STRUGGLE WITHIN THE GOVERNMENT

The most significant struggle over the occupied territories occurred within the ruling parties—the Labor Party and the parliamentary Maarach (Alignment) which it maintained with Mapam (the United Workers' Party), which included a very broad range of territorial conceptions—from extreme hawkish to moderate dovish. (See "Alignment" and "Mapam" in Glossary.) Within the Alignment, which essentially determined Israeli policy, the controversy over the occupied territories was interwoven with internal power struggles, both in the party and in the state.

In the Labor Party, between 1967 and 1973 there were three dominant streams of thought concerning occupied territories. One stream was led by Pinhas Sapir, Secretary of the Treasury, considered the party strongman and controller of its *apparat*, in addition to having a major role in economic decision-making (Salpeter and Elitzur, 1973); another stream was led by Defense Minister

Moshe Dayan, whose charismatic personality made him attractive to many; a third stream, less established as a pressure group, was led by the Minister of Education and Vice Premier Yigal Allon. Each of these streams had interests extending beyond the problem of the territories, but they generally preferred to frame their conflicting interests and struggles for power in terms of an ideological struggle over the fate of the territories. The power struggle focused on the determination of the next Prime Minister. The adoption of the position of one stream's policy concerning the territories would be seen as a gain in the power struggle for the post of Prime Minister. This is not to say that the conflict over the territories was secondary, but rather that in addition to all the other factors noted, Israeli policy on the territories' fate was conditioned by power struggles within the Israeli political system (see *Maariv*, 8/4/72).

Sapir, though he made few public statements on the subject of the territories, was considered to be the main representative of the dovish approach to the Labor Party and the Israeli government. His arguments tended to be pragmatic and to emphasize that Israel should not annex territories whose population would radically change the country's demographic balance. In addition, he wanted the creation of a proletariat of Arab manual workers supervised by Jewish skilled workers and "managers," which Zionism had always opposed. Arie Eliav was considered the ideologue of this stream, and he argued both in terms of the traditional values of part of the Labor Movement (such as Jewish labor and universalistic egalitarianism) and of the rights of the Palestinians to part of the land of Palestine:

> The path Israel should take is to declare her readiness in princi-
> ple . . . to return to the Palestinian Arabs most of the territories
> of the [*West*] bank and the Gaza Strip so that they may establish
> on them and in the territories of the east bank of the Jordan an
> independent and sovereign state of their own. . . . The Jews have
> full historical rights . . . over the whole of Israel . . . but it must
> be said: on this very piece of land, on the very same square kilo-
> meters . . . there are national-historical rights for the Palestinian
> Arabs who live there as well. Who will delude himself and say that
> these Arabs, natives of this piece of land, are "passersby"? These
> "passersby" have been living here for more than 1300 years
> (1972: 153-54).

On the other hand, Moshe Dayan (in a speech delivered on 27 June 1973) argued that the Palestinians had lost their right to political self-determination when they chose to join the Hashemite Kingdom and reject the Partition Plan. They remained refugees primarily because the other Arab countries did not grant recognition to the population "transfer" between them and Israel and did not absorb the refugees. Their leaders wished to turn back the hands of the historical clock and to establish the State of Palestine instead of the State of Israel (*Haaretz*, 6/29/73). Thus, according to Dayan, the Palestinians' right to territorial lands had been nullified because (a) they had relinquished their right in the past, (b) a population transfer had been made, and (c) the claims of the Palestinians were irreconcilable with Israel's right to exist. Conclusions as to the Palestinians' territorial rights can be derived from Eliav's view, but not from Dayan's thesis, since he also acknowledges a "Hashemite entity" with claims to the territories. Dayan's position on the territories can be seen as an attempt to annex the maximum amount political conditions would allow by establishing settlement facts in the tradition of practical Zionism. He sought to solve Israel's demographic problems and the problems of political representation of the territorial populations by formulating a type of dual governance whereby the inhabitants would live on territory administered by Israel (in the future possibly under Israeli sovereignty) while they would have political representation in Jordan (BBC interview, 5/14/73). In the case of the Sinai, Dayan was prepared for an Israeli withdrawal from all the territories "essential to Egypt, for its day-to-day life and security" (*Time*, 7/24/73)—i.e., from the Suez Canal and the Suez Bay—in exchange for a settlement. His approach was anchored in the basic conviction that time is working in Israel's favor and thus the political/military status quo should be preserved.*

In addition to the basic hawk and dove approaches in the ruling party, a third, compromise view was formulated by Yigal Allon—known as the Allon Plan—whose basic points were advanced as early as July 1967. The fundamental principle underlying the Allon Plan†

---

*From the same interview: "For the next ten years Israel's boundaries will remain as they are now, but no large-scale war will take place ... [!] "

†The plan is summarized here on the basis of Y. Cohen (1972) and an address by Allon to a conference on the implications of the 1967 War for Israeli society published in *Yediot Achronot*, 6/4/73.

was *selective annexation* of territories so that (a) the main centers of Arab population would not be included within the territories annexed to Israel, (b) defensible boundaries incorporating most of the strategically important areas (such as the Jordan Valley, Sharm-al-Sheikh, and the Golan Heights) would be assured, (c) the major places considered sacred to Judaism (such as Jerusalem and Hamakh-pela Cave near Hebron) would be included within the annexed territories, and (d) no areas would be annexed which were essential to the Arabs and whose annexation would stand in the way of any future settlement with them. The plan was formulated in very flexible terms, leaving open the options of a settlement with the Hashemite Kingdom and/or with any Palestinian entity. It had two parts—the programmatic part described above and the operative part, which included concrete suggestions for the establishment of areas of Jewish settlement beyond the armistice lines of 1949. These settlements, in accordance with the conception prevalent between 1937 and 1947, would independently determine the physical boundaries of Israel.

The Allon Plan was never accepted by the Israeli government, but its operative part seems to have served as a working consensus for the political system until the May 1977 elections. The plan was not even submitted for formal approval because its acceptance would have disturbed the equilibrium within the ruling party, would have damaged Israel's relations with friendly nations (especially with the United States), and would not have satisfied either the doves or hawks.* However, the operative part of the plan (the settlement of the territories) provided a common ground for doves and hawks: the opponents of annexation saw in it a framework for a future political settlement, while the proponents of annexation viewed it somewhat favorably because it did not bar partial or total annexation. Above all, the plan was seen as having the advantage that "It can be enacted immediately and does not leave a vacuum because of the lack of any Israeli presence" (*Davar*, 12/22/68). The plan's

---

*At the time the plan was presented, a "national unity government" was in power in which the right was participating. This government had been established before the 1967 War but was dissolved on 5 July 1970 in the wake of Gahal's suspicion that it was about to accept a proposal by the U.S. Secretary of State (William Rogers) for a settlement which would entail Israeli withdrawal from most of the territories.

operative part was accepted as a compromise between the ruling party and Mapam, and it acted as a balance within the government coalition between the religious parties, on the one hand, and the moderate Independent Liberal Party, on the other. The actions taken by the government in accordance with the plan placed it midway between the extreme demands of the right for immediate annexation of Judea and Samaria, the Golan Heights, and large parts of Sinai, and the demands of other parties and groups to leave most of the territories free of Jewish population—or even for immediate retreat from some or all of the captured territories without any political compensation from the Arabs.* Thus the operative part of the Allon Plan became, between 1967 and 1977, a sort of balance point for the system as a whole.

The two main implications of selective Jewish settlement in the captured territories for the Jewish-Arab conflict were: (a) it served to create a new territorial status quo while leaving room for future negotiation; (b) it refocused the conflict on the struggle between the Jewish and Palestinian peoples—a struggle which had steadily declined in significance between 1949 and 1967.[†] Between June 1967 and May 1977 seventy-six settlements were established in the territories captured by Israel in the 1967 War (see Table 6.2).

The balance in the political system achieved by the fulfillment of the operative part of the Allon Plan was only temporary, and with the passage of time, public attitudes moved in a "hawkish" direction. Thus, during the formulation of the Alignment's political platform in October 1969, proposals were made (largely under pressures exerted by the Defense Minister) for demanding a more intensive Israeli presence in the territories. In the election campaign, however, only general statements were included in the platform to the effect that "the country's boundaries must be strategic defense boundaries as needed to ensure the State's unchallenged existence, the defense of its peace and the prevention of any future attempts at attack" and "the establishment of security settlements and per-

---

*For example, the Histadrut's Secretary-General, Y. Ben-Aharon, called for a withdrawal from part of Sinai to show "good intentions."

[†]The refocusing of the conflict on the Palestinian Arab problem was a result not only of Israeli settlement activities, but also of the growth of autonomous Palestinian political institutions and guerilla organizations whose political successes intensified their activities.

Table 6.2

NEW JEWISH SETTLEMENTS IN THE OCCUPIED TERRITORIES,
1967-1979

Region	June 1967-May 1977[a]		June 1977-July 1979[b]		Total Number	Percentage of All Settlements
	Number	Percent of Total	Number	Percent of Total		
Golan Heights	25	86 %	4	14 %	29	24 %
West Bank	28	41	40	59	68	55
Sinai and the Gaza Strip	23	92	2	8	25	20
Total	76	62	46	38	122	100

Sources: (1) M. Drobless, Settlement Department, The Jewish Agency, Press conference, 7/25/79; (2) Y. Galili, *Zu Haderekh*, 8/20-8/27/80; (3) *Haaretz*, 9/14/79.

[a]Period of the Labor government

[b]Likud government

manent settlements should be speeded up" (*Maariv*, 8/5/69). However, an appendix was attached to the platform which was known informally as the "oral Bible." It stated the Alignment position on territorial aspirations and security needs in specific terms:

> Israel views the Jordan River as its eastern security boundary [*that is—a boundary west of which foreign military forces may not cross*]; the Golan Heights and the Gaza Strip will remain under our exclusive control, and free navigation from Eilat and southward will be assured by independent Israeli forces which will control the area of the Straits. This area [*the eastern coast of Sinai*] will be attached to Israel by a territorial continuum.*

But this document was not binding and left room for manipulation by the party's factions, each of which could accept or reject it or interpret it as the members saw fit.

*Personal letter from Minister Galilee to the Prime Minister, 7 August 1969; published in *Maariv*, 4/15/71.

The 1973 election campaign (which was postponed due to the war) also focused on an attempt to intensify Israeli presence in the occupied territories. The Minister of Defense proposed the certification of land purchases in the territories by both institutions and individuals (i.e., treating the territories as a frontier).* This would legitimize what had been occurring since the end of 1972, when Jewish entrepreneurs, along with government and "national" institutions, began to purchase considerable tracts of land, particularly in the West Bank.† The process began when:

It became clear that in reality the attitude of the Arab population had taken an interesting turn. While in the past there was nothing more distasteful than the sale of land to Jews, and Israelis were forced to purchase land under the name of unknown companies in Lichtenstein, the ban has been lifted. Some Arabs are willing to sell land to Jews openly and the purchasers come with the seller to his Arab neighbors in order to receive a written certification from them stating the boundaries of the sold area (*Haaretz*, 3/27/73).

This process of the defreezing of lands in the occupied territories was almost identical to the process of the defreezing of Arab lands in the Mandatory Period (see Chapter 2). The flow of capital—both from the national authorities and public institutions, and from the private entrepreneurs and speculators—caused a sharp rise in land prices,** but also stimulated more and more Arabs to convert

---

*Dayan also proposed the establishment of a city (Yamit) and deep-water port in the Rafah Approaches. Establishment of a city at this site would, in the long run, require setting the border deep in Sinai—a deviation from the Allon Plan (*Haaretz*, 8/17/73).

†The official basis of these purchases was Order 25, issued by the Military Government in Judea and Samaria on 18 June 1967: "Any land transaction, whether direct or indirect, is to be undertaken only by permission of the certified authority" [*that is, the military government*]. Official permits were granted to four civilians allowing them to purchase lands in the territories, but no more permits were granted after the matter became a subject of public controversy (see W. Weinstein, *Maariv*, 4/6/73).

**One of the arguments against permitting private purchases was that it would lead to speculation. At first it was possible to purchase land for £P 3-5 per square meter, but the price rose quickly to £P 20 per square meter (*Maariv*, 4/6/73).

land to capital despite the community pressures against sales to Jews. In the West Bank a national committee was established for the purchase of Arab lands which were liable to be sold to Jews (*Maariv*, 4/8/73), and "Jordan's religious leaders announced . . . that anyone selling his land to Israelis is a traitor to Islam and the Arab nation" (*Haaretz*, 4/9/73). The General Manager of the Jewish National Fund was forced to acknowledge that "Since the beginning of the public debate over land purchases in Judea and Samaria, the supply of lands for sale has been reduced" (*Haaretz*, 4/10/73).

Let us assume that the supply of lands for sale grew as Israeli control of the territories was seen as permanent both by landowners and purchasers (who were prepared to invest more as the risk of loss declined and chance for profits increased). After the 1973 War this trend seems to have been reversed. Thus Dayan was in favor of legalizing land purchases to achieve (a) additional defreezing of land by encouraging investment by private individuals, (b) the intensification of Israeli presence in the territories, being aware that changes involving land in the Jewish-Arab conflict are generally irreversible, and (c) enhancement of his political prestige by demonstrating his power to influence policy. For a time it seemed that with the support of the Prime Minister, Golda Meir, Dayan's approach would be accepted by a majority. But Mrs. Meir changed her mind "in the wake of the international uproar" the proposal aroused (*Haaretz*, 4/9/73). She also wanted to prevent speculation by private entrepreneurs: in response to a question by Menahem Begin in the Knesset, the Prime Minister said that when she saw the list of requests for land purchases—requests for acquisition of 50,000 dunams, 15,000, 5,000, 2,000, etc.—she realized that what was involved was land purchase for speculation (*Haaretz*, 4/11/73). However, the matter was raised again in the elections of 1974, and the struggle regarding settlement in the new territories began anew. A compromise was finally arrived at in an agreement known as "The Galilee Document" (named after its author, Israel Galilee, a prominent figure in the Labor Movement), in which Dayan received approval for speeding up the rate of settlement and the construction of a deep-water port "south of Gaza." In the matter of land purchase, the agreement altered the status quo only slightly. Primacy was again granted to a national authority—the Israel Land Authority—in the purchase of lands. (Most of the public land acquisitions were made through a subsidiary company of the JNF—Himnuta—which is registered as a European corporation.) But purchases of land by private entrepreneurs were permitted in cases in which "the Israel Land Authority cannot purchase it or is not interested in purchasing it" (*Maariv*, 8/10/74). In practice, this agreement could not be put into effect before the outbreak of the 1973 War.

Settlements were established on four different types of land. The first type was government lands, owned by the Jordanian and Egyptian governments. In many cases, Arab inhabitants cultivated these lands or claimed the right to them and de facto ownership of them. Until 1973 about 57,000 dunams of this type of land were fenced off in the Raffah area. When the Bedouins living there were evicted in 1972, it became a controversial matter in Israel. Of the 360,000 dunams in the Gaza Strip, more than 55 percent of the lands were registered in the name of the British High Commissioner; this was transferred to the Egyptian military command and later to the State of Israel (*Yediot Achronot*, 3/17/72). The second type of land was acquired—in exchange for payment or for government lands—from Arab owners.* The third type was abandoned lands, particularly in the Golan Heights, where about 35 villages (totalling 70,000 dunams) were abandoned, and in Judea and Samaria, where 37,500 dunams defined as "abandoned" were given over to Jewish settlement. The fourth type was taken by order of the military after the Arab owners refused to sell. Such were the lands given to the settlers of Kiryat Arba (Hebron) and Nahal Gittit. In Akraba (a small village in the West Bank), the agricultural produce was destroyed in order to pressure the owners to sell their lands (*Maariv*, 7/14/72), which also became a subject for controversy. In such cases, the military could keep the area closed to the original owners for as long as it wished in exchange for yearly damage payments.

In East Jerusalem, which was immediately annexed to the State of Israel, the expropriation of lands was undertaken. By August 1970, about 17,000 dunams had been transferred to Israeli ownership—about 25 percent of the total territory (70,000 dunams) annexed to the Israeli city of Jerusalem. The new territories were about half the area of Israeli Jerusalem prior to 1967 (37,000

*About 50,000 of 52,000 dunams of land purchased by the Israel Land Authority in the occupied territories were exchanged for government lands (*Maariv*, 4/6/73).

dunams) and almost three times the size of Jordanian Jerusalem before 1967 (6,000 dunams). According to the original plans, between 100,000-150,000 persons would be settled on these lands. These actions, as well as intensive building activities, were undertaken to establish *faits accomplis* according to Benbenisti (1973:98-288), who until 1971 was in charge of affairs relating to the eastern part of the city. Land expropriation and the other settlement activities in Jerusalem and the other captured territories were undertaken in an almost clandestine manner. In an article entitled "Wall and Tower—1973 Version," a reporter described the settlement of Nahal Gittit as follows: "[They] came to the Akraba lands at night, and prepared and fenced the camp of tents by the next morning. It was worthwhile remembering that the 'wall and tower' period ended 35 years ago" (*Haaretz*, 8/20/73). (See Chapter 4.)

During this period, a new form of settlement was begun—the *mizpe* (lookout)—to strengthen the Jewish presence in the Galilee, where there had always been an Arab majority. Consisting of a small number of families at a selected location (usually on a hilltop which has strategic control of the surrounding area), these settlements do not have infrastructures of schools, medical dispensaries, stores, etc., but are dependent on nearby city or village centers for these services. From this point of view they are extensions of city suburbs. It is still too early to see in which directions the *mizpim* will develop, or how long they will last.

Thus, between 1967 and 1977, when the various governments were in doubt about the fate of the newly acquired territories, they resorted almost ritualistically to patterns of action from the past. These patterns of action were employed because the system's goals were vague and sometimes conflicting (for example, seeking security and peace at the same time), and because of cross-pressures from various groups and components of the system. Between 1967 and 1977 these were constraints to the development of a policy which would (1) freeze the political status quo created after the 1967 War, while (2) promoting Israeli presence by means of settlement, and (3) achieving selective ownership of territories on the assumption that time was operating in favor of the Israeli side. It seems then that the inability to obtain sovereignty was the result of both internal and external constraints.

THE REOPENING OF FRONTIERS: 1967-1982

THE NEW REGIME AND THE PEACE TREATY WITH EGYPT

In May 1977, as a result of the general elections, Israel for the first time ever had a change of government. The reins were transferred to the Likud, a coalition headed by the Herut party (see Glossary), the direct descendant of the Revisionist Zionist party.* There was a general expectation that the new government would harden the Israeli position toward the Arabs—especially in regard to territorial disputes. After all, the Revisionist Party motto was "Both sides of the Jordan—both this side and that belong to us" (from a song composed by Jabotinsky), and it not only did not recognize Arab rule over the western side of the Jordan (i.e, the West Bank), but until 1965 had not accepted the fact that Trans-Jordan had been detached from the territory of Palestine in 1922. The badge of the youth movement of the party—Beitar (see Glossary)—carried a map of "Greater Israel" which included all the territory of Palestine before the first partition.† The Revisionist Party had a clearly defined place in the Zionist spectrum: it was considered an elitist movement with a distinctly right-wing, anti-socialist stand, which gloried in the primordial symbols of Homeland, Blood, Race (in the pre-fascist era), and a single flag.** The leaders of this movement, and especially its founder (Jabotinsky), laid great importance on military bearing and discipline, and they supported a militant underground movement which competed with the semi-legal army of the Yishuv, actively opposing both the British and the Arabs. After the State of Israel was proclaimed, this underground movement accepted democratic principles and became one of the political

*In spite of the general movement rightward within the Israeli political system beginning with the War of 1967 and leading eventually to the change of government in 1977, it appears that it was not the platform of the Likud which brought it victory, but a protest vote against the Labor Party's mismanagement of the 1973 War and the corrupt practices of various party members which had recently been exposed. This protest brought about the establishment of a new party—the Democratic Movement for Change—which entered into a coalition with the Likud and the National Religious Party, changing the Israeli political map.

†The badge was changed in 1978 after the Likud came to power.

**The Revisionists opposed the two-flags approach of the left, which carried a red flag to symbolize social progress as well as the blue-and-white national flag.

parties. For many years its leadership, headed by Menahem Begin, was composed of the former leaders of the underground—the Irgun Zvai Leumi—and it began receiving the votes of the new immigrants who had come from the Middle East (i.e., the Oriental Jews), who were on the periphery of the social and political system. Herut was thus a social protest party, in spite of its nationalistic stress. The ideology of the leaders and the aims of the constituents were linked through a number of populist appeals, with ties to the land being central. On the other hand, Revisionist Zionism did not consider "creating facts" (or what we have referred to as presence) as important to the achievement of territorial aims as did the predominant sector of the Zionist movement.

It was expected that soon after the Likud took over the government, Israel would announce the annexation of all the territories, or most of them, or—at the very least—the areas referred to in the Bible as Judea and Samaria (i.e., the West Bank), in accordance with its election platform and its official ideology. The government did not announce any immediate annexation, however, or even any such intention,* though at the very beginning it took steps which meant the rejection of the Allon Plan (selective settlement of the West Bank) and the intention of creating facts by means of presence even in areas densely populated by Arabs.

It is hard to imagine what would have happened had there not been an unusual combination of events. First, almost immediately after the Likud came to power, Egypt announced its willingness to make peace with Israel in exchange for the evacuation of lands conquered in 1967; second, in the last year of the term of office of the Likud, it seemed very likely that the Likud would not be reelected, which meant that the Alignment would be returning to power.† These two developments influenced the policy of the Likud toward the territories.

---

*The non-annexation of the territories, as long as negotiations were in progress, was a condition laid down by Moshe Dayan for joining the Likud government. Only after the 1981 elections did the Likud government extend Israeli rule to the Golan Heights.

†This was the forecast of all the public opinion polls in 1980. It was primarily due to serious failures in the economy, which had brought Israel an annual inflation rate of about 130 percent, and the image of a government which could not function, especially after it had suffered a number of major setbacks.

Peace with the Arabs or, to be more precise, obtaining recognition and legitimation of the existence of a Jewish state in the Middle East was always a central desideratum in Israeli society (see Chapter 7), and it was one of the most basic aims of the Zionist movement, especially after the State of Israel was proclaimed. The longer the period that elapsed from the War of 1947/48 without peace with the Arabs, the more that aim began to appear as semi-utopian, or for future generations only, to much of the population. But it is one of the central beliefs of those who are dovish that it is possible to achieve peace, and that Israel can influence the Arabs to agree to it.

When President Sadat arrived in Jerusalem (19-21 November 1977) and proposed peace, his proposal could not be opposed (in terms of public policy) either externally or internally. Added to this was a belief, widely shared among the Israeli leadership, that Egypt was primarily interested in the return of its territories (the Sinai Peninsula and possibly the Gaza Strip), and would be willing to accept a formula which would permit the continued control by Israel of the West Bank (and possibly the Golan Heights), provided that a degree of political independence was given to the inhabitants of these areas. This was the background for the formulation of Israel's proposal of Palestinian autonomy which was agreed upon at Camp David. It appears that that agreement was sufficiently vague to satisfy both the Israeli and Egyptian interpretations. The Israelis understood autonomy to mean self-rule in internal matters (education, health, welfare, employment, etc.), while land, water, and internal and external security would all be under Israeli supervision. This would apply for the transitional period of five years; no indication was given as to what would occur after that. The Egyptian interpretation, on the other hand, of the words "establishing the elected self-governing authority . . . in order to provide full autonomy for the inhabitants" included the establishment of an Arab Palestinian state in the West Bank and Gaza Strip within the transitional period.* The contradiction between these two interpre-

*See "Letters Accompanying the Peace Treaty" from Menahem Begin and Anwar Sadat to Jimmy Carter, *Treaty of Peace between the Arab Republic of Egypt and the State of Israel*, 26 March 1979. Washington: US Department of State, Bureau of Public Affairs, 1979.

tations is clear, but each side hoped that time would eventually work for its view. The Egyptian side hoped that the internal dynamic created with the establishment of a self-governing authority in the West Bank and Gaza, coupled with international pressure, would force Israel to recognize a sovereign Palestinian state (or one with a federative tie with Jordan). On the other hand, the Israeli leadership hoped that during the transition it would be able to so entrench the Israeli presence in these territories that political control would have to remain in its hands. In other words, Israel hoped to exchange control of Sinai for greater Israeli control over the West Bank, an area to which the Jewish collectivity is attached by deep sentiment (see Chapter 8).

From the pinnacle of popularity it attained in March-April 1979 as a result of signing the peace treaty with Egypt, the Likud's popularity rating fell drastically, and by the middle of 1980 it seemed that in the coming elections there would probably be a change of government, with the control returning to the Left, which does not share the Likud's views regarding the territory in the West Bank. Despite the results of the polls of early 1980, the Likud won the elections, but at that period it was afraid that its whole territorial conception, upon which it based the Israeli agreement to the Camp David accord (whereby it relinquished control over the entire Sinai peninsula and accepted a peace settlement which seemed to carry a high price tag) would collapse. From that time on, the government began acting differently. But to understand the processes involved, we must analyze an additional phenomenon within the Israeli sociopolitical system.

GUSH EMUNIM: FROM SETTLERS TO INHERITORS*

Gush Emunim came onto the Israeli political map on 26 July 1974, when a group of about a hundred people, accompanied by about 2,500 supporters, camped in an old railroad station—Sebastia—in an area densely populated by Arabs and considerably beyond the territory the Allon Plan had envisioned for Jewish settlement. After three days of deliberation, the government decided to forcibly evacuate the place (which by then had been renamed *Elon Moreh*

*This analysis is based mainly on Raanan (1980), Sprinzak (1981), O'Dea (1978), and conversations with Gideon Aran, who prepared a Ph.D. thesis on this subject at the Hebrew University.

in Hebrew). The settlers offered passive resistance. During 1975 the members of Gush Emunim tried on five occasions to return, but the military government again and again evicted them. They tried again on the festival of Hanukkah at the end of 1976, accompanied by about 2,000 supporters. This time there were also voices of support from the activist left and from a number of Jewish leaders throughout the world. The government negotiated with the settlers, and reached a compromise under which thirty families, including about fifty children, plus another twenty singles were transferred to a nearby army base. There they began building a settlement, using private funding. In May 1977, Prime Minister Begin visited the base and announced that "there will be many more Elon Morehs." But the establishment of the settlement was delayed (meanwhile the government had begun its peace talks with Egypt), and the group again began a series of protest actions. In June 1979 the government resolved to establish a permanent settlement in a nearby area, but a number of local residents appealed to the Supreme Court, claiming that parts of the settlement would be located on their land. The Supreme Court restricted itself to deciding if the location of the settlement was based on security considerations or was politically motivated.* The Court decided that the site selection was politically motivated and ordered the area evacuated within thirty days. A short while later the settlement was moved to another location. Elon Moreh was the symbol for the struggle of Gush Emunim to change the map of Israeli presence on the West Bank, and, since 1977 a total of thirty-three settlements, which the settlers refer to as *hitnahluyot* ("inheritances"), have been set up. The establishment of another forty-four settlements in the area is planned by the middle of 1981 (either close to or within areas densely populated by Arabs), with a total of about 25,000 Jewish residents (*Haaretz*, 2/2/81). Not all these settlements belong to the Gush Emunim (the *Amana* settlement movement), but Gush Emunim is

---

*According to the Hague Convention, a conquering power is forbidden to make any changes in captured territory prior to the signing of a peace treaty except for security reasons. Israel claimed that the various settlements served its defense needs, but in this case the Court ruled against it. (As regards the West Bank, Israel does not consider itself a conquering power because it did not recognize the legitimacy of the annexation of the West Bank by Jordan.)

171

clearly the driving force in this settlement process and in applying political pressure.

WHAT IS GUSH EMUNIM?

The Gush Emunim movement began its development in the 1950s within a Jerusalem *yeshiva* (a senior institution for Jewish studies)— Merkaz Harav—which belonged to the Zionist-Nationalist wing of the religious sector. The students, on the whole, came from established middle-class families, and they sensed a dissonance between their religious commitment and their elite family backgrounds. In Israeli society, in spite of its many religious elements (see Chapter 7), the major social decisions were made by people who were secularists. While there were religious political parties (the Zionist Mizrahi and non-Zionist Agudat Israel), they concerned themselves primarily with maintaining the religious sector and meeting its needs. They usually did not become involved in other political questions dealing with foreign policy or internal affairs. Thus the religious sector remained on the periphery of the society, which deeply affected the national-religious middle-class youth.

The first important step by this group to enter the mainstream was to serve in the Israeli army. Defense and service in the armed forces are central components of Israeli society (see Horowitz and Kimmerling, 1974), and combining military service, primarily in the elite forces (paratroopers and armor), with Talmudic studies kept the group together while bringing it into a more central place in Israeli society (see Kimmerling, 1979a). Military service also gave the group organizational skills, contact with the subculture of non-religious Israeli youth, experience in handling the mass media, etc. which would later be useful in its political struggle (see Raanan, 1980 and Sprinzak, 1981). This step was taken at about the same time as the encounter of the Israelis with Judea and Samaria. If this confrontation was a shock to the secular population of Israel, for the religious population it was "divine guidance." They summoned up all the references in Jewish religious literature to the sanctity of the land and the responsibility of Jews to redeem it and safeguard it from non-Jews. With the active pressure of Gush Emunim (led by a group of rabbis headed by the dean of the Merkaz

Harav yeshiva) the Israeli political system became mired in theological arguments which paralyzed its ability to make decisions.

As a result of the 1973 War, Gush Emunim became a political force independent of the National Religious Party, under whose aegis it had operated since 1967. It emerged as part of a general protest against what was perceived as the failure of the political leadership to foresee the coordinated Arab attack on Israel and to lead the nation in a time of crisis. Also contributing to the formation of Gush Emunim was the new balance of forces revealed in the 1973 War, which brought about a reevaluation by most of the community in Israel of Israel's capacity to retain the land conquered in 1967 (see below). Gush Emunim reacted along two planes: (1) ideological and (2) political.

On the ideological plane, it formulated a policy which stressed that no land should be surrendered within the boundaries of the land promised to Abraham ("from the River Euphrates . . . in the north to the river of Egypt [*the Nile*] in the south, and from the Great [*Mediterranean*] Sea in the west to the desert in the east"). While the Jewish religion has never had universal agreement on the validity of these boundaries or the time period in which they will be achieved, the leaders of Gush Emunim (and some of the leaders of the National Religious Party) translated these verses to political demands in the *here* and *now* (Raanan, 1980:81). Even more, they saw the unity of the land as part of the unity of the cosmic order, and a necessary condition for the final redemption, while most others saw Israel as acquiring these lands as a *result* of the final redemption. Thus surrendering any land became a violation of religious law, while preventing the surrender of land became a religious commandment, which completely ignored the realities of the political situation and relied on the hope that somehow all the problems could be solved by some miracle. The escape from reality was accompanied by a rejection of Western culture, which was blamed for the Holocaust and all the Israeli troubles, including the pressures for Israel to retreat from the occupied territories. The immediate Arab environment was seen in xenophobic terms, including rejection and hatred.

On the political plane, the members of Gush Emunim began to "create facts" of Jewish presence in areas of the West Bank—primarily in those areas with a dense Arab population where they

173

feared land might be returned under the Allon Plan. This followed the classic Zionist practice of pioneering settlements, used in setting up the Jewish quarter of Kiryat Arba near Hebron. As in the case of Hebron, the Jewish community found it difficult to withstand pressures from such settlements.

Thus from 1977 there was a combination of (1) a nationalistic right-wing government, with a reservoir of populist supporters, which annulled the settlement policies of the left, and (2) a messianic religious group which was rapidly becoming politicized, and which had adopted the tactics of the Zionist left and the central symbols of pioneering, asceticism, and settlement in an openly conflictual context. This combination brought about a marked pioneering movement in the occupied territories. It was no longer referred to as settlement, however, but rather as *hitnahlut*, with the implication that this was a form of "inheriting" the land in accord with the divine promise made to the Children of Israel. This new terminology was soon widely accepted and became part of the standard political lexicon.*

"PEACE NOW"

A political group which was formed immediately after the visit of President Sadat to Jerusalem and the beginning of peace negotiations between Egypt and Israel was the Peace Now movement. Its leaders and activists were very similar in background to those of Gush Emunim—that is, young men and women of the middle class and upper middle class elite, most of whom were academics, college students, and officers in the Israeli army reserve who had served in elite units in the 1973 War. They began organizing after the publication of an open letter from a number of reserve officers to the Prime Minister which demanded that the territory conquered by Israel in 1967 be returned for the sake of peace. Their motto was "Peace [*shalom*] is preferable to the whole [*shelema*] of Israel."

Within a short time this group was able to bring out tens of thousands of people for demonstrations of unprecedented size in

---

*Gush Emunim was a major participant in the movement for halting the withdrawal from Sinai, and in the violent clashes with the authorities during the evacuation of the settlements of Raffah Approaches and the town of Yamit in March-April 1982.

Israel, which were a counterbalance to the pressure of Gush Emunim and the other political extremists. Peace Now saw itself as a continuation of protest groups which had emerged as a result of the 1973 War and had brought about the resignation of Golda Meir. The program of Peace Now was phrased in vague terms so that it could attract all the dovish elements in the country, and it took no stand whatsoever on two central issues of the Arab-Israeli dispute: control over East Jerusalem and recognition of the Palestine Liberation Organization (PLO). After the signing of the peace treaty with Egypt in 1979, the activities of Peace Now died down to a large extent, and by the 1981 elections its leaders were split up among several political parties. Peace Now's activities were renewed during the Lebanese war of 1982, demanding the immediate withdrawal of the Israeli armed forces from Lebanon.

PUBLIC OPINION

A detailed breakdown of Israeli attitudes concerning territorial concessions from 1968 to 1979 is provided in Figure 6.1, from which four broad generalizations can be drawn. (1) In general, there was a tendency not to return the land conquered in 1967. Those who wished to return *all* the territories were always a distinct minority in comparison to those who wished to return only part or none of the territories. (2) Public opinion made differentiations between territories. Thus, for example, while only one percent was willing (in February 1968) to return the Golan Heights in exchange for peace, 41 percent was willing to return the Sinai peninsula. (3) Public opinion was subject to extremely sharp swings. Thus, for example, while only 6 percent of the population was willing to return the whole of Sinai in July 1973, 60 percent was willing to do so in November 1977—a dramatic change by any measure! (4) There was a tendency to be more willing to return territories (on a selective basis) as time went on.

This increasing willingness to return territory stemmed primarily from (a) the 1973 War and (b) the visit of President Sadat to Jerusalem, where he announced his readiness to make peace with Israel. Several turning points are evident in Figure 6.1. Immediately after the Six-Day War (1968), a substantial minority of the people were ready to return the territory in the Sinai, while keeping the

Figure 6.1

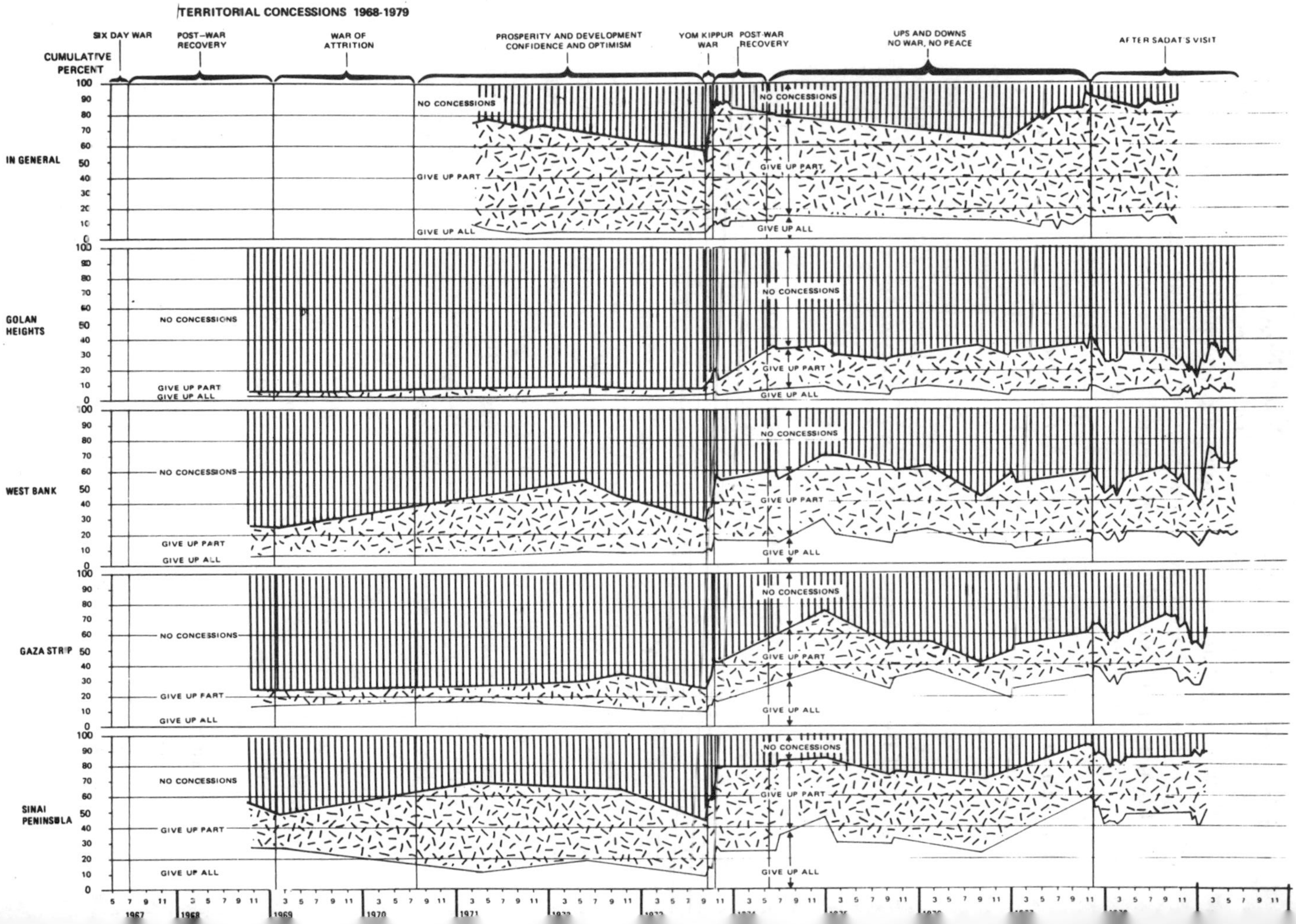

TERRITORIAL CONCESSIONS 1968-1979
SIX DAY WAR
POST-WAR RECOVERY
WAR OF ATTRITION
PROSPERITY AND DEVELOPMENT CONFIDENCE AND OPTIMISM
YOM KIPPUR WAR
POST-WAR RECOVERY
UPS AND DOWNS NO WAR, NO PEACE
AFTER SADAT'S VISIT
CUMULATIVE PERCENT
IN GENERAL
GOLAN HEIGHTS
WEST BANK
GAZA STRIP
SINAI PENINSULA
NO CONCESSIONS
GIVE UP PART
GIVE UP ALL
1967
1968
1969
1970
1971

other areas. When it was seen that peace was not a realistic hope, this readiness declined. At all times thereafter (except July 1973), however, there was readiness by most of the population to return all or part of the Sinai peninsula. As a result of the 1973 War, those who stated that none of the West Bank should be returned declined from 67 to 42 percent, while those who were willing to return the entire West Bank went up from 8 to 18 percent. This tendency continued, so that by February 1975 those wholly opposed had decreased to less than a third of the population. But the percentage favoring no return went up again, reaching 57 percent by September 1976.

The visit of President Sadat did not change public opinion in regard to the West Bank and the Golan Heights: Egypt's readiness to make peace with Israel changed only the feelings about the Sinai peninsula. There was least change of position in regard to the Golan Heights. Up to the 1973 War, 90 percent of the population believed that nothing should be returned. As a result of the war there was a moderate increase in those favoring partial return, with those believing that nothing should be given back ranging from 65 to 75 percent. As for the West Bank, there was always a sizable element which believed in selective annexation.

How can these changes in public opinion best be explained? After the 1967 War, when Israel had won a decisive victory, it did not appear to be logical to forego any territories. Not only was the cost of keeping them low and the gains to be derived from keeping them obvious (as time went on, becoming even more evident)* but also Arab behavior, as expressed in the Khartoum Declaration,† offered no incentive for Israeli concessions. Figure 6.1 shows the lack of national consensus as regards Israeli control of the West Bank, the "holy places," the "original homeland," etc. The readiness to make territorial concessions varied among the members of the different Israeli governments (including that of the Likud), which had a significant impact on the national consensus, since public opinion is influenced to a great extent by the messages the government

*As detailed at the beginning of this chapter.

†In September 1967 the leaders of the Arab world, meeting in Khartoum on the invitation of President Nasser, resolved "three noes": "no peace, no negotiations, and no recognition of Israel."

177

transmits to the populace—both direct (declared policy) and indirect (the decisiveness of policy and the extent of agreement within the government). But it is difficult to make a sharp differentiation between public opinion and the opinion of the government because, to a large extent, they are exposed to the same reality and share the same basic values.

CHANGES IN TERRITORIAL POLICY: 1979-1982

For the first two years, the new regime which came to power in 1977 acted in quite a different manner than had been expected. It negotiated a peace treaty with Egypt and signed an agreement for complete withdrawal from the Sinai peninsula. In this agreement it also recognized that the Palestinians have "rights" (without defining what these rights are)—a basic change in some of the components of the Arab-Israeli territorial conflict. But the regime did not make any concessions which would hinder efforts to increase Israeli control over the territories of Judea and Samaria. To some extent as a result of the pressure of Gush Emunim and in reaction to changes in Israeli public opinion, but primarily because it believed that its time was running out, the Likud government moved rapidly to create facts of Israeli presence in the territories which would make it more difficult to withdraw from parts of "the whole Israel" and perhaps prevent any implementation of the Allon Plan (see map, p. 240). What were the main points of these actions?

First, there was a drastic change in priorities in order to strengthen Jewish presence on the West Bank. An estimated 8 percent of the 1980-81 national budget was allocated for the maintenance and development of hitnahluyot,* but if one adds the supports not included in the budget, such as tax exemptions for those living in development regions, the salaries of government workers who deal primarily with the settlement of these areas, subsidies for transportation, etc., this figure rises to 12 to 15 percent of the national budget (excluding interest on loans and military expenditures, which represent about half the total budget), and probably even higher. The fact that this amount was spent at a time of economic crisis during which cuts were made in welfare services shows that the government was willing to bear the political costs of allocating major

*See Zvi Shuldiner, "The Real Cost of the *Hitnahlut*," *Haaretz*, 7/25/80.

resources for aims on which there was no public consensus. In Jerusalem and other places in November 1979, there were demonstrations demanding that funds be allocated for meeting social problems (primarily a shortage of housing for young couples) instead of investing them in the hitnahluyot.*

Second, there were drastic changes in policy in regard to retaining control over the territory of the West Bank. Lands which had belonged to the government of Jordan were seized. The area of these lands was about 700,000 dunams, or one-eighth of the area of the West Bank.† Apart from these lands registered in the name of the Jordanian government, up to 1967 only about one-half of the rest of the territory had been legally registered. The remaining land was available for bargaining between the government and individuals because proving ownership was very difficult in most cases. In addition, about half the land legally registered was registered to absentee owners, and its administration had been transferred to custodians. Much of this land, primarily of that classified as belonging to the government, was awarded to the hitnahluyot. Between October 1980 and February 1981, 20,605 dunams of land were seized for this purpose (*Haaretz*, 2/26/81). Until 1979 only large tracts had been taken, creating a certain territorial continuity, but from then on any land which could be obtained was seized, even if it was surrounded by land under private Arab or communal Arab ownership, and an attempt was made to demonstrate presence on it (*Haaretz*, 2/11/81).

Third, beginning in March 1981, some hitnahluyot were awarded the status of local authorities, and courts were established in some of them. Based on the traditions of Mandatory Palestine, local authorities have considerable authority over local matters, and some of the *mitnahlim* (lit., "inheritors"—the settlers in the hitnahluyot) tended to interpret this as partial Israeli sovereignty over those areas under their control.**

*See *Haaretz*, 11/23/79. In response, the government tried to combine social needs with its ideological aims by offering extremely cheap housing in the West Bank (*Haaretz*, 9/14/79), but the demand for housing was greatest in settlements near the cease-fire lines of 1948/49, which were seen as safest from return to Arab control.

†See *Haaretz*, 10/26/79; based on research by Arie Eliav.

**Yehuda Litani, "The Territories Have Already Been Annexed,"*Haaretz*, 3/8/81.

At the same time, something quite different occurred which could have major implications for the future. As a result of the peace treaty with Egypt, the government was forced to take down Israeli settlements which had been set up in Sinai, along the entire Gulf of Aqaba (to Sharm-el-Sheik), and in the Raffah area. These settlements were not closed down without serious internal strife among the settlers and their supporters. Those settlers who were evacuated were granted compensation exceeding the real value of their property,* which made them accept the evacuation without a major political struggle. However, this evacuation had far-reaching significance—for the first time in the history of Jewish settlement, Jewish presence was seen to be reversible. One assumes that the students of the school of Jabotinsky, who did not see settlement as the practical expression of Zionism, found it far less difficult to take such a step than did the members of the Labor parties. A precedent was created which puts into question the effectiveness of the Israeli government's efforts in this period to bolster Jewish presence on the West Bank.

Fourth, in the beginning of 1982 the Israeli government asserted the extension of Israeli rule over the Golan Heights, which meant the annexation of the area to Israel. The main reasons for this step and its timing seem to have been: (a) it was the last stage of the withdrawal from Sinai, and the unprecedented evacuation of the Israeli settlements (especially the towns of Yamit) created a more favorable international atmosphere for such an action. (b) the Likud government needed to demonstrate to its constituency that it had not betrayed the hard line in the Jewish-Arab conflict; (c) there was relatively high public support for the Golan Heights annexation (as indicated in Figure 6.1 above). The only real opposition to the annexation came from the sparse Druse population of the area (about 8,000 people in five villages), who were primarily concerned about

---

*The high rate of compensation was intended to serve as a precedent, but in the event the next government wishes to evacuate settlers, it will not be able to afford to do so, because the Sinai peninsula and the Gaza Strip included a few hundred families, while the West Bank includes thousands of families who have become mitnahlim. The compensation for the territories evacuated at this point is equal to about half of what Israel is spending on welfare! It has aroused great anger and stirred public debate, and those leaving the settlements have been labelled "peace profiteers" (see *Haaretz*, 12/23/80).

their possible compulsory enrollment in the Israeli armed forces and the confiscation of their lands and water sources for new Jewish settlements.

SUMMARY

In the relatively short period of time between 1967 and 1982, a great number of very dramatic changes occurred in the territorial context of the Arab-Israeli conflict. The Israelis acquired control over vast new areas of land, some of which were densely populated and others of which were desolate. At the beginning of this period it was hoped that it would be possible to convert most of these territories in exchange for recognition of the legitimacy of the State of Israel by the Arabs to trade land for peace. As these hopes dwindled, the readiness to give up these lands decreased—especially those areas for which there were strong sentiments derived from Jewish mythology and Zionist ideology. Because these sentiments were strong from the very beginning with respect to Old Jerusalem, it was annexed immediately by Israel.

But the conquest of these new lands stirred up a dispute in Israel in regard to their degree of frontierity—i.e., the degree to which they were a resource for territorial expansion. Taking into account the political constraints, to what degree could control of these lands be increased by adding a settlement presence and ownership (public and/or private) to the military presence, so that thereafter sovereignty could be imposed upon them? The major obstacle to Jewish control over these territories was the dense Arab population in the West Bank and Gaza Strip. The dispute about the degree of frontierity of these lands to some extent broke down the national consensus which had existed in regard to the management of the Arab-Israeli conflict, but there was general agreement concerning the strategic-defensive value of these territories.

As a result of the 1973 War, the Arabs' opposition to Israel's continued occupation of these territories was strengthened, and they were prepared to pay a high price to gain control of these lands, which meant that Israel might have to pay a high price to retain them. The cost-benefit balance of keeping these territories was no longer so favorable for the Israelis. In response to the Egyptian readiness to exchange peace and recognition of Israel for ter-

181

ritory, the Israeli government tried a different approach: to obtain peace and recognition by exchanging territory (the Sinai) for territory (continued control over the West Bank). In the process, it was willing to create a precedent of the reversibility of settlement presence.

Considerable quantities of land on the West Bank passed to Israeli control, but it is very difficult to determine how much was involved. Based on an estimate by the government of Jordan of February 1979, 27.3 percent of the lands of the West Bank passed to Israeli control,* but this appears to be highly exaggerated and includes the area of Jerusalem annexed by Israel.

With this background, factional rivalries in Israel were intensified. A radical, fundamentalist group—Gush Emunim—appeared which was largely divorced from political reality and rejected the values of Western culture. In its efforts to strengthen Jewish control over territory, it managed to move the entire system to a certain extent in its direction. As a result of its initiative, and with the economic and political support of the government, the extent of control in the occupied territories was raised considerably by means of presence, and the new area began to become more and more regarded as a frontier.

From June 1982, following the Lebanese War, the prestige as well as the effective social and political control of the PLO collapsed in the West Bank. One of the consequences is that large tracts of land which were frozen have begun to be sold by Arab owners, mainly to private investors. The frontierity of the West Bank has risen sharply, and many private land purchasing and development companies have begun to supply large settlement projects in the area, competing with the governmental projects. They promise housing and a high quality of life, not far from the metropolitan centers, at relatively low prices. According to some estimates, by the end of 1982 about 200,000 dunams will have been purchased or expropriated by governmental agencies, and an additional 20,000 to 100,000 dunams by private investors (*Haaretz*, 12/17/82).

But the struggle within the Jewish community in these matters is far from decided, and it is possible that it will only be decided as a result of the intervention of external forces.

---

*See "Research Material," *Journal of Palestine Studies* 32: 95. In testimony before a committee of the U.S. Congress, the estimate was even higher, and was set at about one-third of the land of the West Bank (Ruedy, 1978).

Chapter Seven

THE SEARCH FOR LEGITIMACY

About ten years ago, a young Israeli columnist wrote about a "midsummer night's dream" in which an old Arab came to his home and found the traces of his own past:

> He removes my grandfather's picture [*the grandfather was a prominent figure in the Second Aliya*], and underneath it reveals a picture of his [*the Arab's*] grandfather. . . . For a long time I have been feeling that this house is not mine. And lately I have had another feeling, which is very characteristic of the average Israeli adolescent: I feel that someone lived in this house before we came (Y. Geffen, *Maariv*, 11/8/72).

From the beginning of the modern Jewish settlement in Palestine to this day, the settlers have had ambivalent feelings based on their perceptions about (a) the relationship of the Jewish people to the Land of Israel, or Zion, (b) the relationship of the local Arab residents to the land of Palestine, and (c) the relationship between the new Jewish settlers and the local residents. Common to their perceptions of each of these three relationships was that they felt *ill-at-ease*. Sometimes this feeling was latent; at other times it was openly manifest. It no doubt stemmed from the fact that the immigrant-settlers, who sincerely believed they were returning to the land of their fathers, found themselves in a land which was already populated with inhabitants who had their own claims and rights. The result was a confrontation between claims and counterclaims, between competing rights of two peoples. No matter what answer the individual settler might give to this problem, he could not ignore it.*

In the previous chapters we have reviewed the problems which confronted the Jewish settlers in transferring land in Palestine from

---

*Attempts to ignore the problem were a type of answer.

the possession of one national entity to another, and their methods of dealing with these problems. In this chapter we will review the moral and existential problems this process of land transfer created for the Jewish settlers, and show how their response influenced the society and its institutions.

THE RELATIONSHIP OF THE SETTLERS TO THE LOCAL ARAB POPULATION

We have already reviewed the relationship of the Jewish people to the land of Israel. It was comparatively uniform among the different streams of Zionism, and has changed little over time. On the other hand, there was no consensus among the settlers about their relationship to the local Arabs or about the relationship of this Arab population to the land they also saw as a homeland. The perceptions and positions among the Jews on these topics were many and varied, and within this framework we can discuss only the more important ones.

1. *The Arabs as relatives.* This perception was the dominant one among the first settlers who came to Palestine. The Arabs were regarded as Semitic relatives who greatly resembled "our forefathers." It followed that if the Jews were returning to the land of the forefathers and wished to renew their ancient culture, they should selectively imitate the customs of the Arabs in clothing, food, work methods, agrarian technology, personal relationships, etc., and should be integrated to a certain extent within the Arab culture. At the same time, they felt they should influence Arab culture by bringing it into contact with the advances and advantages of Western culture. Implicit in this approach was the belief that there were no important differences in interest between the settlers and the local inhabitants, and whatever disagreements there might be were transitory and the result of misunderstandings. The most radical exposition of this view was given by David Ben-Gurion, who as a young man in 1917 tried to prove that the fellaheen in Palestine were remnants of the ancient Jewish nation who had remained to guard the land for the rest of the Jews (1931:13-30). (Somewhat later Ben-Gurion changed his views on this issue.)

2. *The Arabs as natives.* This view was not often propounded. It implied that Zionism was part of the colonizing movement of white men going to live among the non-whites. Holders of this view openly acknowledged the conflict of interests between the settlers and the local inhabitants. It was the view held by Jabotinsky, who said in 1933:

> Every native race, whether it is culturally advanced or backward, sees its land as its "national home," where it wishes to live and remain forever as the *sole owner*; and such a nation will not willingly agree to have new owners, and not even to have partners to this possession (1953:253; emphasis added).

From this perspective, not only did the Arabs want to remain the sole owners, but they could not be expected to freely agree to the realization of Zionism in exchange for the cultural and economic benefits it might bring them.

> One can of course bribe individual Arabs, but that does not mean that all the Arabs of Palestine are prepared to sell that patriotic zeal which even the Papuans do not sell. Every aboriginal nation fights settlers as long as there is the slightest hope of ridding itself of the danger of foreign settlement. Thus they act, and that is the way the Arabs of Palestine will act (*ibid.*).

This view did not make light of the Arabs, nor did it ignore them (as did some of the early colonialists), but it saw Palestine as a frontier upon which Jewish settlement should be imposed by force. Though this view of the Arabs as natives is seldom openly expressed among Zionists, the conviction that only by force could Zionism achieve its aims became one of the most widely shared perceptions in the Jewish collectivity.

3. *The Arabs as Gentiles.* This view saw the relationship between the Jews and the Arabs (the Palestinian Arabs, in particular) as one in which the Jews were pursued by the Arab *goyim* (i.e., Gentiles).* Thus the riots in Palestine in 1920/21 and 1929 were seen as "pogroms," and the later efforts of the Arab nations to destroy the

*This perception was greatly encouraged by the Arabs' adoption of many anti-Semitic images and expressions taken from classic European anti-Semitic tracts (see Harkabi, 1972).

State of Israel were regarded as part of a racist Nazi policy to eradicate all Jews. From this point of view, any Arab success was a return to the Holocaust. The advantage of perceiving the relationship between the Jews and the Arabs as rooted in anti-Semitism was that it made the situation familiar and meant that the existence of the conflict was independent of the actions of the Jews in Palestine (or later in Israel). The great disadvantage was that it undercut the Zionist claim of eliminating anti-Semitism by the implementation of Zionism.

The hatred of non-Jews for Jews (though not labelled as anti-Semitism) and the return of that hatred by the Jews was a central motif in the writings of Y. H. Brenner, who described the situation in Palestine in 1913 as follows:

> In small Palestine, in addition to its other inhabitants, there are no less than six-hundred thousand Arabs, who are, in spite of their low station and lack of culture, the actual owners of the country and are recognized as such, and we have come to penetrate into their midst and to live among them, because we are forced to do so. There is already hatred between us, and this must be so—and will be so. They are stronger than we in every way, and they can turn us into earth that can be trampled. But we, the Jews, are already used to living as the weak among the strong, and here too we must be ready for the results of hatred and must use all the means available to our weak hands in order to be able to exist here as well. After all we are accustomed to this—to be surrounded by hatred and to be full of hatred—yes, full of hatred, that is what we must be! (Cursed are the weak ones who love!)—and that is the way we have lived since we became a people (1956:323).

At base, this perception is a feeling of weakness and inferiority when confronted by the *goyim*, but with the Jews having certain "relative advantages": the feeling that there is no other choice (the Hebrew slogan of *Ein Breira*—"There is no alternative"—keeps recurring in the Jewish-Arab conflict) and prior experience as a form of preparation against persecution. But this perception also includes a belief that in the relationship between Jews and non-Jews, the Jews are morally and physically superior because of their capability to suffer and survive.

4. *The Arab as Canaanite.* This is a relatively recent perception which received its major impetus after the 1967 War and is held by

only a few of the national-religious elements. It sees an analogy between the present situation and the Hebrew tribes' conquest of Canaan, when they were given a divine order to destroy the idolaters and take over the land as an inheritance. In this view the settlers are the Hebrews and the Arabs the Canaanites. Thus the Arabs' claims to the land have no validity when juxtaposed with the divine command. Under present political conditions, this view cannot be implemented, but its underlying principle is that of Gush Emunim and its supporters. Gush Emunim does not have a position regarding what is to be done with the Arabs in the conquered territories. It is concerned only with creating a massive Jewish presence in these areas to prevent their return to Arab control. It appears that Gush Emunim expects the future of the Arab residents to be resolved in some miraculous manner.*

The reverse of this view—an attempt to formulate a pan-Semitic Canaanite ideology based upon new definitions of the boundaries and natures of both sides to the dispute—emerged among a fringe element of Jewish artists and intellectuals in the 1940s. This movement clearly arose in response to the pressures of the conflict with the Arabs, and the major group within it proposed to resolve the conflict by assimilating the Arabs within the "Hebrew nation," whose members would be all those born within the borders of the "Land of the Euphrates," and which would be freed from the pathological past by the "Hebrew force." Thus a Pax Hebraica would be achieved by what would in essence be an inclusive frontier (see Ratosh, 1976).

5. *The Arabs as an oppressed class.* This view prevailed for many years within the dominant stream of the Zionist settlers—the left. It attempted to explain the Jewish-Arab relationship within a Marxist framework. The source of the Arabs' hatred for the Jewish immigrants was that their immigration endangered the feudal and exploitative pre-capitalistic regime existing in Arab society. Therefore the traditional Arab leadership, to protect itself, incited the Arab masses against the Zionist settlers. As Jacobson put it in 1912:

---

*In the Zionist history the Balfour Declaration (1917) was perceived as a miracle, as well as the appointment of Sir Herbert Samuel as the first High Commissioner of Palestine (1920). The results of the 1947/48 and 1967 Wars were also explained as divine intervention in history on behalf of the Jews.

187

"The reason for the hatred against us in Palestine is because we aid the fellaheen and therefore cause damage to the interests of the effendis" (Assaf, 1970:69). There was no real conflict of interests between the Arab masses and the Jewish settlers, who ought to be building a just and equalitarian society which would serve as a model for the Arabs as well. Cooperation between the Jews and Arabs would come with a socialist revolution among the Arabs, and it was the duty of the Jews to aid those Arab elements who would further revolution. Ben-Gurion argued that "We must seek the approval and understanding only of the Arab worker, and only a covenant between the Hebrew and the Arab workers will establish and preserve the covenant between the Jewish and the Arab nations in the country" (1931:85). On the other hand, Yitzhak Tabenkin, one of the founders of the Labor Movement, at a conference of Ahdut Haavoda in 1924, insisted that the rights of the "inhabitants of the land [*the Arabs*], who [*were*] reactionary by nature," should be transferred to the revolutionary Jewish *avant-garde* (1967:353).

6. *The Arabs and Jews as two national movements.* Within various segments of the Jewish community, a perception slowly developed that, in opposition to the Jewish national movement (Zionism), an Arab national movement was being created in Palestine. Whether the development of such an Arab movement would be at the expense of the Jewish national movement, or both movements could develop side-by-side, would lead to very different political conclusions. The Jews who saw the development of two national movements as a "zero-sum" situation concluded that the Arab movement must be throttled in its infancy. (This was Jabotinsky's view.) On the other hand, those who saw the developing Arab national movement as unavoidable (and any efforts to stop it as unethical) sought ways to reconcile the two movements. The two methods most often proposed were territorial division and the division of political authority. The idea of territorial division was first raised in 1937 (see Chapter 2), and was essentially an attempt to gain legal, political, and ethical sanctions for conditions as they were. The idea of dividing authority — or of establishing a bi-national state — came primarily from a group of intellectuals in the 1930s and 1940s, and was the program of Hashomer Hatzair (see Hattis, 1970). Some Zionists sought even further compromise with the Arab national movement.

Ahad Haam, for example, proposed that Palestine be made a spiritual center, which meant the Jews would forsake any demands for political sovereignty in exchange for the possibility of developing communal and cultural autonomy.

Regardless of how these six views have been expressed at different times by different segments of the population, in almost every instance there has been a tension between a particularistic approach, focusing on the problems of the group, and a universalistic approach, based on humanitarian values. Even those who perceive the Arabs as Canaanites, and regard the land as promised to the Jews by divine will, did not ignore the powerful universalistic principles to which the Jewish religion, based on tribal beliefs, has become committed over the centuries. The tension between the particularistic and universalistic approaches, present to some extent in all these views, is heightened by the tension caused by the discrepancies between Zionist ideology and practice.

This continuing tension, aggravated by everyday reality in Palestine, created a problem of self-legitimation for the Jewish polity. The immediate issue was the conflict between the right of the Jewish people to own all or part of the territory of Palestine as compared to the right of the local Arab residents to own the same land. It was not that Zionism did not have any answers: it had many answers it could and did give. Thus Ben-Gurion in 1928 stated that

> According to my ethical beliefs, we do not have the right to deprive even a single Arab child, even if by means of that deprivation we will achieve our goal [*our national demands*]. Our work [*the Zionist enterprise*] cannot be built upon the deprivation of even a single person's rights (1931:150).

Jabotinsky agreed with Ben-Gurion that the conflict of rights existed, but he related its existence to vestiges of the "diaspora mentality" which "the new Jew" had to rid himself of:

> Ask the French farmer if France is his country; if it is proper that it should be an independent country. For [*the French farmer*] these are axiomatic, and not "problems." Only those with crippled spirits, with a diaspora psychosis made these [*questions about the*

189

right of the Jews to Palestine] into a "problem" which must be investigated and proved (1972:221).

CONFLICT AND ANOMIE

Even when sovereignty was achieved by the State of Israel, the problem of the legitimation of the system, including establishing ownership and presence, did not disappear; if anything, it became more severe. The Israelization of the Arab lands which had been abandoned or had been classified as absentee land, the fact that the borders now extended beyond those assigned by the UN, the continued Arab enmity (accompanied by military and paramilitary action, including periodic wars), the problem of the newly created refugees, and especially the problem of the territories captured in 1967, with their sizable populations—all these contributed to the continued existence of the problem of establishing Israel's legitimacy.*

Even when the question of the legitimation of the collectivity was not apparent on the surface, it continued to be a problem. The clash of universalistic values with particularistic elements in the Zionist ideology, along with the clash between Zionist ideology and practice, continued to create a system of cross-pressures producing a state of anomie within the system—in other words, the weakening of the norms which bound the members of the collectivity to the societal order.

When Durkheim coined the term *anomie* in 1897, he made the level of suicides the measure of anomie. If, as argued here, the conflictual context was a factor in the legitimacy of the system, thereby creating a certain amount of anomie, then there should be a statistical relation between the intensity of the conflict and the suicide rate. This was indeed the case: there was a statistically significant correlation between the salience of the Arab-Israeli conflict and the suicide rate in Israel in the years 1949-1966 (see Table 7.1). In addition, there was a statistically significant correlation between the salience of the conflict and the amount of mental illness in the

*In the first years of the state, the problem of absorbing the mass immigration took precedence over all other problems.

Table 7.1

CORRELATION COEFFICIENTS BETWEEN THE SALIENCE OF THE USE
OF FORCE ACCORDING TO THE IDENTITY OF THE INITIATOR
AND SUICIDE RATES ACCORDING TO SEX, 1949-1966

	Initiator of Use of Force			
	Arabs	Israel	Other[a]	Total
Total suicides	.049	.372	.240	.182
Male suicides	.136	.250	.259	.006
Female suicides	.306	.400	.180	.369

Source: Kimmerling (1974: 76).

[a]Most of the incidents classified as "other" are incidents in which the initiator cannot be clearly specified ("Gunfire broke out between an Israeli Defense Force patrol and a Jordanian patrol . . .," etc.). About 11 percent of the incidents fell into this category, but most of them were of low salience.

country (Kimmerling 1974).* This correlation applies to all phases of the conflict, and not only those involving the use of force, but when the Israeli side initiated the use of force, the suicides went up measurably. Thus it is not the direct pressure of the conflict that increases the suicide rate, but (1) the sum total of the problems involved and (2) Israeli initiatives.

THE DIFFERENCE BETWEEN A RIGHT AND AN ATTACHMENT

As a result of the Israeli victory and territorial conquest of 1967, the question of the Jewish right to the land became very salient. As noted earlier (Chapter 6), not only were the physical borders of the collectivity expanded, but also questions which had appeared to be resolved were asked anew in the wake of the encounter of the Israelis with territorial expanses which were of historic and symbolic significance and with a population which classified itself as "Palestinian."

*It is interesting to note that the suicide rate in Israel is also affected by the amount of immigration and the degree of unemployment. These two variables have a multiple correlation of .733 with the suicide rate or, in other words, can predict 54 percent of the variance.

The problems which this encounter engendered have already been reviewed in Chapter 6, but here we should note that the questions with which the Jews were confronted in regard to specific territorial areas were easily generalized to include all of the territory. The members of the Whole Eretz Israel Movement held that whoever questioned the right of Jews to Judea and Samaria also questioned their right to the rest of the land. This failure to differentiate between specific areas and the entire area of the collectivity was a factor in arousing doubts about the legitimation of the entire collectivity, especially when it became involved in a direct conflict with the Palestinians and their rights.

There are no objective criteria for determining the rights of the Jews as compared to the rights of the Palestinians, but the researchers of the Israel Institute of Applied Social Research (see Katz et al., 1972) investigated Jewish attitudes regarding the rights of the two peoples. In a representative sample of the Jewish population of Israel, it was found that 45 percent of the respondents believed that the Palestinians had some rights to the land. In a separate study, Israelis were asked why they felt the Jews had rights to the land. They were offered the following choices:*

1. [*The right to*] refuge and protection which the State of Israel grants every Jew (81%).
2. The Zionist settlement in the country (66%).
3. The longings of all generations to return to their homeland (61%).
4. The right of the [*Jewish*] forefathers, dating back to the biblical period (59%).
5. The military conquests, beginning with the War of Independence (56%).
6. The decision of the United Nations (40%).

Perhaps the most significant finding is that one of the choices was cited by 81 percent of the respondents. About 85 percent cited several justifications (Katz et al., 1972:163).

It appears that religiosity is the most important factor in determining the answer patterns regarding the source of legitimation (see Table 7.2). The more religious the person, the more emphasis he places on historical and traditional factors, and complementing

*The figures in parentheses indicate the percentage of those agreeing that each is a basis for Jewish rights.

Table 7.2

REASONS GIVEN FOR JEWISH RIGHTS TO THE LAND BASED ON
RELIGIOSITY AND EDUCATIONAL LEVEL
(*in percent*)

Religious and Educational Group	Rights back to Bible	Longing of all genera- tions to return	Zionist settle- ment in country	Military conquests since War of Inde- pendence	UN reso- lution	Refuge and protection which Israel gives each Jew
Religion: Attends synagogue at least on Saturdays and festivals						
Education:						
0-4 years	84%	68%	52%	58%	33%	73%
5-10 years	83	73	65	61	40	81
11+ years	86	81	61	54	33	76
Religion: Sometimes attends synagogue on Saturdays and festivals						
Education:						
0-4 years	74	67	59	69	45	67
5-10 years	68	72	68	65	51	86
11+ years	56	58	72	52	40	82
Religion: Sometimes attends High Holiday services						
Education:						
0-4 years	70	74	73	77	53	92
5-10 years	57	64	68	58	40	79
11+ years	45	51	69	55	42	86
Religion: Never attends synagogue						
Education:						
0-4 years	68	71	39	39	29	71
5-10 years	49	55	65	51	38	79
11+ years	39	47	64	45	39	80
TOTAL POPULATION	59	61	66	56	40	81

Source: Katz and Gurevich (1973:322).

these, factors related to force and military conquest. If age is kept as a constant, the historical factor declines as educational level rises (see Table 7.3), but there is a tendency for this factor to be more important as age increases. The most frequently cited justification—regardless of religiosity, age, or education—was that Israel was a place of refuge for Jews. Even among the non-religious, however, the religious-traditional argument plays a prominent role, with 49 percent of those with a secondary education and 39 percent of those with a higher education giving this reason.

It appears that the Zionist settlement still plays a prominent role in giving the system legitimation, while the reason least often cited is international recognition. The listing by 56 percent of the sample population of military conquest—the right of power—as a basis for legitimation suggests that a considerable portion of the population is troubled by the question of the Jews' right to the country. The right of power was slightly more salient among the younger age groups, but declined with the rise in educational level.

The conquest of Judea and Samaria created tremendous problems among that segment of the population which did not believe in the annexation of these areas, whether their reasons were practical, ideological, or both. This was because it opened anew a number of the questions with which the Jewish settlement had grappled in the past. It was necessary to again deal with the question of the Jews' right to the entire country, which was linked with the right to the conquered territories.

An interesting proposal was made by S. Avineri to adopt the concept of *attachment* in place of *right*. While a right has a quasi-legal connotation, and is interpreted as being equivalent to a title, which cannot be divided, an attachment is a type of spiritual relationship—a feeling of closeness—which does not necessarily involve any operative consequences. The advantage of this concept is that two attachments to the same place need not be mutually exclusive:

> In terms of an attachment, there is no doubt that [*the Jews*] have an attachment to all of the territory of the historical Land of Israel, and the Land of Israel . . . does not only include Judea and Samaria and Gaza, but also areas which are out of our control at present. Is our attachment to Mount Nebo and to Amman less than our attachment to Nablus? But not every place to which

Table 7.3

REASONS GIVEN FOR THE JEWISH RIGHT TO THE LAND
(in percent)

Reasons	Number of Respondents	Very important	Important	Not overly important	Not at all important	No answer or opinion
Refuge and protection which Israel gives to every Jew	2055	78%	14%	2%	1%	5%
Zionist settlement in the country	2054	63	26	4	1	6
Longings of all generations to return to the homeland	2056	58	27	6	2	7
Right of [*Jewish*] forefathers dating back to biblical period	2058	57	25	9	3	6
Military conquests, beginning with War of Independence	2056	53	25	12	4	6
Decision of UN	2057	38	24	19	12	7

Source: Katz and Gurevich (1973:320).

the Palestinian Arabs have an attachment must be under their control. It is difficult to ask nations to forego a right [*but on the other hand*] different attachments may live together (*Maariv*, 6/5/73).

Uriel Simon, a religious thinker, makes a similar distinction in arguing with Gush Emunim:

There is no doubt that a Jew as I myself, who believes in the holiness of the Land of Israel, feels a basic conflict between his faith and his ethical feelings, that the revival of Israel cannot take place at the expense of the freedom of another nation. The way out of this ethical contradiction is to be found in differentiating between our religious right to the land and the legal-political right which may be actualized in practice. . . . Abraham made sure to pay full value for the Cave of Makhpelah [*even though the country had been promised to him*] because the religious right cannot simply be translated into legal ownership (Quoted in Raanan, 1980:99-100).

The fact that such attempts are made to find semantic, legalistic, or other formulas to solve the problem of legitimation shows that the problem which Epstein pointed out in the Zionist Congress of 1907 and Motzkin in the Congress of 1898—that the Arabs also live in Palestine, and they demand their right to the land—is still part of the social system's struggle over its identity (Yehoshua, 1980).

MECHANISMS OF CREATING LEGITIMATION

Faced with the problem of legitimation which arose as a result of the mutually exclusive claims of the Arabs and Jews, and in light of the tensions within the Zionist movement's ideology between particularism and universalism and between theory and practice, institutional mechanisms were created to deal with the problem. In Chapter 1 we noted that the problem of legitimation has two dimensions: the acquisition of recognition from the outside (from the Arabs or the world) and the acquisition of internal recognition of the justice of the Zionist enterprise. The two dimensions are reciprocally related, with the consequence that at least some of the efforts at gaining external recognition were undertaken primarily to strengthen internal support, and *vice-versa*. In addition, a number of the institutional arrangements and mechanisms whose manifest function had no connection with legitimation had a latent function (in the sense of Merton, 1957:19-84) of legitimizing the system. (I use this concept because, like Robert Merton, I believe that "armed with the concept of latent function, the sociologist extends his inquiry in the very directions which promise most for the theoretical development of the discipline" [66].)

Some of the primary arrangements and mechanisms within the system which were meant to answer the problem of the self-legitimation of the collectivity are analyzed below.

A. THE DEFINITION OF THE CONFLICTUAL SITUATION AND THE DEFINITION OF THE IDENTITY OF THOSE INVOLVED IN THE DISPUTE

Underlying the justification of Zionist claims to the outside world there have almost always been two principles: first, the contention that the Jewish-Arab dispute is not a zero-sum situation; second, the limiting of all aspects of the dispute to the material plane, while downplaying the political and primordial dimensions. This approach has a long tradition within Zionism, and was adopted by Herzl himself. In his *Alteneuland*, which appeared in 1902, a son of an Arab notable tells how he gained from Zionist settlement:

> Those who had nothing, and who therefore could lose nothing, obviously gained. And they did indeed gain: employment opportunities, a livelihood, good conditions . . . and when [*the Jews*] drained the swamps in the country, irrigated it and planted the eucalyptus trees, they improved the land, they used these local workers, the strong ones, and they paid them a fair wage . . . . These hapless people have been made far more fortunate than they were before. They earn a decent wage, their children are healthy and are studying. No one has harmed their ancient religion and customs. Only good has come from them (Herzl, 1960:17).

In most of their contacts with the Arab leadership (see, for example, Sela, 1972/3) or the British government and its officials, the Jews stressed the increased opportunities which would result from the economic development of Palestine—primarily modernization of agriculture, including the change from extensive to intensive cultivation and from subsistence crops to cash crops. It was the Zionist claim that the inflow of the capital and expertise of the Jews would enable the Arab population and the millions of Jews to live side-by-side in Palestine. It was easy to show how Jewish capital had already brought about economic growth among the Arab population and the development of new industries, such as citrus crops and manufacturing (Boneh, 1938:255-77), and how the Mandate, as an economic framework, drew primarily from the developed Jewish sector to supply services to the undeveloped Arab sector.

But it appears that even the Jewish leadership was aware that, in terms of the sum-total of Jewish-Arab relationships, this type of argument carried little weight. As Ben-Gurion reports:

> The assumption which was accepted in the Zionist movement then was that we were bringing a blessing to the Arabs, and therefore there was no reason why they should oppose us. In the first talk I held with Musa al-Alami [in 1933] . . . this assumption was undermined when Musa al-Alami told me: "I would prefer that the country remain poor and desolate for another hundred years, until we, the Arabs, will be able, by our own efforts, to make it bloom and develop it." I felt that he was a patriotic Arab and was entitled to say that (1967:19-20).

While these claims were directed primarily at the British and the Arabs, and thus were part of Zionist foreign policy, they also played a role in constructing a self-image of the Jewish collectivity in Palestine. The perception of the situation as zero-sum had political implications which led to attempts to find alternative ways of defining the collectivity. The proposal for the establishment of a bi-national state or the cantonization of Palestine, which was favored by Brit Shalom between 1925 and 1933 (Keydar, 1967; Hattis, 1970), along with some of the leaders of the Mapai party in the early 1930s (see Ben-Gurion, 1931:189), and was eventually adopted by Hashomer Hatzair (Cohen, 1970:282-90), no doubt stemmed from these attempts. The idea of the partition of Palestine was eventually accepted by the leadership of the Yishuv based on the perception that this was the best that could be obtained under the existing political conditions. When Ben-Gurion, who saw partition as "the most desirable solution at this time [1947]," sought to explain to his son what had brought the British to propose partition, he argued that it was the British who invoked the concept of *justice*:

> The English were dismayed .... On the one hand, they knew that England had obligated itself to the Jewish people to aid in the establishment of its national home in Palestine . . . but on the other hand, the English saw that the Arabs had not just arrived in the country, but had been there for about a thousand years, a longer time than the existence of the English state itself, and that they had arisen again and again against the "national home" and against the British Mandate . . . . The demands of the Arabs appeared to them to be logical and just. This is their land, they have already been living on it for hundreds of years, and they do not want foreigners to live in it and take control over it (1968:177).

By making the dispute over Palestine a territorial-national struggle extending beyond the issue of the land itself—i.e., the entire Arab nation against the Jewish nation—the Jews could negate one of the factors contributing to the perception of the struggle as a zero-sum situation: the limited and given quantity of the land resource. As Jabotinsky put it in a speech he made in 1914:

> We must make this matter [*our right to Palestine*] not a "question" between the Jewish nation and the *Arab nation*. The Arab nation, which has about thirty-five million people, has [*an area equal to*] half of Europe, while the Jewish nation, which has about ten million people, wanders throughout the world and has no place of its own (1972:220; emphasis added).

Ben-Gurion spoke in similar terms in 1936 to the Arab historian Antonius:

> I deny the assumption that the aspirations of the Jews and the Arabs are not mutually reconcilable. There is no necessary and unavoidable contradiction. As a starting point, one should take the assumption that the question is not between the Jews of Palestine and the Arabs of Palestine—*in this limited area there is indeed a contradiction which it is hard to reconcile*—but one should see the Jews as a global unit, and the Arabs as a global unit. And I believe, that between the national aspirations of the Jewish nation and the national aspirations of the Arab nation, there are no contradictions, because we are only interested in this land, and the Arabs are interested not only in this land but in the whole territory of the

Middle East. And whatever will happen in Palestine will not change the global status of the Arab nations (1967:48; emphasis added).

Placing the dispute in such a perspective not only decreased the importance of Palestine for the Arabs, but allowed the Zionists to assert the justice of their demands, which was needed to make their self-image acceptable:

Justice means that everyone will receive what he is entitled to, and especially — that the one who has nothing, will at least receive something . . . one of the two: if Zionism is not just, let us leave . . . . But if it is just, if its demands are just ones, that of this vast territory, which is half the size of Europe, and which has a population of 37 million people who speak Arabic (the richest race in territories in the world!) — that of this fantastic and almost unused property, 1/170 should be set aside for a nation which has nothing in the entire world (Jabotinsky, 1972:224).

These examples do not reflect all the definitions of the conflictual situation within the Jewish community, but they provide a representative sample of the claims made for "external consumption" (and sometimes for "internal consumption"as well) which (1) illustrate the different reactions to the cross-pressures within the system and (2) place the conflict within a world order (as used by Shils, 1965) which is familiar and understandable.

B. ZIONIST TERMINOLOGY

There is a significant link between the cross-pressures on the social system and the tendency to define processes related to the dispute in non-conflictual terms, or place them in a framework outside the Jewish-Arab relationship. This can be seen in the language employed to analyze the three major areas of the dispute: the struggle for the ownership of land, the struggle for numerical superiority between the Jews and the Arabs, and the struggle for employment opportunities at all levels of the Mandatory system. Another tendency was to define the opposition in the struggle as other than the Arab — as another element in the Jewish sector, as the British government, as nature, or as human nature.

The struggle for employment opportunities occurred within two contexts: (1) a class struggle within the Jewish community —

i.e., the competition with Arab workers for jobs in the Jewish community's economy, and (2) within the self—i.e., the development of the ability to engage in physical work and "the transformation of work into an inherent value," in accordance with the "labor religion" doctrines of A. D. Gordon, whose views were influential in the development of the "pioneer economy" (see Schweid, 1970:174; Kimmerling, 1982, ch. 1). The struggle over immigration was never included as part of the Jewish-Arab conflict. The changing of the status quo to the extent of creating a Jewish majority was desirable, but only after the White Paper of 1939 was published was it connected to the dispute, and then it was in the context of the struggle against the British Mandate.

At the same time, the struggle for land was defined, not by accident, as "the redemption of the land"—a phrase with a double meaning. Not only was the land to be redeemed from non-Jewish ownership to Jewish ownership, but it was also to be redeemed from its desolation and from nature. As early as 1907 Epstein advanced the claim that would consistently be used as part of the Zionist argument—both for external and for internal consumption: "We will again conquer, by means of science and sweat, what our fathers conquered by the sword and spear. And we will redeem the land, not from the Arab fellaheen, but from drought, from desolation and from neglect" (1907:29). Again, it was not by accident that many of the sources stressed that "the large tracts of land which were redeemed by the JNF in the valleys were almost all desolate and covered with malarial swamps" (Olitzur, 1939:138-39). But transferring the issues which were at the center of the Jewish-Arab conflict to the internal-Yishuv arena had implications beyond more convenient semantic definitions in terms of strengthening the sense of identity, self-image, and belief in its right to exist of the Jewish collectivity.

C. THE STRUGGLE AGAINST NATURE AS PART OF ZIONIST IDEOLOGY

The conjunction of the demand for redeeming the land from its desolation and the need to change the self-image and life patterns of people who were not "natural laborers" helped to create the Zionist ethos. The role which became its symbol was the pioneer (*chalutz*), described by Eisenstadt in these terms:

This is a person who is willing to make do with little, who is willing to live as an ascetic. This willingness to forego material benefits is not asceticism for its own sake, even though the ascetic principle became quite strong, but was meant primarily to enable the pioneer to implement an important task for the whole, and especially for the future society which would come about . . . . The second central principle regarding the image of the pioneer [is] . . . the stress on agricultural work—or physical work in general—and in not exploiting anyone else, as the most primary means of renewing the youth of the nation and the creation of "new" people and a new national unit (1967:14).

The creation of these "new" people was essential because "The Land of Israel will not be Jewish, even if Jews settle in it and buy land, unless they work the land with their own hands. For the land is not really that of its owners, but of its workers" (Schweid, 1970:173). The pioneer struggled both with his own nature and with nature in general. It was he who drained the swamps, removed the rocks from the soil, and later made the wasteland bloom. The pioneer gave the answer to the basic problem faced by the Jewish settlers when they were convinced that the land—and especially the land which they saw to be uninhabited—was cultivable.

Another aspect of the image of the pioneer was the striving to build a special type of communal life, which would lead to the development of a just society (Eisenstadt, 1971). That, together with the willingness to live a spartan existence, gave the pioneer an "ethical image," as described by the poet Chaim N. Bialik in 1921:

Tell me, where was this sight ever seen elsewhere. For a revolutionary spirit to blow through the land and to draw with it the youth in order to revolutionize the nation, to change it from a nation which tended the spirit to one which works physically— this must be the first time in history [that such has occurred]. If there is any hope that new ideas will triumph—they will first come from that place [the kibbutz] and from the hearts of these youngsters. They will fulfill with their lives the great dream of mankind not with the power of the fist nor with an army, but by deeds and work (1940:104).

The Yishuv adopted the image of the pioneer as its self-image and as its symbol to the outside world. By this adoption it transferred the ethical character of the pioneer to the Yishuv: such a society cannot be unjust.

The struggle with nature in which the pioneers were involved, the changing of the landscape, the improvement of the land and the climate—all these would strengthen their right to settle the land. The local residents did not care about making the land bloom, and sometimes even damaged the landscape and ruined the climate, but now, after the "heroic Hebrew pioneers" had come, they were returning and reviving the land. This motif was repeated many times in Zionist mythology. The struggle with nature took several forms:

1. *The Jews built cities on the sandy coast of the sea.* This claim was made before the Peel Commission, concluding as follows:

> If the immigration of men and money continues to supply the demands of production and consumption alike, new towns, it is foretold, will spring up along the sandy coast, where no one can assert, whatever may be said inland, that a Jew coming in means an Arab going out (1937:115).

2. *The Jews dug water wells.*

> The vast majority, or 96 percent [*of 338 drillings from 1924 to 1936*] were made by Jews, either by the settlement corporations connected to the Zionist Federation, by PICA, or by private companies or individuals, and only 4 percent were carried out by others, including the government. As a result of this extensive drilling, the added quantities of water brought about an expansion of the irrigated land in the country (Granovsky, 1938:224).

3. *The Jews drained the swamps.* This was the central component in the Zionist epic. Bein describes one of these cases—the draining of the land in the Jezreel Valley in 1922—as follows:

> In extreme heat to which they were unaccustomed—Beit Alfa is 70 meters below sea level!—with miserable economic conditions, while struggling constantly against malaria, when there were often occasions when they would have to stand up to their chests in the vile-smelling swamp water, the children of a nation which had been city dwellers for many generations worked there—performing the tasks that in most colonial countries are only performed by the natives. A number of those who performed the work fell as victims in these heroic undertakings, some of them suffered poor

health for the rest of their lives, and almost all of them endured years of want and disease (1970:239-40).

4. *The Jews changed the face of the land and its climate by planting forests.* By planting forests, whose instrumental value was marginal, the pioneers symbolically expressed their struggle with nature and the conquest of the land. In a well-known story by a contemporary Israeli author, A.B. Yehoshua, an analogy is drawn between the forests and the Zionist enterprise. A forest is planted on the ruins of a destroyed Arab village which no one remembers anymore. Only a speechless old Arab and his eccentric daughter remain in the village ruins. The old man gathers cans of kerosene in order to burn down the forest, but the forest is eventually destroyed by the Jewish hero of the story, who evidently cannot withstand the pressure of the confrontation between the past and the Zionist present (1970).

Thus the Jewish settlement was struggling with nature (and with human nature) to prove (1) that the resources in the Jewish-Arab conflict were not zero-sum, and (2) that the Jewish settlers had a right to the land as a result of the combination of their present deeds and their past.

D. RELIGION AS THE RIGHT OF THE PAST

Zionism was an essentially secular revolution. It was one of the forms of rebellion agains the social structure of traditional-religious Judaism, which was seen as a major cause of the persecution the Jews had suffered while they had been exiled from their homeland. The most militant opposition to Zionism was from the religious camp, which saw it as a false messianic movement which might be more dangerous than secularization itself because it projected many motifs which were based on religion (Friedman, 1977). There is, however, no basis for the claim of Elmessiri (1977) that Zionism was in opposition to the Jewish religion. While Zionism was a revolt against specific institutional, political, and social expressions of the Jewish religion, as well as against specific religious leaders, it included many components which were borrowed from the Jewish religion.

Not only did most of the Zionist groups include religious motifs, but the leadership of the Yishuv was willing to guarantee the maintenance of religious customs and religious services for the entire population, and even to allocate material resources and make ideological compromises which were clearly inconsistent with the beliefs of the Zionist mainstream. At the 18th Zionist Congress in Lucerne, in 1935, where for the first time the left was assured of hegemony, a number of the conditions of the Mizrahi for being part of the Zionist administration were agreed to by Ben-Gurion:

> To guarantee the observance of the Sabbath and the Jewish festivals in the work in the field and in the vineyards, commerce and industry . . . . Complete Kashrut in the public kitchens . . . . To guarantee for the Mizrahi in advance a fixed suitable percentage of the immigration of pioneers and craftsmen . . . . To guarantee a suitable percentage [of funds] for the Orthodox settlement . . . . To guarantee for the Mizrahi a suitable number of the officials in the Zionist institutions (Ben-Gurion, 1968:125).

These concessions by Ben-Gurion appear to support the determination by Friedman that

> Zionism is the only secular movement [in Judaism] which tried to come to an agreement with Orthodox Jewry. The reason for this was not only practical . . . but possibly, and maybe primarily, ideological. It is connected to the problem of legitimation of the Zionist movement, for while in every "normal" national movement, the link between the territory and the nation is natural and is not cast in doubt, as far as the Zionist movement is concerned, the link between Palestine and the Jewish nation is not based on a living reality; in other words, the residence of the Jewish nation in Palestine is not based on actual reality but on historical memories, links, and sentiments. These memories and sentiments are an essential part of Jewish tradition, which Orthodox Jewry represents, both in the eyes of the secular Jews and in the eyes of the non-Jewish world. It was most essential for the Zionist movement to gain to its side at least part of Orthodox Jewry, and to prevent the Orthodox camp from standing in opposition to it (1971:118).

Thus a complex system of exchange developed within the secular majority willing to accept a considerable number of restrictions upon itself, such as having the Sabbath and Kashrut observed and having Jewish religious law apply in all areas of personal law,* guaranteeing the religious sector a sizable portion of the material resources and access to political positions within the Yishuv system. In return, the participation of religious Jewry in the Zionist collectivity strengthened the ties between the Jewish settlement and the Land of Israel. The most succinct definition of this exchange system was expressed by a Minister of Religions many years later: "The Jewish Codex [*the Halacha*] is our *constitution as well as our charter* in terms of our right to the Land of Israel."[†]

A central figure in this linkage between religious Jewry and the Jewish settlement in Palestine was Rabbi Abraham Isaac Kook, who was the rabbi of Jaffa and the colonies of that area from 1904 to 1914, and from 1919 to his death in 1935 Chief Rabbi of the Ashkenazic community and the head of the Rabbinic Appeals Court. Rabbi Kook was torn between his attachment to the anti-Zionist Orthodox camp and his feelings for the new Yishuv (see Friedman, 1977), but he was perceived as lenient and innovative and a person to whom one could speak. One of the major motifs in his philosophy was a belief in the centrality of the Land of Israel in the Jewish religion: *there is no Judaism without the Land of Israel*—the actual land, not the messianic one—and there is no Jewish existence in the Diaspora unless it is anchored in the Land of Israel (Avineri, 1981: 187-97).

In this regard, two simultaneous processes took place which complemented one another: (a) the inclusion of segments of religious Jews within the Zionist movement and within the federative structure of the Jewish community in Palestine, and the development of a *modus vivendi* with them, with each side compromising somewhat, and (b) the selective absorption of elements of religion and tradition into the Zionist culture and symbolic system. The principles which were accepted and became central within the national identity and the Hebrew culture were comparatively marginal within the framework of traditional Judaism, but were seen as significant in making the connection between the nation and the land. The need for this linkage was not initially derived from the confrontation between the

---

*Jurisdiction in personal law was awarded by the British government (continuing the situation as it had been under Ottoman rule) to the various religious authorities in the country, who enjoyed almost total autonomy in this sphere.

[†]Radio broadcast, Galei Zahal, military broadcasting station, 12/16/71; emphasis added.

Jews and Arabs in Palestine. It stemmed from the problematic nature of the Zionist solution to the Jewish question, and only in the course of time did this problem include the dimension of rights.

A clear example of such a process is the central place the Bible played in the ethical and cultural system of the Jewish community which was being established. While the Bible is an integral part of the Jewish legal heritage and traditional Jewish scholarship, over time it was shifted into the fringes of the culture. The stories of the Bible were taught as "moral tales" in the schools for younger students (the *heders*), but at the higher levels they were no longer taught as part of the curriculum and were replaced primarily by Talmudic scholarship. The Jewish Enlightenment movement began rediscovering the Bible—primarily the Pentateuch and the Early Prophets—which merged well with the streams of returning-to-the-earth in the nineteenth-century Russian populist movements of the *narodniks*. The novels of Abraham Mapu, the father of the modern Hebrew novel, were based on the biblical stories, and they became an integral part of the future image of the Hibat Zion movement (which made up the First Aliya) after the anti-Jewish riots and decrees in Eastern Europe in the early 1880s.

The Bible occupied an even more central position with the Second Aliya, for whom (unlike the members of the First Aliya, who had not forsaken religion and adopted modern ideologies) the connection between them and the Land of Israel was not self-evident. Rahel Yanait Ben-Zvi tells of the many hikes she and her friends took throughout the country, with the Bible in their hands, compulsively seeking to find the remnants of ancient Jewish history, trying to identify ancient Hebrew settlements from the Arab names of villages. When they reached Nablus, they passed a well: "I stayed at the mouth of the well for a long time. I sought the riddle of my people in its waters, the memory of our father Jacob, the youth of our nation." On another occasion, she visited the grave of the matriarch Rachel, leaving the place only after her friends called to her: "One of them was astonished by my wet eyes, and I solved the problem for him off-handedly: 'Don't be afraid—my socialism has not been affected by my contact with the grave of Rachel'" (1964:110).

In the curriculum of the schools of the new Yishuv, the Bible occupied a prominent place, side-by-side with a shift away from the traditional studies, as in the heder and yeshiva, and the bringing in of secular studies into the schools. Thus, "in the schools in the colonies they studied the Bible, Talmud, Hebrew language and Jewish history as major subjects, even after they had introduced French, and these enjoyed a great deal of attention and most of the time was devoted to them" (Azaryahu, 1929:57-112). Already in 1892 a small group of teachers had tried to organize a teachers' assembly in Palestine and to formulate a uniform curriculum where about a quarter of the time would be devoted to the Bible. This tendency continued, although with a slightly greater emphasis on general studies, in the curriculum which the Teachers' Federation later formulated in 1907 (see Ozarkovsky, Yehiel, and Kriesski, 1907).

E. THE INSTITUTIONALIZATION OF HIKING IN THE COUNTRY

Above we described the hikes of Rahel Yanait and her friends, who roamed throughout the country linking the places they were walking with the names that appeared in the Bible. As the Hebrew educational system developed, the institutionalization of organized hikes in the country increased. Eventually it became one of the most important activities of the youth movements, as did the custom of the yearly hike, which appears to be a specifically Israeli custom. In a radio talk by Azarya Allon, he explained why it was important to hike throughout the country, even when there were security tensions in the air:

1. Our link to the land is less than that of other nations, and there is no better way than hiking, and especially when there is this tension in the country, to strengthen this link.

2. There are important sections of the country which are not inhabited by Jews and they are in danger. Hiking is thus a tool for displaying Jewish presence in those areas (Israeli Broadcasting Service, 1/9/74).

The efforts expended in trying to locate old Hebrew settlements by their modern Arabic names and the naming of new settlements using the ancient Hebrew names is part of this same process, referred to in Zionist jargon as "the redeeming of names." In an introduction to a book published by the JNF in 1937, which summarizes the research which had gone into the use of a hundred names which had been "redeemed," the author says:

And the [*following*] generations will then look into our souls and will see how we tried to *link* the times in which we are living with those times which preceded them by thousands of years, when we renewed the settlements and their names . . . names, each single one of which, and all together, express *our right* and our link to this country (Arikha, 1937:6; emphasis added).

There are other phenomena connected with the desire to stress the link between the past and the present. One is the prominent place which archaeology occupies, and another is the demand by Israel's most prominent leader, David Ben-Gurion, to be considered not only a statesman and social reformer, but also a patron of the spreading of the Bible and an interpreter of the Bible.

F. INSTITUTING HEBREW AS THE LANGUAGE USED BY THE SYSTEM

More than anything else, the cultural process which demanded the greatest social investment was establishing the Hebrew language as the official language of the system, and making it the basis for an independent Israeli culture. It was an aspect of nation-building in which the teachers played a decisive role. The transition to Hebrew—from Yiddish and the tradition it represented—was an inseparable part of the struggle of the pioneer with nature (Eisenstadt, 1967:14). The Hapoel Hatzair party took as its platform from the very first that: "Our world stands upon three elements: on Hebrew land, on Hebrew labor, and on the Hebrew language" (Even-Shoshan, 1963: 255). The adoption of the Hebrew language was another link in the chain which was perceived as connecting the Jewish settlement with its historical past in the country. Thus one of the arguments given for the adoption of the Sefaradic pronunciation (as opposed to the Ashkenazic one) was that "this was the characteristic way our ancient fathers expressed themselves in this language" (Yellin, 1905:4). Jabotinsky later tried to express this in political terms, but one can assume that here the dynamic of presenting the matter for external consumption came into play:

The revival of the Hebrew language in the gentile world adds honor to Zionism, and increases its political power. Carry out this experiment by yourselves, if you find occasion to do so. Take a simple non-Jew, let him hear a conversation in Hebrew, wait until he asks you "What language is that?" Answer him briefly: "The language of the Bible"—and listen to what the next question will be. It will be: "What do you hear from the Land of Israel?" (*Doar Hayom*, 1/8/31).

The transition to Hebrew did not come about without an internal struggle, because the alternative of using Yiddish was very attractive. Yiddish was the language of almost all those who came with the first immigration, and it was a living language with a rich modern cultural and literary tradition. In addition, the use of Yiddish was seen as linking the small Yishuv with the major Jewish centers who served as the reservoirs of material and expressive resources (including manpower). Added to this was the internationalist orientation which brought Poalei Zion, when it first became active in the country, to formulate a Yiddishist ideology, and to publish its first newspaper (*Der Onfang*) in Yiddish. "Only years later did they accept the Hebrew language as the national language" (Braslavsky, 1966:122). Even Hapoel Hatzair, in spite of its Hebrew orientation, found difficulty in bringing about the conversion to the Hebrew language.

The argument that Hebrew would unite the Yishuv—i.e., that it would bring about the use of a common language by all the Jews, including the traditional Sefaradic Jews, was used especially at the time of the First Aliya, when the Sefaradic community was predominant in the Yishuv, and provided the link between the new Yishuv and the local Arab elite, as well as political protection through its close ties to the Ottoman rulers.

The idea that Hebrew would be a unifying force was forgotten as the power of the Sefaradic community declined, and as the Ashkenazic community became dominant with the Second and Third Aliya waves. In addition, as the Ottoman power waned (and eventually disappeared) the Sefaradic community no longer played a prominent role as intermediary between the Jews and the central government. From that time on, until the great waves of immigrants from the Oriental lands after the State of Israel was proclaimed, Hebrew was almost never presented as being a unifying force, but, if anything, as a socially divisive one. Nevertheless, in the "language *kampf*" between Yiddish and Hebrew which reached its peak in 1914, Hebrew emerged victorious.

SUMMARY

The tensions which were created in the Jewish system as a result of the existence of the Arab adversary who demanded sole control of the same area of land involved two types of problems:

1. Activities which had significance in the context of the Jewish-Arab dispute were not in accord with the universalistic values which held sway in the collectivity, but were nevertheless seen as essential for the building of the nation.

2. The granting of unconditional legitimacy to the existence of the collectivity was problematic—not only because of the conflict with the Arabs, but also because that conflict added other dimensions to it.

The system did not formulate a direct and complete response to these problems, but a number of symbols, activity patterns, and institutions were created within it which lessened the tensions along three planes: (a) extra-conflictual contexts and significance were given to a number of the activities involved in the management of the conflict; (b) activities were carried out to demonstrate that the competition for resources about which the struggle revolved was not a zero-sum situation, and that scarcities could be overcome; (c) priority was given by the ethical and cultural system of the collectivity to those symbols which linked the settlers with the land, and by this means emphasized the legitimacy of the settlement.

These symbols, activities, and institutions were not created to solve the problems the conflict had raised, but one may assume that during the process of crystallization of the Israeli social system, those institutions which could offer solutions were reinforced, just as settlement patterns were adopted which could contend with the conflictual situation. As the system grappled with the problems of its own legitimacy, it developed particularistic orientations and approaches, some of which were spread by various socializing agents, including the educational system.

Chapter Eight

SENTIMENTS AND POWER

The story of Zionist settlement in Zion is not ended. For a long time after this book is published, that unique story will continue to intrigue the international community and stir up controversy. The sides which are directly involved will almost certainly continue to play according to the rules laid down long ago, but they will on occasion depart from them. Almost anything is possible in the Middle East, where everything is temporary, and there is nothing more permanent than change. The time has come to try to summarize our account. The summary must be constructed on two planes: on one plane, how a group of immigrant settlers behave given a very low degree of frontierity; on the other plane, how Jewish settlers behaved in the specific case presented here.

Before beginning this summary, we must discuss another dimension of social behavior related to territory—i.e., the different kinds of orientations toward territorial expanses.

TYPES OF ORIENTATION TOWARD TERRITORIAL EXPANSES

An attempt to construct a conceptual framework for analysis of orientations toward territorial expanses has been undertaken by Eric Cohen (1976) and developed by Kimmerling (1979). Cohen posits four basic orientations, each including two sub-orientations with mechanisms for regulating the territory in accordance with the principles implicit in the orientation. These four basic orientations are:

1. Instrumental Orientation. This orientation perceives of territorial space as the source of the resources which an optimal use of land would yield—i.e., the crops that can be grown, the water and minerals that can be produced, the people that can settle on it, and

212

the tourists to whom the landscape can be sold. Cohen identifies two regulative sub-orientations. One is a *technical* sub-orientation: the know-how a culture has at its disposal. (Animals living in a territory may use its resources intensively, but they have a limited view of the available resources.) A quasi-parallel to this sub-orientation can be seen in the efforts of the British (and the Jewish response) to establish the absorption capacity of Palestine—i.e., the resources available for possible Jewish immigration (see Friedlander and Goldscheider, 1979: 63-81). The other sub-orientation is *economic*: it relates to land in terms of the potential profits to be derived from ownership. The land market becomes a regulative mechanism as nature is turned into property. Orienting to land solely in economic terms was a Jewish tactic in the pre-sovereign period for managing the conflict between Jews and Arabs (Kimmerling, 1974).

2. Territorial Orientation. This orientation relates to territorial space in terms of its control in accordance with the values of a specific culture. It has two sub-orientations—*strategic* and *political*.

The *strategic* sub-orientation relates to the territory in terms of the possibilities of military control, from either an offensive or defensive perspective. Thus in the Mandatory period some Jewish settlements in Palestine were set up primarily to contribute to the collectivity's defense and security (see Kimmerling, 1974). This continued after 1948, and especially from 1967 through 1977. Locating settlements according to defensive needs is a well-known practice, manifest from ancient cultures (Chagnon, 1968: 109-59) to the present day (Whittlesey, 1971).

The *political* sub-orientation relates to territory in terms of legitimate control, leading to sovereignty. The political organizer— i.e., the government—is the ultimate authority which determines how territory is to be allocated to individuals, groups, and institutions (Soja, 1971). It also determines the boundaries of the collectivity. Political control is usually based on previous strategic dominance, as was the case of the territories added to Israeli control following the 1967 War (see Nissan, 1978). In the bargaining period of 1977/79 with Egypt, Israel attempted to convert strategic control over some of the occupied territories partly into Arab recognition (peace) and partly into greater political control over some of the other territories (the West Bank). On the other hand, political claims may be raised for territories outside the strategic control of the collectivity (such as the Revisionists' early claims for all of biblical Israel, on both sides of the Jordan River, which were later abandoned).

3. Sentimental Orientation. This orientation relates to territorial space in terms of emotional attachments to certain areas, which may give rise to a sense of belonging among individuals and groups, on the one hand, or a sense of separation, on the other. The former feeling is rooted in what Cohen refers to as a *prestige* sub-orientation.

The *primordial* sub-orientation is the most profound expression of the sense of belonging, usually on the basis of "blood connections" to family, tribe, and nation. Places have special value for an individual or group, regardless of their instrumental or symbolic value, because they serve as a common basis for the community to which the individual or group belongs. Thus, in various peasant societies, land is the primary source of feelings of security and collective identity. Töennies defines *gemeinschaft* society as one where the common ties of its members to the land are the basis of solidarity (1955). Many developing countries are characterized by social and political groups drawn together on the basis of *landsmannschaft*, as the populations flowing into cities settle where they do on the basis of places of origin and also form social and economic relationships on the basis of village origins and the shared hope of future return.

A dramatic example of this is provided by some second- and third-generation Palestinian Arabs who were reared mainly in refugee camps, but for whom their "home villages," most of which no longer exist, are the basis of their self-identity, as well as the subject of a myth of return which is a central cultural motif (Harkabi, 1972: 5). A similar orientation was evident in Zionist ideology—the idea of the return to Zion in Palestine, for which there was no acceptable substitute.

According to Cohen, one's orientation may be affected by the *prestige* of a particular territorial space. Territories can be organized in a hierarchy according to the prestige accorded them, in particular by the individuals with whom they are identified.

4. Symbolic Orientation. This orientation relates to territorial space according to the symbolic values it has for individuals, groups, or societies. Places gain symbolic value when they express or represent human values—meanings which are attributed to them by culture.

The less institutionalized (and less important here) sub-orientation is the *aesthetic* one, where the territory is classified as beautiful
or ugly, attractive or repulsive, etc. The more institutionalized *moral/
religious* sub-orientation may be crucial. Man may organize physical
space by its distance from a sanctified symbol-laden center, and any
harm to the center violates the cosmic order. It may be a geographical
place where the supernatural and the material unite (Eliade, 1958:
314-19). Palestine is conceived of as the Holy Land for both Muslims
and Jews (and of course Christians), and one of the ideological disputes between the Jews and Muslims has revolved about the degree
of holiness each side attributes to the country. Specific places, such
as the Wailing Wall and the area of the Temple-Mount (i.e., the great
mosques in Jerusalem), the Cave of Makhpela in Hebron, etc., are
holy to both sides. Other places which are considered holy by only
one side have nevertheless played a role in the conflict, especially in
mobilizing support for the struggle. For instance, the annual local
Islamic celebration of Moses, which is held at his reputed (by Muslims)
tomb near Jericho (Nabi Mussa), in which Arab delegations from
various parts of Palestine gather for a week-long festival, frequently
culminates in anti-Zionist demonstrations as the celebrating Muslims
return to Jerusalem.

The moral/religious orientation to the territory of Palestine has
been essential to the Arabs, particularly in the initial stage of the
Jewish-Arab conflict, when the Palestinian-Arab identity was not
crystallized and the Arab leadership was in need of mobilizing symbols. Throughout the conflict, the Islamic religion and territoriality
have been closely related because, according to Islam, the entire world
is divided into the Land of Islam (*Dar al Islam*) and the land of war,
whose conquest is demanded by religious law through holy war (*jihad*)
(Lewis, 1974: 245). (Within any territory under its control, Islam
seems to be very tolerant of the "unfaithful.") Since jihad is employed
to expand the boundaries of Islam, it is even more obligatory when
Islam is threatened with forced retreat (Harkabi, 1972: 129)—a threat
which became a reality in the course of the Jewish-Arab struggle. The
question of the right of the Jews and/or the Arabs to the land of
Palestine has occupied both sides in the conflict, and it is likely the
religious sub-orientation has fulfilled a similar function for both
adversaries (Harkabi, 1972: 135). It is interesting to note the parallels
in this sub-orientation by both sides toward Palestine: (1) the entire

expanse, as well as parts of it, has moral or religious value *per se*; (2) the religious sub-orientation serves as a means for legitimizing both sides' claims in their struggle for the same territory.

One can assume that there is no "pure" orientation toward territory, and thus orientations are likely to be mixtures of instrumental, sentimental, etc. The significance of the orientation is determined by the degree of its expression in the system. An internal order governs these orientations and constitutes a sequence that extends from the instrumental pole (the technical sub-orientation) to the most expressive one—the moral or religious sub-orientation. Omitting the aesthetic and the prestige sub-orientations, the rest can be arranged on a scale of expressiveness:

> A wide spectrum of phenomena could conveivably be summarized by the extent of the collectivity's readiness to pay for the achievement of what seem to be two kinds of consistencies within the system: (a) consistency between the three components of the patterns of control of territorial expanses—ownership, presence and sovereignty—so that the existence of one makes the others desirable [*see Chapter 1*]; (b) consistency between the patterns of control over, or the amount of "frozenness" of a territorial space and the orientation towards it. The less fluid a space is, the more expressive an orientation it requires, and *vice versa*. But within the system one or both kinds of inconsistencies can persist, because there are almost always internal and external constraints that can prevent the attainment of consistency (Kimmerling, 1979).

There is no connection between the degree of frontierity of a territory and the expressive relationship to it because expressive orientation is a quality of the immigrant population, while frontierity is a quality of the target territory, but we have seen (Chapter 1) that there is a connection between the degree of control over a territory and its frontierity.

CHARACTERISTICS OF THE JEWISH-ARAB CONFLICT

The territorial conflict between the Jewish and Arab social systems can be divided into four main periods. The first is the pre-sovereign period, when the area of potential control (ownership and/or presence) was very vaguely defined. As time passed, the borders would become more and more limited by social and political realities (see maps, pp. 237-38). The second is the period when the Jewish system achieved sovereignty (following the 1947/48 War), when the boundaries were clearly defined from the Israeli standpoint, and the struggle focused on gaining recognition for these boundaries from the Arab neighbor states and the world-at-large. (Attempts continued to raise the level of control *within* the borders and in the secondary frontiers— e.g., the Negev and the Galilee.) The third is the period following the 1967 War when Israelis perceived that the frontiers were partially reopened, but were uncertain of their ability to increase control over new areas (see maps, pp. 239-40). This potential expansion of the borders broke the consensus as to the goals of the conflict management. Some reverted to advocating the gaining of maximum territory and the security it provided rather than pursuit of the goal of achieving recognition and legitimacy. The fourth period is when legitimacy seems to have been at least partially reached. As a consequence of the general election of 1977, and the takeover of the government by the Revisionist Zionists, a peace treaty was signed between Egypt and Israel.

Asymmetry: In the first period, the Arabs controlled most of the resources over which the struggle took place. Their population was greater than that of the Jewish community, as were their economic opportunities and land ownership. The Jews, therefore, struggled for changes in the status quo, while the Arabs fought to maintain it. The Jews adopted a policy which would promote the defreezing of Arab lands, enabling this resource to enter the economic market. To achieve this end, they minimized the political significance of the land. However, after the land was transferred to Jewish ownership, its ownership was given "national" meaning. In the second and third periods, the asymmetry in land ownership was reversed; the Arabs struggled to change the existing situation, while the Israelis sought to maintain it.*

Goal Postponement: The ultimate goal of both sides was the attainment of exclusive political control over the contested identity

---

*Another kind of asymmetry was the perception that only one side (the Arab) had the potential ability to win a total victory by the physical destruction of the Jewish community. Israeli acquisition of nuclear weapons would eliminate this asymmetry.

("South Syrian," "Palestinian," "Secular-Democratic," or any other Arab identity, on the one hand; "National Home," "Commonwealth," or "sovereign Jewish state," on the other). In the first period, the Arabs could not achieve their basic goals because of the restrictions imposed upon them, primarily as a result of the acceptance of the British Mandate (Zureik, 1979: 59-74), but also because of their internal social, economic, and political weaknesses (Porath, 1977). The Jews, on the other hand, could not achieve their goals because of their relatively small numbers when compared to the Arab population. Thus the Jews had to create conditions which would give them time to accumulate strength before they could seek their ultimate goal. As a result, the conflict was focused on secondary goals, whose sole purpose was to permit the accumulation of power by one side at the expense of the other.

In the first period, both Jews and Arabs exerted pressure on the Ottoman and British governments to act in accordance with their respective interests. From the early nineteenth century, the Ottoman government had placed restrictions on Jewish land purchases. To a certain extent these restrictions remained in force under the British, culminating in the prohibitions and limitations on land purchase imposed in 1940. Despite these restrictions, the Jews acquired enough land to establish several areas of settlement which in time created a continuum of Jewish territory. This included most of the coastal plain and the valleys, while the mountain areas remained under Arab ownership almost exclusively. Thus, with respect to land, the government, while promoting its own interests, acted in such a way as to give the Jewish community the postponement it needed in order to change the status quo.

While in the first period both sides were forced to defer their goals, in the second period, after the destruction of the Palestinian-Arab community as a social and political entity, and the transformation of the conflict from an intercommunity to an interstate conflict, only the Arab side was forced to defer its goals.* In the short run, the Arab states' goal was to prevent Israel from achieving additional territorial expansion, which was seen as an inherent characteristic of

---

*The Arab states—except Jordan—froze the Palestinian Arabs in the status of refugees, sometimes within *landsmannschaft* frameworks, and attempted to foster a myth of return to the usurped lands.

the Zionist state, with the fate of the Palestinian Arabs as a vivid example. In the long run, their aim was to maintain warfare on a controlled level until they were strong enough to regain control over the entire territory.

Between 1949 and 1967 Israel perceived that its major goal of control over a considerable amount of territory had been achieved, but that its complementary goals of Arab recognition of the Jewish state and the termination of the conflict were unattainable. Thus Israel postponed its complementary goals, and was content with the realization of three secondary goals: (1) maintenance of its security in the face of periodic guerrilla activities, (2) intensification of control over the territory already under its control (through increased Israeli presence), and (3) accumulation of strength by continuing the process of nation-building and by increasing military power.

During the third period, no important changes took place in the goals of the belligerents. But Israel now held considerable additional Arab territory, some of which was densely populated and some of which was near important Arab centers, which improved Israel's bargaining position. The Israeli bargaining strategy aimed at two seemingly conflicting goals: to return some territories in exchange for recognition, and to maintain some territories under Israeli control. For the Arabs, the immediate goal was removal of Israel from the 1967 occupied territories either by force or by making peace, but this did not mean relinquishing their ultimate goal.*

Zero-Sum: There was a tendency on both sides (but especially by the Arabs) to perceive the conflict as a situation where one side's gain was the other's loss (and *vice versa*), even if the gain or loss did not stem from interaction between the sides. This approach, which assumes that the resources in dispute are permanently limited, is referred to in game theory as "zero-sum" (see, for example, Rapaport, 1969: 39). The limited resource was the area of Palestine, which was further limited by the 1922 White Paper which put Trans-Jordan outside the boundaries of Palestine. In this framework, every piece of land taken over by the Jews—whether purchased or conquered from nature, whether or not previously settled or cultivated by Arabs—was a gain for Zionist settlement and, by definition, a loss for the Arab community.

---

*Both sides' goals were presented in simplified form as systemic goals disregarding the internal disputes among different factions of the two communities.

The conflict continued to be perceived as zero-sum in the second and third periods, with some exceptions. The salient exception of the second period was the complex relationship between the Hashemite Kingdom of Jordan and Israel. The two countries were declared enemies, but between 1948 and 1967 each needed the assistance of the other against the ex-Palestinian Arabs. Both administered territories originally allocated by the 1947 Partition Plan to the Arab-Palestinian state, and both were interested in the absorption of the Palestinians into the Jordanian political and social system to hasten the end of the Palestinian-Arab identity. In exchange for Jordan's resolving the Palestinian problem for Israel, Israel tacitly agreed to protect the regime and political existence of Jordan. This mutual need seemingly ended when Israel took control of the West Bank and the vast majority of its population, but Jordan remained strategically valuable to Israel as a potential ally against the Palestinians—the major opponent in the zero-sum game (Y. Cohen, 1972).

In the third period, the conflict between Israel and the various Arab participants became more complex. Still, any territorial gain by Israel was an equivalent loss for the Arabs. The costs of territorial gains were increasing, however. The West Bank and Gaza Strip areas captured in 1967 were densely populated by Palestinian Arabs. Maintaining this population under Israeli administration, by stopping the process of their absorption by Jordan, initiated a reverse process of "re-Palestinization," strengthening the Palestinian-Arabs' claim to be recognized as a political entity.* The rights of the Palestinians are usually perceived as a challenge to the rights of the Israelis, which meant that gaining control over the West Bank and Gaza Strip territories (at least in the period between 1967 and 1977) tended to undermine Israel's legitimacy. These paradoxical outcomes of conflictual situations contributed in the third period to the breakdown of the internal consensus concerning territorial expanses (see Isaac, 1976).

Awareness: The situation not only brought about clashes based on objective conflicts of interests (see Kriesberg, 1973: 4-5), but also

---

*This process of re-Palestinization is also beginning among the Israeli Arab population (see the secret memorandum published by *Al-Hamishmar*, 9/7/76). In March 1976, for example, a countrywide Israeli Arab protest movement was organized for the first time against expected new land expropriations.

involved conflicts based on the perceptions of both national groups about each other.

On the Jewish side, land was the central factor in both direct and indirect management of the conflict. Direct management of the conflict involved creating roles, organizations, and institutions to respond to the other side's actions relating to the land. In the first period, land purchase organizations were created and the roles of land buyers and brokers were institutionalized to mediate between the Jewish community and elements in the Arab community (Doukhan-Landau, 1979). Direct management also involved adapting organizations and roles to withstand the conflict. For example, special patterns of settlement were developed to meet Arab opposition to Jewish settlement.

The indirect management of the conflict by the Jews was expressed in the processes of development and institution-building to expand the power of the Jewish collectivity to be used in the struggle.

The picture presented above presents the general framework within which the struggle over land took place. However, there were considerable deviations from this model:

(1) The consciousness of the two sides that they had conflicting interests, and their perception of the conflict as zero-sum, were parts of a process which intensified through the first period within both communities. We must distinguish between awareness of the nature of the conflict and the readiness to acknowledge such awareness. One aspect of the conflict focused on the definition of the situation. The Jewish side refused to define the situation in Palestine as a zero-sum conflict. The Jews claimed that there were enough lands for both communities with a changeover to intensive cultivation and the draining of swamps, and that by "making the wilderness bloom," the absorption capacity of the land would be almost unlimited. On the other hand, the Arabs defined the situation as an acute conflict of interests, claiming that "for every Jew who enters, an Arab must leave" (Abu-Lughod, 1971).

(2) The two sides did not always play a "rational game"—i.e., did not always act in their own best interests. Indeed, an interesting aspect of the conflict—both from the strategic and sociological standpoints—is the extent to which both sides acted rationally.

(3) In the first period, the model assumes the existence of two subsystems under the superstructure of an external government,

acting in opposition to one another as whole units, but the relations were much more complex because of the lack of consensus within each of the two subsystems as to the nature of the conflict and its management (see Horowitz, 1982). It was made even more complex by the low level of control of the two subsystems over their members in contacts with the other subsystem. The Jewish side exploited the inability of the Arab side to control its members—especially in making land purchases in the first period (as well as the third and fourth).

CHANGE AND CONTINUITY IN THE ZIONIST
ORIENTATIONS AND POLITICS

As Palestine's Jewish community attained sovereignty over part of Palestine, the attitude of the collectivity toward the land changed when compared to the period when it had been limited to struggling for ownership of land (Kimmerling, 1977). Under sovereignty, the internal impact of the Jewish-Arab conflict was expected to diminish. However, several factors combined so that the situation continued to be defined as a conflictual one, although with an improved bargaining position for the Jews. These factors were:

A. The 1947/48 War, in which the Jewish community attained sovereignty, was not ended by peace but rather by shaky armistice or cease-fire settlements, with occasional use of military force by both sides (Khouri, 1968: 180-204). According to Allon (1968: 15), Israel was forced to regard itself as being in a state of active warfare. As a consequence of this no-peace, no-war situation, the Arabs refused to recognize Israeli sovereignty, and varying degrees of recognition were accorded by the rest of the world (particularly with reference to sovereignty over the region of the New City of Jerusalem). This non-recognition, accompanied by expressions of extreme hostility and the use of force, demonstrated the problematic nature of Israel's sovereignty, creating the need for continued ritualistic conflictual behavior to strengthen Israeli sovereignty over the territories within the state's boundaries (e.g., Birim and Ikrit; see Kimmerling, 1977).

B. Sovereignty over the territories was not clearly understood by all Israelis, which resulted in a continuing series of legitimacy crises, calling into question the collectivity's very existence. These crises operated in various spheres in different ways: some strengthened the system's conflictual responses, while others limited its reactions.

C. Although the vast majority of the lands had been transferred to the collectivity's sovereignty and ownership, there was still an Arab agrarian population controlling lands within the State of Israel. This population had previously been part of the opposing side in the conflict, and its very existence—despite its new definition as part of the collectivity—stimulated the continuation of hostile attitudes toward the Arab inhabitants of Israel (see Geries, 1969: 95-116).

D. The transition to a sovereign state did not bring with it a dramatic change in the institutional structure of Israel's political system or in the basic perceptions which guided it (see Horowitz and Lissak, 1978). There were very few changes in personnel of the political elite and the major decision-makers until 1977. Under such conditions it is not surprising that many patterns of reaction learned in the pre-sovereign period continued.

In the wake of the 1967 War, there was a resurgence of direct confrontations over lands between the Arabs (Palestinians and some of the Arab states) and Israel. As a result of the war, Israel obtained military control over extensive new territories (see map, p. 240). This control was perceived as temporary because of a variety of political and social constraints stemming from external factors (e.g., the inability to translate military strength into international political power), as well as internal limitations (e.g., the inability to absorb a large Arab population into Jewish society). This temporary occupation could end in different ways for different territories. The territory could return to Arab control (as occurred after the capture of Sinai in 1956); there could be *de jure* imposition of Israeli sovereignty (as in East Jerusalem in 1967 and Golan Heights in 1982); etc. The temporary occupation was perceived as a stage in a continuum of situations which might move toward permanence.

In order to transform the temporary into the permanent—until sovereignty could be imposed on the territory—use was again made of the ownership pattern of control. Before 1948 ownership had served as a substitute for sovereignty. Now the ownership was reinforced by Israeli presence. Between 1967 and 1982 there was a partial return to the pattern of the Jewish-Arab conflict which prevailed in the first period as a result of the return to a direct conflict with the Arab population over land, along with pressure from other nations which created a new sense of uncertainty as to the collectivity's ultimate physical boundaries.

It is not surprising that a social system with strong continuity, facing a situation similar to one it faced in the past, will react in a similar way. Thus the sovereignty vacuum in the occupied territories again created the "Yishuv situation," in which not only the collectivity's physical scope but also its ethnic content and political identity were problematic. It had seemed that this situation would not arise again for the Jews after the 1948 War, as a result of which most of the Arab population was uprooted from the territories captured by Jewish forces. This perception of the renewed situation stimulated reactions learned in the past, such as land purchase and settlement, which were central in Zionist ideology.

Between 1967 and 1977 Israel aimed at preserving the territorial status quo, while both sides saw that the Arab interest lay in changing it. Time was perceived as acting in Israel's favor. However, in the sum total of power accumulation by both sides, the effects of time were not clear.

In the fourth period, the followers of the Revisionist Zionist ideology took over the leadership in Israel and began the dramatic peace negotiations between Egypt and Israel. As a result of the combination of the new rulers' ideology and the peace talks, the attitude toward different territorial expanses was changed. The remote territories became less important and more expendable; the more central ones became more important and less expendable. The primordial and moral-religious orientations toward Judea and Samaria were increased, and the centrality of the strategic orientations toward the Sinai was decreased. But the change was even more fundamental when, for the first time in Zionist policy, presence was not irreversible, and settlements were not perceived as determinants of *faits accomplis*. This was consistent with the original ideology of Revisionist (and Political) Zionism, which downplayed the role of settlements *per se*— the core value of Practical Zionism—and emphasized more general political processes, which were seen as more crucial in determining the fate of the Jewish nation. As a consequence of this new orientation, when Egypt offered peace and official recognition in exchange for all or most of the territories occupied in the 1967 War, Israel agreed to exchange the more remote territories but not the more central ones.

THE MOUNTAIN AREA

The territorial expanse around which the Jewish-Arab conflict focused until 1967 could be divided into two areas: (1) the central mountain area and (2) the coastal plain and great valleys. From 1967 on, a third area was added: the Sinai peninsula. Historically, the major primordial symbols of the Jewish collectivity and its holy places have been linked to the mountain area of biblical Judea and Samaria (including the city of Jerusalem). However, the mountain area was less available to the Jewish settlers and the land buyers because it was densely populated, and the land was predominantly owned by many smallholders, extensively cultivated, and sometimes consecrated to God (Baer, 1971: 66-72). It is not surprising that in the formative period the Jews were essentially unable to purchase land in the mountains, and the area remained devoid of Jewish control, except for the district of Jerusalem. But despite the lack of Jewish control, this area was viewed as an integral part of Palestine as a political entity, and the Jewish community, as well as the world Zionist leadership, would not relinquish its claim for future control over the whole territory.

This claim was an integral part of the political management of the conflict with the Arabs. The Jewish community maintained its religious and primordial orientations toward the central mountain area, but the political orientation predominated along with the instrumental. After the acceptance of the 1947 Partition Plan, followed by the 1947/48 War, the central mountain area seemed to be excluded from even the potential control of the collectivity (see Gabbay, 1959). It was located outside the physical boundaries, and except for the Old City of Jerusalem, the area was not explicitly included in the national system of symbols. But it remained part of Jewish mythology and was emphasized in the school curricula as a result of the intensive teaching of the Bible. The stigmatized right wing attempted to transform this territory into a primordial symbol for the whole collectivity in an effort to mobilize the community to fulfill nationalist goals and to challenge the nation's rulers—the so-called "pragmatic left." The pressures to include this area in the orientation of the collectivity, and to relate it in primordial or moral terms, was behind the ideological cleavage between hawks and doves that developed in Israel when control over this territory was suddenly attained in 1967 (see Isaac, 1976). As for the Old City of Jerusalem, the system moved without delay to exert control over the "holy place" and annex it, at the same time expending considerable effort to establish a strong presence and ownership. There was a strong consensus in the collectivity for these actions.

For the rest of the mountain area, however, the situation was different. A standstill in military and settlement presence, accompanied by an apparent strategic (or political) orientation, was the outcome of a mixture of perceptions of external constraints and different orientations toward this area. On the one hand, there was hawkish pressure to increase the level of control and to translate military victory into sovereignty. This was usually justified in terms of primordial and religious orientations (sometimes accompanied by strategic arguments). On the other hand, there were moderate and pragmatic suggestions (e.g., from Moshe Dayan) to open the area to private entrepreneurs, who would create a flow of capital and renew the process of land accumulation similar to that which prevailed in the first period of the conflict. The demographic problem would be solved through a complex differentiation between territory and population, which is the basic premise of the proposal for autonomy of the Arab Palestinian population offered in the fourth period (as well as the third period proposal for a division of sovereignty between Israel and Jordan). The Israelis would have control over the territory while the population would be allowed self-rule or come under Jordanian rule.

The doves did not demand immediate withdrawal from these territories or deny their emotional significance for the collectivity. The dovish approach was aimed at preparing the collectivity for future relinquishing of control over the occupied territories. Their predominant orientation toward the territory captured in 1967 was political, and the mountain area (excluding Jerusalem) was regarded as a convertible resource, to be exchanged either for Arab recognition (i.e., peace) or for legitimating and consolidating control over those territories occupied after the 1947/48 War (Kaplowitz, 1976: 293-95).

An alternative approach to the hawks and doves was to argue that in a situation where two national movements had conflicting "equally legitimate" claims to a territory, the only solution was division in which both sides could preserve their sentimental attachments to the whole territory, without granting control to one side at the expense of the other. This readiness to accept limited or divided control over territory to which there is a strong emotional attachment seems, in the Zionist ideological context, to be a profound social change, not just a redefinition of the situation.

THE COASTAL PLAINS AND THE GREAT VALLEYS AS FRONTIERS

In contrast to the mountain area, the coastal plain has few Jewish primordial symbols. In the biblical period, the coastal plain was populated more by non-Jews than by sons of Israel. At various times, however, especially in the Second Temple period, some of it was under Jewish control. From at least the beginning of the British Mandate, the area was included as an integral part of the political entity of Palestine, and thus became an object of Zionist aspirations. The major attraction of this area, as well as of the great valleys and some parts of the southern mountains of the Galilee, was its sparse population, which comprised primarily poor tenants or nomad Bedouin tribes, and its ownership by absentee landlords. These were the lands with highest frontierity in Palestine, and during the first period of the conflict, many plots of these lands were purchased by the Jewish National Fund, by societies, and by private investors. On these lands a relatively dense network of Jewish settlements was established (see Orren, 1978), creating a territorial continuum with a sociopolitical infrastructure. Soon the area was viewed as the core territory of the Jewish collectivity. The process of land acquisition was relatively slow because of a shortage of financial resources on the Jewish side, as well as political and administrative barriers set up by the Ottomans and the British and, in some instances, the tenants' resistance to the transfer of lands that they worked.

There was a rapid transition from instrumental orientation toward the coastal area (i.e., farming for economic profit) to the perception of settling on lands having primordial meaning, rooted in the predisposition to relate to these lands as the "homeland." This was due in part to the immense emotional and physical efforts involved in settlement. Overcoming the difficulties of conquering the land from nature, when nature included not only sand and swamp, but psychological, social, and political obstacles as well, gives the settler a deep emotional attachment to the land and a feeling of entitlement to it. Defining the struggle as primarily one against nature rather than against men or sociopolitical forces was necessary in order to give self-legitimacy to the Zionist activities.

In the coastal plain and the great valleys, the combination of ownership and presence-by-settlement in the formative period was the functional equivalent of sovereignty. It was accompanied by self-administration (e.g., municipalities), included in a territorial continuum that was more or less politically homogeneous, subordinate to a Zionist quasi-government (see Horowitz and Lissak, 1978). These processes reinforced the expressive orientation toward these areas.

As long as neither party to the conflict could achieve a decisive advantage, the mountains and the coastal plain, plus the valley area, were "naturally" divided between the belligerents long before partition plans were proposed to give this division political institutionalization. Neither side could achieve its final territorial goal, but the struggle was continued by the Israelis to achieve greater control over marginal areas (e.g., elimination of the Arab presence in the coastal area after the 1947/48 War, establishment of Israeli presence along the western Jordan Valley and the Gaza Strip after the 1967 War, and annexation of the Golan Heights in 1982).

ANALYZING TWENTY-THREE CASES OF CHANGE IN CONTROL

The symbolic place in the system of a given territory may change. That is, the collectivity may change its orientation toward a given territorial expanse, or its degree of control over it, or both. To illustrate this point, I shall present four basic possible *territorial outputs*—that is, the combination of the major orientations of a collectivity toward a space, and its actions to achieve (or increase) control over the space. The territorial outputs are: (1) territories which the collectivity does not aspire to or control; (2) territories desired by the collectivity but over which it has no control; (3) expanses that are under the collectivity's control but have instrumental value only—peripheral territories; (4) territories over which there is strong control combined with fundamental expressive orientations—core territories.

Each of the four could be either initial territorial outputs or attained outputs. Thus there are twelve logically possible patterns of change or fluctuation (see Table 8.1). In analyzing twenty-three sample cases, I found only ten patterns of change in outputs of socioterritorial behavior. There were no cases of change from (a) uncontrolled

Table 8.1

MAJOR CHANGES IN THE OUTPUTS OF SOCIO-TERRITORIAL BEHAVIOR–PRINCIPAL SPACES

Initial output	Attained outputs			
	No control and undesired territory	No control but desired territory	Peripheral territory	Core territory
No control and undesired territory			Sinai Peninsula (1949)[a] Golan Heights (1967) Jordan Valley (1967) Gaza Strip (1967) Sinai (1956)[a] Sinai (1967)	Negev (1948)[b]
No control but desired territory	Trans-Jordan (1922)		Mountain region (1967)	Coastal plain (1890-1947)[d] Galilee (1890-1947)[b]
Peripheral territory	Horan (1948) West Sinai[e]	Mountain region (1948)[c] East Sinai and Rafah area settlements[e]		Territories attained in 1947/48 War[f] East Jerusalem (1967) Golan Heights (1982)
Core territory	Palestinian Arab state (1947) Beit-Haarava (1947) Gush-Etzion (1948)	Hebron (1929) East Jerusalem (1948)		

[a] Returned shortly to initial output
[b] Low Jewish presence and ownership
[c] Excluding Jerusalem and including the Jordan Valley
[d] Including the Jezreel, Heffer, and Beisan Valleys
[e] According to the peace treaty between Egypt and Israel
[f] Additional to the Partition Plan of 1947

and undesired to uncontrolled but desired territory, or of change from (b) core to peripheral territory.

From Table 8.1 it is clear that it is possible to convert territorial expanses from regions of no control not only to peripheral territorial zones (e.g., Sinai three times—1949, 1956, and 1967, and the Jordan Valley), but also to core territories (e.g., Negev, which Israel annexed as a result of the 1947/48 War though it had been excluded from the collectivity's orientation when the 1947 Partition Plan was accepted by the Jewish community). Movement in the opposite direction is also possible. Large areas moved from control to no control zones (e.g., the Sinai peninsula during the implementation of the peace treaty between Egypt and Israel). The drastic transitions which occurred as a result of the inner dynamics of the Jewish-Arab conflict were most clearly manifested by cases of spaces that moved, after 1949, from zones of no control to some degree of control. In all these cases (excluding the Negev), control over the space was achieved only as a by-product of military or political needs, with territorial expansion not an end in itself. But after the attainment of control, there were tendencies to define the spaces as necessary to the existence of the collectivity (mainly in strategic terms—like the Golan Heights) and/or to revive the potential expressive orientations toward them. The boundaries of expressiveness have been affected by perceived possibilities of controlling the space in terms of domestic (social and political) and international constraints.

On the other hand, considerable territories dropped from the collectivity's orientation and desire for control and moved toward the zone of no control (including no orientation). These threw the scarcity of the territorial resources claimed by both parties into relief and heightened the acuteness of the conflict.

There was only one case in which territorial space controlled by the system through ownership and dense settlement-presence, and perceived as an integral part of the collectivity's space, was abandoned. This was Gush-Etzion, a relatively isolated group of settlements in the mountain area which was destroyed by Arab forces in 1948. What is important in this instance is not so much that a relatively centrally located territory was abandoned as a direct result of a change in the local power balance, but that the space was apparently cognitively abandoned as well. The reversibility of a territory located in a semi-central zone is thus not impossible. An additional point abandoned in 1948, without any attempt to retain it despite its obvious strategic location, was kibbutz Beit Haarava.* These cases seem to demonstrate that the system was not ready to pay *any* price to maintain control over a relatively centrally located territorial space when the perceived probability of success was low. Thus it is probably injudicious to refer to fragmented central territorial spaces as irreversible. That is to say, the system tended to pay higher (but not unlimited) costs to keep its level of control when (a) the territory was already under the control of the system, and when (b) the orientation toward it was expressive. This conclusion is, of course, appropriate only for specific and limited areas and not for the whole territory of the collectivity. One would assume that for the whole territory, or for a considerable portion of it, or even for expanses perceived as necessary for the existence of the collectivity, the system would be ready to pay any price.

In three cases the collectivity lost control of specific areas but did not expel them from its cognitive map (orientation zone). The first occurred in 1929, when the ancient Jewish community of Hebron was destroyed and many of its members massacred. Hebron was transformed into a symbol, not only because a Jewish community was destroyed, or because it was a holy place (the Cave of Makhpela), but mainly because its fate was perceived as foreshadowing the fate of the whole Jewish community in the event of an Arab victory (equivalent to the function of Deir Yassin in the Arabs' interpretation of Jewish intentions). The second case was the fall of the Jewish Quarter in the Old City of Jerusalem, as well as the whole eastern part of the city, to the Arab Legion in 1948. This included the most holy place for the Jewish people—the Wailing Wall—and was described by Ben-Gurion as a "misfortune for many generations." Israel proclaimed West Jerusalem its capital in 1948, despite its strategic vulnerability and the political costs. (Most nations do not recognize its status because Jerusalem was destined for internationalization according to the Partition Plan of 1947.) The system was ready to pay these costs, as it was ready to bear the costs of annexation of the eastern city in

---

*Kibbutz Beit Haarava settled in an area north of the Dead Sea in 1939, and its members tried to integrate agricultural work with working for the phosphate plant in the production of various minerals. The place was completely isolated, and every objective strategic evaluation concluded that it was impossible to defend. As a result, it was abandoned in early 1948.

1967. It seems that the strong expressive orientation toward this area was not sufficient to initiate measures to take control over it, but when control was accidentally gained, the system acted promptly to incorporate it into the core zone.

CONCLUSIONS

One may arrive at conclusions along two planes from this research. The first is the "practical" plane—how it was possible to establish an immigrant-settler society on a territory which had an extremely low level of frontierity; the second is the "theoretical" plane—the causal relationships between sentiments, perceptions, and ideologies and economic, political, and social behavior in a given territorial situation.

It is clear that it is possible to build an immigrant society even under conditions of low frontierity. The proof of this is the fact that Israel was established, has existed as a sovereign state since 1948, has developed into a regional power, has developed a modern economy, and has a regime which is one of the most democratic in the world—for the Jewish citizens at least. In the recent past its legitimacy has even been recognized by the largest and most highly developed Arab nation—Egypt. In spite of the continual conflict in which Israel has found itself, it has developed a system of social mechanisms which have prevented it from taking on the characteristics of a besieged social system (see Kimmerling, 1979b).

But Israel is not entirely a success story. It has not succeeded in persuading a majority of the world's Jews to move to Israel, or in preventing sizable segments of its own population from leaving the country.* It has not been accepted as legitimate by most of the countries in its region, and it remains dependent on massive external aid.

*In every country of immigration, there is perpetual emigration. Ben-Gurion noted more than once that most of the members of the Second Aliya, with whom he arrived in Palestine, left the country. In 1927 (as well as in 1982) there were more emigrants than immigrants. But it appears that Israel is the only democratic country which sees emigration as a threat to its existence. In Zionist terminology, emigration is called *yerida*, which means to fall, to deteriorate, or even to lose part of one's holiness or sanctity, while immigration is *aliya*, which connotes ascending, increasing one's sanctity, or a pilgrimage. Zionists tried to make yerida a stigma, but were evidently unsuccessful. It is estimated that between 350,000 to 500,000 people have left the country.

It has had only limited success in absorbing mass immigration and in closing the social, economic, and cultural gaps between Jews who came from developed countries and those who came from developing countries (see Smooha, 1978; Peres, 1971; Kimmerling, 1982). There are internal struggles over the nature of Israeli society—between the religious and the secular, between socialists and capitalists, between those with universalistic beliefs and those with particularistic beliefs—which are far from being solved, and there is not even a consensus about the principles governing the struggle. One cannot attribute all the successes and failures in this partial list directly (or even indirectly) to the Arab-Israeli conflict, even though the conflict has affected all these processes to some extent. However, these issues were not at the heart of this study.

The concrete question which was asked here is: How did this society deal with a situation of very low frontierity, and what were the implications of this frontierity and the way the society dealt with it for the content and social praxis of the society?

As we have seen, the society developed very elaborate patterns of control which helped it accumulate territory and preserve the territory over which it had gained control. The sophisticated use of all three components of territorial control—presence, ownership, and sovereignty—permitted it to be very flexible in acquiring land and to be successful in maintaining most of what it had acquired. This approach should not be seen as a universally valid one which would work in all situations. It was an *ad hoc* method which was developed in response to specific conditions, including (1) low frontierity, (2) acute conflict with the environment, where (3) military power could not guarantee the irreversibility of territorial gains, or (4) the recognition and acceptance of these gains by others, as a result of which (5) crises of legitimacy occurred within the society and (6) fears were aroused as to the complete failure of the Zionist settlement.

Some of the concepts used in this work—such as presence and ownership—found institutional expression, such as the settlement system, the Jewish National Fund, and the Israel Lands Authority. These institutions were partially the products of a specific immigrant society acting in circumstances of limited frontierity in opposition to political forces and external constraints almost no other immigrant society has had to endure. We may argue that the Turnerian thesis may be applied—but conversely, with the lack of frontierity being decisive—in understanding the Israeli case. One can show that a number of the components and patterns of activity of Israeli society were determined by the need to establish an immigrant society in circumstances of a shortage of land.

As to the question of the causal relationships between the degree of control over territory and the collective emotions it evokes, we may be able to provide a tentative answer on the basis of the twenty-three cases of territories moving from one pattern of control to another. What in the long run determines the level of control over a space when the power relations between opposing sides are held constant? Is it (1) the level of control itself, (2) the degrees of expressiveness, or (3) a previously existing orientation in the system toward the territorial expanse? It seems necessary to consider the question in two different contexts: (a) the territory of the country as a whole, and (b) distinct spaces or regions within the country.

The expressive orientation toward Zion was a necessary but not a sufficient condition for the creation of a Zionist ideology and immigration and settlement. The various alternative territories proposed at different times as a national homeland to solve the so-called Jewish problem had no mobilizing appeal. However, Zion was a vague territorial concept. The gap between the semi-metaphysical concept and actual political boundaries left the interpreters of the concept with a great degree of freedom—the mountain area or the coastal plain, one or both sides of the Jordan River, or "from the Dan [River] to Beersheba" *versus* from the Littani River to Akaba beach (to give but two biblical definitions of the boundaries). Thus most orientations toward the future homeland did not prescribe either a distinct territory (apart from Jerusalem) or a definite level of control over it. Actual Jewish control of specific territory was attained mainly where and when the opportunities were favorable or, later, when political or strategic needs required it. All the available evidence indicates that the Jewish achievement of control over the territories captured in the 1967 War was accidental (or at least unplanned). The sentiments toward distinct territorial expanses were expressed only after control was attained: only a general expressiveness toward them existed previously. The major function of these expressive orientations, which clearly manifest themselves only after control over territory is attained, is to grant the system some self-legitimacy in maintaining control. More important, they are an integral part of the absorption of the space into the collectivity's self-image, which then reinforces control. In sum, the kind of orientation maintained toward a distinct territorial space seems to be a result of the degree of control achieved over the space; there is no evidence from this case that orientation determined the achievement of control over a defined territorial expanse. But when a minimal degree of control (at least military presence or ownership) was attained, an interaction between the type of orientation—on the instrumental-expressive continuum—and the pattern of control can be observed, with each tending to reinforce the other.

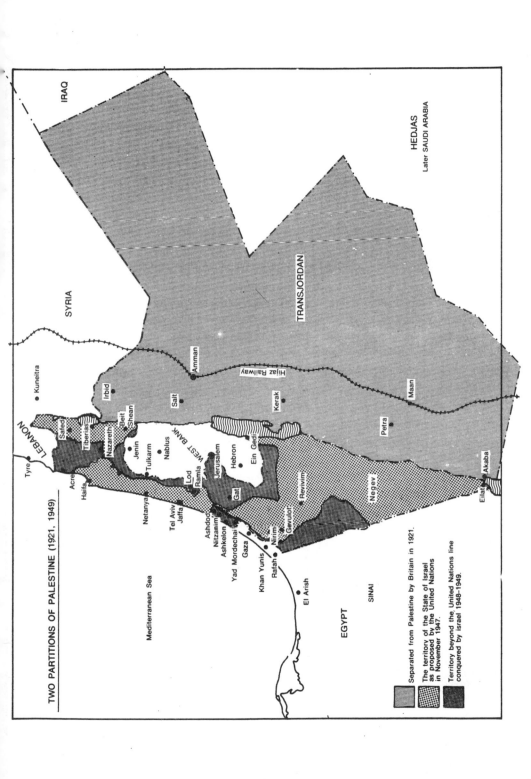

TWO PARTITIONS OF PALESTINE (1921, 1949)

IRAQ

SYRIA

LEBANON

Tyre

Kuneitra

Safed

Acre

Haifa

Tiberias

Nazareth

Beit
Shean

Irbid

Jenin

Tulkarm

Nablus

WEST BANK

Netanya

Tel Aviv

Jaffa

Ramla

Lod

Jerusalem

Salt

Amman

Hijaz Railway

Mediterranean Sea

Ashdod

Nitzanim

Ashkelon

Yad Mordechai

Gaza

Khan Yunis

Rafah

El Arish

Gat

Nitzanim

Gevulot

Nirim

Revivim

Ein Gedi

Hebron

Kerak

Petra

Negev

Eilat

Akaba

Maan

TRANSJORDAN

HEDJAS
Later SAUDI ARABIA

EGYPT

SINAI

Separated from Palestine by Britain in 1921.

The territory of the State of Israel
as proposed by the United Nations
in November 1947.

Territory beyond the United Nations line
conquered by Israel 1948-1949.

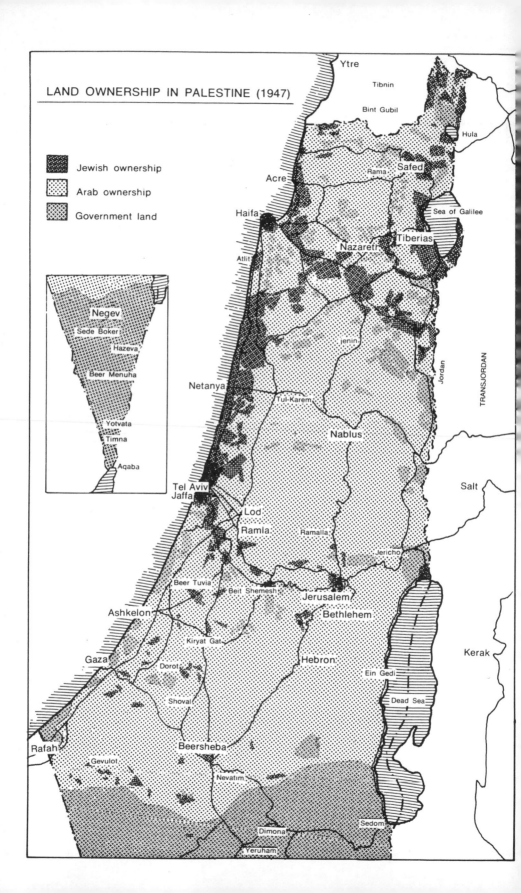

LAND OWNERSHIP IN PALESTINE (1947)

Jewish ownership
Arab ownership
Government land

Negev
Sede Boker
Hazeva
Beer Menuha
Yotvata
Timna
Aqaba

Ytre
Tibnin
Bint Gubil
Hula
Rama
Safed
Acre
Sea of Galilee
Haifa
Tiberias
Atlit
Nazareth
Jenin
Jordan
Netanya
Tul-Karem
Nablus
TRANSJORDAN
Tel Aviv
Jaffa
Lod
Ramla
Ramalla
Salt
Jericho
Beer Tuvia
Beit Shemesh
Jerusalem
Ashkelon
Bethlehem
Kiryat Gat
Hebron
Gaza
Dorot
Ein Gedi
Shoval
Dead Sea
Kerak
Rafah
Beersheba
Gevulot
Nevatim
Dimona
Sedom
Yeruham

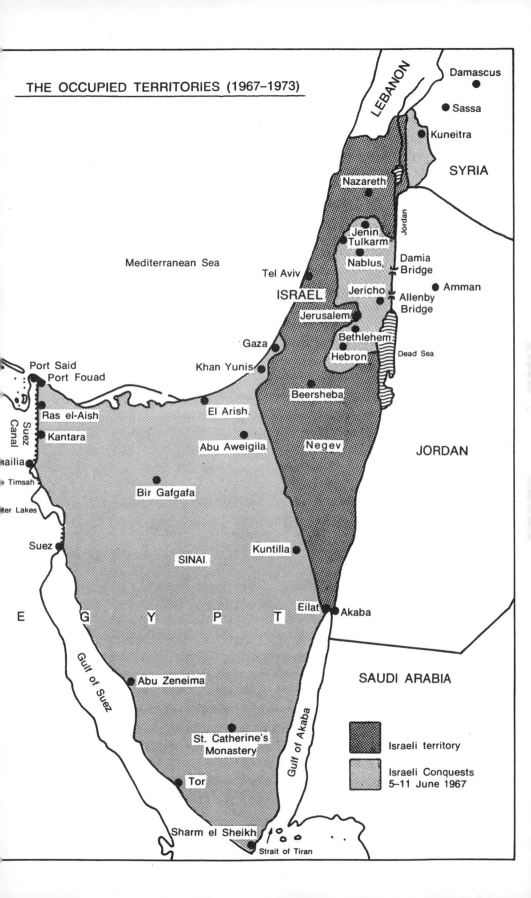

THE OCCUPIED TERRITORIES (1967–1973)

LEBANON

Damascus

Sassa

Kuneitra

SYRIA

Nazareth

Mediterranean Sea

Jenin
Tulkarm

Nablus

Damia
Bridge

Jordan

Tel Aviv

ISRAEL

Jericho

Amman

Jerusalem

Allenby
Bridge

Gaza

Bethlehem

Hebron

Dead Sea

Khan Yunis

Beersheba

Port Said
Port Fouad

JORDAN

Ras el-Aish

El Arish

Kantara

Negev

Suez
Canal

Abu Aweigila

...ailia

Timsah

Bir Gafgafa

...ter Lakes

Suez

SINAI

Kuntilla

E   G   Y   P   T

Eilat

Akaba

SAUDI ARABIA

Gulf of Suez

Abu Zeneima

Gulf of Akaba

St. Catherine's
Monastery

Israeli territory

Tor

Israeli Conquests
5–11 June 1967

Sharm el Sheikh

Strait of Tiran

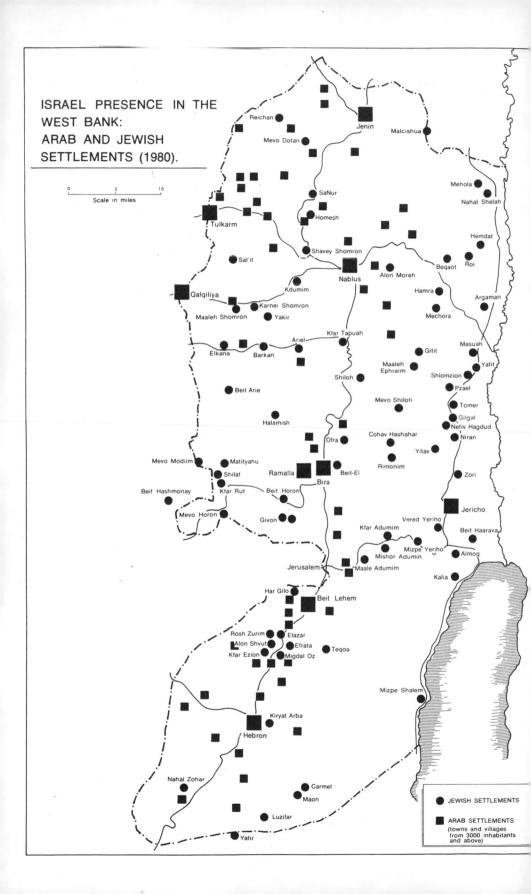

ISRAEL PRESENCE IN THE
WEST BANK:
ARAB AND JEWISH
SETTLEMENTS (1980).

Scale in miles
0   5   10

GLOSSARY

AGUDAT ISRAEL

A worldwide political orthodox organization founded in East Europe in 1912. Up to World War II, it vehemently opposed Zionism. Within the *Yishuv*, it was particularly active among members of the East European "Old Yishuv." On the basis of its opposition to Zionism and the establishment of a Jewish state, and in its pursuit of ethnic and religious autonomy in Palestine, it made several attempts to establish contact with the Arabs. In Israel, Agudat Israel is a political party that has frequently participated in the government as a member of the ruling coalition. It is the only political party in Israel that maintains a private educational system.

AHDUT HAAVODA

A socialist-Zionist party founded in 1919 when *Poalei Zion* merged with other groups. In 1930 it merged with *Hapoel Hatzair* to form the largest leftist party within the Jewish community in Palestine—*Mapai*. In 1942 it separated from Mapai, and in 1948 merged with *Hashomer Hatzair* to become a Marxist-Zionist party—*Mapam*. During the years 1954-1965 it acted as an independent party (Ahdut Haavoda-Poalei Zion). In 1965 it formed a new alignment with Mapai, and in 1968 the two united with Rafi to form the Labor Party. Throughout its history, Ahdut Haavoda has adopted activist attitudes in the Jewish-Arab conflict.

ALIGNMENT: [Hebrew: MAARACH]

1965-1968: An alignment between *Mapai* and *Ahdut Haavoda* which made them the largest bloc in the Israeli Parliament (*Knesset*). Following the Six-Day War, the two merged with Rafi to form the Labor Party. As of 1968: an alignment between the Labor Party and *Mapam*.

ALIYA: Jewish immigration to Palestine and Israel.

First Aliya (1882-1903): The first wave of immigrants—members of the Hovevei Zion organization in Russia and Romania, who came to Palestine in the wake of the 1881 pogroms directed against most of the Jewish communities in Eastern Europe. They founded the first agricultural settlements in Palestine; their goal was a future Jewish society based on agriculture. Some Yemenite Pilgrims joined this wave.

NOTE: This section is intended to serve not only as a detailed Glossary, but also as a condensed presentation of the institutional arena of Palestine/Israel for the foreign reader. Italics indicate cross-references to other Glossary entries.

241

Second Aliya (1904-1914): The wave of immigrants who came from Russia mainly in the wake of the abortive revolution of 1905. It consisted of young people with Marxist and socialist orientations, most of whom came to Palestine with the desire to organize the working class and initiate the class struggle against the members of the *First Aliya*.

Third Aliya (1915-1924): The wave of immigrants who came to Palestine following World War I and the 1917 Balfour Declaration. It consisted of young people who were willing to undertake any hard work, adopting the chalutz (pioneer) figure as a model.

Fourth Aliya (1924-1929): The wave of immigrants who came from Poland as a consequence of the anti-Semitic policies of the Polish government.

Fifth Aliya (1932-1939): The wave of immigrants who came from Germany in the 1930s in the wake of the increasing power of the Nazi movement. (The fourth and fifth aliyot resulted in a marked increase in the flow of capital into Palestine.)

ARAB EXECUTIVE COMMITTEE

Elected during the third *Palestinian Convention* (Haifa, 1920) as a political body representing the Arab population of Palestine. At first the Mandatory Government refused to recognize it, but as early as 1922 it was given de facto recognition by the government as the representative of the Arabs. Ruled by the *Hussainies*, it played a central role in the 1933 Arab revolt against the British. As the revolt ended, the Executive Committee was replaced in 1936 by the Supreme Arab Committee.

BEITAR

The youth movement of the Revisionist Zionists, and later of the *Herut* movement in Israel. Founded in Riga in 1923, by 1931 it had become a world-wide organization headed by Vladimir Jabotinsky. Beitar called for national orientation, evoking primordial myths and rejecting socialist Zionism. During the *Yishuv* period, it participated in the breaking of strikes. It was structured after paramilitary organizations, with emphasis on ceremonies and uniforms, and was the major reservoir for the *Etzel* and *Lehi* organizations.

BRIT SHALOM

A political society founded in 1926 by Jewish intellectuals to promote understanding between Jews and Arabs. As of 1930 it had adopted the notion of a bi-national state as a solution to the Jewish-Arab conflict, and some of its members were ready to accept limitations on Jewish immigration in return for a treaty with the Arabs. The society was originally sponsored by the *Jewish Agency*, but because of its radical proposals it was banned by the organized *Yishuv*, and in 1933 it became inactive. It reemerged in 1942 under the title Haihud; in addition to the original Brit Shalom members, others from *Poalei Zion-Smol* and *Hashomer Hatzair* joined. During the years 1927-1933 it published a periodical—

Sheyifotainu. There have been a limited number of Arabs among its members.

COMMUNIST PARTIES

From the *Second Aliya* onward, the waves of immigrants coming to Palestine included elements with a distinct Communist orientation. The majority of them subsequently emigrated as a result of material hardships or social ostracism, while others, particularly the leaders, were expelled by the British aided by the organized *Yishuv.* The first organized Communist party was a faction of *Poalei Zion,* which in 1919 founded the Socialist Labor Party [Hebrew: Mifleget Hapoalim Hasocialistit]. In 1922, after the party had undergone several metamorphoses, it split into *Poalei Zion-Smol* and the Palestine Communist Party (PCP). By Mandatory law the party was outlawed, but it continued as a faction in the *Histadrut* until it was expelled in 1924. In 1924 the PCP was accepted as a member of the Comintern, which saw the acceptance of the PCP in the Arab community as the basis for Comintern expansion in the Middle East. The PCP fought against the "conquest of labor" and the "conquest of the land." At that time the party consisted of an Arab section, which openly supported the Arab revolt in 1936, and a Jewish section, which condemned the revolt as a "fascist rebellion." However, the Jewish section soon returned to the fold, and in 1940 hailed the White Paper as the greatest accomplishment of the national Arab liberation movement. In 1945 many Jews broke away from the PCP to form the Hebrew Communist Party (HCP) in protest against the extreme pro-Arab line of the PCP. Following the USSR's recognition of the State of Israel, the HCP became the Israeli Communist Party (ICP). In 1948 all of the Communist factions in Israel merged with the ICP [Hebrew: MAKI]. In 1949 the ICP reverted to the old tough anti-Zionist line; consequently, the Hebrew Communists withdrew from the ICP and joined *Mapam.* In 1953 a faction was driven out of Mapam and rejoined MAKI; twelve years later, MAKI split into two parties—one with a Jewish majority and one with an Arab majority, which was later named Rakah. From then on, MAKI adopted a growing pro-Zionist line, whereas Rakah undertook to represent the national Arab position. In 1973 MAKI merged with a group that dissented from Mapam (Blue-Red, or Siyah) to form Moked, which defines itself as extreme Zionist left (but not Communist). Since 1977 it has included some Oriental ethnic groups and taken the name Hadash.

ETZEL [Acronym for IRGUN ZEVAI LEUMI: National Military Organization]

(1931-1937): A group that dissented from the *Hagana* organization, demanding a more activist defense policy and protesting the left's predominance in the Hagana. It was joined by an armed group from *Beitar* and gained some sporadic support from rightist elements. In 1936 an agreement was signed between Etzel and V. Jabotinsky making the chairman of the Revisionist Zionists organization Etzel's commander-in-chief. However, a split occurred in 1937, with about half of the members rejoining the Hagana, and the rest carrying on as an independent organization (1937-1948). In 1937 Etzel began its first activities against the Arabs, which met with some strong reactions from the British government backed by the organized Yishuv. Etzel reacted by using terrorist tactics against the British government, but with the outbreak of World War II declared a cease-fire. One group within Etzel—*Lehi*—opposed the ceasefire and continued its anti-British activities throughout the war. In 1945 Etzel resumed its activities as part of the "insurrectionary movement" in coordination with the Hagana and Lehi; these activities went on even after the Hagana withdrew from the movement in 1946. When the 1947/48 War broke out, the Hagana and Etzel once again reached an accommodation: on 1 June 1948 Etzel was abolished and its members joined the Israeli army. The hard-core nucleus of the *Likud* party—*Herut*—is the political manifestation of Etzel.

GAHAL

The electoral alignment between the *Herut* party and the Liberal Party that merged the two largest factions of the right on the eve of the 1965 elections. During the years 1967-1971 it participated in the broad-based government set up on the eve of the 1967 War. After the 1977 general election, it took over the leadership in the framework of the right-wing coalition known as *Likud*.

GENERAL ZIONISTS: [Hebrew: ZIONIM KLALYIM]

A central party in the World Zionist Movement and the *Yishuv*. Between 1931 and 1945 it had two factions, and in 1948 some of its members in Israel left it to join the Progressive Party, which in the early 1960s merged with the General Zionists to form the Liberal Party. However, the Progressives withdrew from the Liberal Party in 1965 and merged with *Herut*, giving rise to *Gahal*. Until the merger with Herut, the General Zionists held moderate views concerning the Jewish-Arab conflict. They participate in *Likud*—the right-wing coalition in power since 1977.

HAGANA

The illegal military organization of the *Yishuv* set up in 1920 following the convention of the *Ahdut Haavoda* party. It was initially subordinate to the *Histadrut* and was dominated by the socialist left, although it declared itself open to any Jew and the defender of the entire Jewish community. (Hagana is Hebrew for defense.) Until the 1936-1939 Arab revolt it was a federative organization of local bodies; however, during those years it became a national organization. As of 1931 it had a central headquarters, with equal representation of the Histadrut and the right wing. Its organizational and political subordination to the Histadrut then shifted to the *Sochnut* and the *Vaad Leumi*. In 1939 its General Staff was set up with differentiation between the military-operative wing and the political leadership. Participation in the Hagana was voluntary, with only 4-7 percent of the total eligible Jewish population enlisted in it. Until the late 1930s the organization adopted policies that were basically defensive of Jewish settlements and assumed British involvement, but later on it undertook the defense of roads and launched retaliatory actions. In 1936 the Hagana created its first units trained in mobile guerilla warfare; with the help of British training, these units were expanded and used to suppress the Arab revolt. The semi-official military cooperation between the Hagana and the British government was intensified during World War II, but came to an end in 1942 with the British victory in El Alamein. Between 1945 and August 1946, the Hagana participated in terrorist activities directed against the British government in collaboration with *Etzel* and *Lehi*. From 1946 until the end of the British Mandate, the Hagana concentrated its anti-British activities on smuggling illegal Jewish refugees from Europe into Palestine. In November 1947 it was awaiting the Arab invasion with plans prepared in advance by its General Staff, and in May 1948, when the regular army was formed, the Hagana supplied the organizational frame and the basic command staff.

HAKIBBUTZ HAARTZI-HASHOMER HATZAIR

An alliance of all the *kibbutzim* that belong to the *Hashomer Hatzair* movement, formed in 1927. The first kibbutzim to join this alliance were established in the early 1920s; at present, the alliance is made up of 75 kibbutzim with a total population of approximately 35,000. The alliance puts heavy stress on the combination of socialism and Zionism, the class struggle, and ideological collectivism. In 1946 it became a political party which merged in 1948 with *Ahdut Haavoda* to form the *Mapam* party.

HAKIBBUTZ HAMEUCHAD

A *kibbutz* organization formed in 1927 by a number of kibbutzim, notably those which separated from the *Labor Legion*. Its ideological orientation has been socialist, with emphasis on national Jewish objectives. It is known for its efforts to promote the cause of Jewish labor during the *Yishuv* period, and for its important contributions to the Jewish-Arab conflict (settling the frontiers, participating in military organizations in the pre-sovereign period, etc.). Hakibbutz Hameuchad considers itself descended from the historical *Ahdut Haavoda*; at present it includes over 60 kibbutzim.

HAPOEL HAMIZRAHI

An orthodox political party in the Zionist organization and Palestine/Israel composed mainly of workers and farmers who sought to blend Zionism, socialism, and Jewish Orthodoxy, founding several collective settlements. It merged with *Mizrahi* in 1956 to form the *Mafdal*.

HAPOEL HATZAIR

A Zionist labor party founded in 1905, its objective was the "conquest of labor" in the Jewish settlements, totally rejecting the Marxist approach and the class struggle. In 1930 it merged with *Ahdut Haavoda* to form the *Mapai* party.

HASHOMER

A clandestine organization founded in 1919 by members of the *Second Aliya* (most of them members of *Poalei Zion*) to defend the Jewish settlements. The Hashomer was the first attempt to build an armed Jewish force in Palestine, and it soon took over the defense of the Jewish settlements in Galilee and in parts of central Palestine. It participated in activities aimed at establishing Jewish presence, and in struggles over the ownership of lands (particularly in the Valley of Esdraelon area). During its eleven years it came to include approximately one hundred members (plus hundreds of candidates and hired guards). To its members, it was an elite, vanguard organization not subject to external authority. It thus managed to antagonize several of the *moshavot* which needed its services, as well as the labor parties, who disapproved of the fact that the organization set forth its own political objectives. This antagonism led to a decision by *Ahdut Haavoda* in 1920 to dissolve Hashomer and replace it with a new organization—the *Hagana*. In 1922 the ex-commander of Hashomer left the Hagana to head a rival organization (hakibbutz) made up of several leftist factions of the *Labor Legion*.

HASHOMER HATZAIR

A worldwide youth movement formed by the merger of two youth movements (the scout organizations Hashomer and Zeirei Zion) in 1916. The members were urged to immigrate to Palestine and join the communal experience of the *kibbutz*, combining it with familiar scouting elements. Hashomer Hatzair attacked the principle of "Jewish labor" and until 1948 supported the idea of a bi-national state as the only solution to the Jewish-Arab conflict.

HERUT

A political party founded by members of *Etzel* after Etzel had been dissolved as an underground movement following Israel's independence. Since 1949 it has been affiliated with the world organization of the Revisionist Zionists, and since 1963 has been represented in the *Histadrut*. In 1965 it formed an electoral alignment with the Liberal Party—the *Gahal*. Herut's program is based on an Israel which includes both banks of the Jordan River. In the economic sphere it favors free enterprise and binding arbitration in settling labor disputes. Since 1977 Herut has been the nucleus of the right-wing bloc—the *Likud*—that holds the ruling power in Israel.

HIGHER ARAB COMMITTEE

The ultimate authority of Palestine's Arabs created in 1936. Dominated by the *Hussainies*, it served as the instrument by which they sought to gain control over the Arab community. After it led the 1936 Arab revolt, it was dissolved in 1937 by the British government; all its members were deported (with the exception of the *Mufti of Jerusalem*, who escaped abroad). In December 1945 it resumed its activities, and in 1947 participated in the riots that began the 1947/

48 War. With the collapse of the Arab struggle within Palestine, it began to operate under the auspices of the Arab League and the Egyptian army. In September 1948 it was reorganized as the Palestinian government based in Gaza (later in Cairo).

HISTADRUT

The General Federation of [Jewish] Labor in Palestine/Israel, founded in 1920 with an eye to furthering both class interests and national interests. It is a combination of a trade union and an economic, settlement-oriented, cultural complex. It sponsors the largest medical insurance program in Israel, and it owns large industrial plants, cooperatives for marketing and consumption, a bank, an insurance company, cultural institutions, including a publishing house, a daily newspaper (*Davar*), and so forth. During the *Yishuv* period the Histadrut was a central instrument in the struggle for exclusive Jewish labor within the Jewish system. Since 1959, Arabs have been admitted as members, and have been granted professional protection on equal terms. In 1966 the word *Jewish* was officially removed from the name of the organization.

HUSSAINIES

A family of Palestinian nobles who have held the post of the *Mufti of Jerusalem* since the middle of the nineteenth century, in addition to other high administrative posts in Palestine, including that of the Mayor of Jerusalem and representative in the Ottoman parliament. In the course of its struggle for power the Hussaini family was organized as a political party (1935)—a common development in the Arab Palestinian community—known as the Arab Palestinian Party (Al-Hizb Al-Arabi Al-Falastini). Haj Amin El Husseini, Mufti of Jerusalem, was the most prominent figure in the family.

IHUD HAKVUTZOT VEHAKIBBUTZIM

An organization consisting of *kibbutzim* with a social-democratic inclination founded in 1951, following the merger of two kibbutz organizations—Hever Hakvutzot and Ihud Hakibbutzim. It has been politically linked with *Mapai* and the Labor Party, and comprises 85 member kibbutzim.

JEWISH AGENCY [Hebrew abbreviation: SOCHNUT]

The executive branch of the World Zionist Organization in Palestine/Israel founded in accordance with Item 4 of the 1922 Mandate Commission from the League of Nations to Britain. The Jewish Agency was set up to represent the Jewish people in working out with the British government a plan for a national Jewish home in Palestine. Together with the *Vaad Leumi*, it has been the dominant governing authority in the *Yishuv*. Its main power rested upon (1) its control over national funds, which supplied the material resources for developing the country, (2) its power to grant visas (according to immigration quotas), and (3) its control over the *Hagana* (as of 1931). With the establishment of the State of Israel, the powers and spheres of responsibility of the state were divided between the Agency and the central government. The Agency has undertaken to handle and promote Jewish immigration to Israel and its absorption, the setting up of settlements, and the fund-raising abroad via the United Jewish Appeal.

KIBBUTZ [plural: KIBBUTZIM]

A collective settlement wherein the means of production are collectively owned by its members. Initially these means of production were agricultural, but today many kibbutzim are based on industry and services. The ultimate authority rests with the members' general assembly, with the daily management handled by an elected secretariat. The tendency is for specialization in the various areas of activity, along with an ideology of job rotation. The nuclear family is maintained, although many of its roles (child-rearing, patterns of consumption, and entertainment) have been handed over to the collectivity. The first kibbutz was founded in 1909, and at present the kibbutz population makes up approximately 3 percent of Israel's total Jewish population. In its early days, there was a bitter controversy over its optimum size. Some of the founding fathers called for the *kvutza* pattern—a small and intimate collectivity—assuming that only a small grouping of several score members could ensure a genuinely egalitarian collectivity. Nowadays the distinction between a kvutza and a kibbutz has been lost. Despite their small percentage of the population (from 7 percent in 1947 to 3 percent in 1982), kibbutzim have been very prominent in the Israeli social system. Their members' participation in management of the Jewish-Arab conflict has always been great (they have provided approximately 25 percent of the soldiers in elite units), and most of the kibbutzim have been frontier settlements which protected the borders and established presence on territories. While they are internally egalitarian, the kibbutzim are outwardly elitist, with a marked selectivity in admitting new members, which may help to explain why they have derived little benefit from the growth of the population in Israel following independence.

KNESSET

The Israeli Parliament, formed in 1949. Its members are elected every four years (unless it dissolves itself) by nationwide, secret, and direct elections. It is comprised of 120 members representing all political parties that have gained at least 1 percent of the vote.

LABOR LEGION [Hebrew: GEDUD HAAVODA]

A pioneer organization founded in 1920 for the purpose of setting up a general commune for all the Jewish workers in Palestine who were building the new society. The legion undertook to drain the marshes and build roads; it also established a number of *kibbutzim*. Differences of opinions within the legion and between it and the central labor leadership (the *Histadrut*) brought about a split that eventually led to the legion's collapse. The first group of dissenters broke away in 1923 and formed the nucleus of *Hahibbutz Hameuchad*. In

December 1926 the legion split into two groups—the Zionists and the leftists, who were ideologically akin to the Communists. In 1927 the leftist group split up, with several of its members emigrating to the USSR, and in 1929 the Zionist group merged with Hakibbutz Hameuchad.

LABOR PARTY. See MAPAI and ALIGNMENT.

LAW OF RETURN

One of the basic laws of Israel, which essentially grants to all Jews the right to emigrate to Israel. Passed in the parliament on 5 July 1950, it is the legislative implementation of the central assumption of the Zionist ideology—namely, that every Jew potentially belongs to the collectivity. The numerous obstacles which bar non-Jews from joining the collectivity, although not stipulated in the law, have given rise to a bitter controversy concerning the criteria used for defining the term *Jew*. It is between those who demand strict exclusivity and those who favor a less restrictive definition.

LEHI [Hebrew acronym for LOHAMEI HERUT ISRAEL]

Israel's Freedom Fighters (also known as the Stern Gang), founded in 1940 for the purpose of carrying on the anti-British activities suspended by *Etzel* during World War II. As of November 1945, its activities were coordinated with those of the *Hagana* and Etzel under the umbrella of the "insurrectionary movement." Between November 1947 and May 1948, Lehi's targets were the organizational centers of the Palestinian Arabs; in May 1948 it joined the forces of the Israeli army. When the war was over, Lehi split into two factions: "leftist" and "rightist."

LIKUD

The dominant political bloc in Israeli politics since 1977, formed from the hard core of the *Herut* party, the Liberals (*General Zionists*), and other right-wing factions, under the leadership of Menachem Begin. After the Camp David agreement (1979), an extreme right-wing faction—the *Thiya*—separated from the Likud, protesting against the concessions granted to Egypt under terms of the peace treaty. The Likud's constituency is a combination of the traditional rightist elements in Israeli politics and the newly arriving Oriental immigrants, who support the Likud's hard line in the Jewish-Arab conflict and oppose the traditional Western (so-called Ashkenazi) establishment.

MAARACH: See ALIGNMENT.

MAFDAL [Acronym for MIFLAGA DATIT LEUMIT: National Religious Party]

A religious-Zionist party founded in 1956 with the merger of *Hamizrahi* and *Hapoel Hamizrahi* movements. It seeks to promote the religious character of Israeli society according to the orthodox Jewish law (Halacha). It has its own educational subsystem within the public school system, but with its own curriculum, as well as women's, youth, and sports organizations and a university (Bar-Ilan) under its auspices. Until 1967 it had no specific policy with regard to the management of the Jewish-Arab conflict, and was largely identified with the moderate elements of Israeli society, but since the 1967 War it has become more deeply involved with some groups calling for a more activist approach and opposing any pullback from the territories conquered in 1967. Following the Lebanese War, several groups in Mafdal called again for a moderate approach.

MAKI: See COMMUNIST PARTIES.

MAPAI

A socialist-Zionist party founded in 1930 when *Hapoel Hatzair* merged with *Ahdut Haavoda*. In 1944 it split up, with Ahdut Haavoda reestablished as an independent party. In 1965 an alignment between Mapai and Ahdut Haavoda was formed; in the same year, however, a faction (Rafi) led by D. Ben-Gurion separated from Mapai following some bitter disputes. In 1968, Mapai, Ahdut Haavoda, and Rafi united to form the Labor Party. From the outset Mapai has been a major political force in the Israeli political system, and all the government coalitions in the pre-state and the early post-state period were centered around it. It is considered a centrist party that can bring together diverse interests, including the bourgeoisie, and despite its socialist orientation, has shown a strong pragmatic sense and capacity for change. Its positions on the Jewish-Arab conflict have been flexible and relatively moderate. Since 1959 Mapai in its various forms has declined, until in 1977 it lost power to a right-wing coalition dominated by *Herut*.

MAPAM

A political party with a Marxist orientation founded in 1948 when *Hashomer Hatzair* merged with *Adhut Haavoda-Poalei Zion*. As a result of internal struggles sparked by the Prague trials, in which some central Jewish figures in Czech politics were convicted for participation in a "capitalist-Zionist conspiracy," the leftist faction was ousted in 1953. The internal disputes persisted, and by 1954 Adhut Haavoda separated from Mapam. Those who remained were Hashomer Hatzair members, most of *Poalei Zion-Smol*, several *kibbutzim* affiliated with *Hakibbutz Hameuchad*, and several hundred Arab members. In 1968 Mapam formed an alignment with the Labor Party. It has always taken very moderate stands on the Jewish-Arab conflict, and until 1948 proposed a binational solution to the conflict. It is the only Zionist party that has Arab members, and kibbutz members of Hashomer Hatzair have always protested against what they perceived as the dispossession of the Arabs.

MATZPEN

The Israeli socialist organization, it adopted *Matzpen*—originally the name of its bulletin—as the official title of the organization in Israel and abroad. Matzpen was founded in 1962 by ex-members of *MAKI* who were ousted from the party because of their dissenting views on the Jewish-Arab conflict, the Cuban revolution, and Sino-Soviet relations. A number of Jewish and Arab Trotskyists and pro-Chinese joined the organization (and later withdrew). In 1965 it joined Haolam Hazeh (a liberal and dovish-oriented political group) for a short period, after which it was forced to leave. Matzpen considers itself part of the revolutionary new left, who believe that world revolution is to be carried out through the struggle between the underdeveloped and developed countries, with the latter gradually being transformed into socialist societies. However, it is Matzpen's attitude toward the Jewish-Arab conflict that is the basis for the hostile reaction against it in Israel. It calls for the de-Zionization of Israel (conceived as an ally of imperialism) so that it will be able to participate in the worldwide revolution. In the wake of the 1967 War, Matzpen gained considerable notoriety by breaking the rule that Israelis are not supposed to criticize Israel abroad. The organization has remained a very small group, with its original leadership scattered around the world.

MIZRAHI

A religious Zionist political party founded in East Europe in 1902; later (from 1918) a political party in the *Yishuv* and Israel. Since 1956 it has been united with *Hapoel Hamizrahi* (as *MAFDAL*).

MOSHAV [plural: MOSHAVIM]

A settlement-pattern of individual smallholders operating farms of equal size with the means of production equally distributed among them. The nuclear family is the major production and consumption unit in the moshav, with marketing, credit, and other economic activities regulated by the moshav. The moshav also has considerable political control over its members. A variation is the "moshav shitufi," wherein all lands are collectively cultivated and owned. Most of the moshavim (approximately 250) are members of the Moshavim Movement, while others (approximately 100) are affiliated with various other organizations (Haoved Hazioni of the Liberal Party, Haovdim Haleumiyim of *Herut*, *Hapoel Hamizrahi*, etc.).

MOSLEM-CHRISTIAN ASSOCIATIONS

Political associations founded by local Moslem and Christian notables for voicing their opposition to Zionism. The first such associations were set up in Jaffa and Jerusalem in November 1918, and were soon followed by others in other Arab communities in Palestine. Formally, these associations were part of a national framework centered in Jerusalem, but in reality each was autonomous.

MUFTI OF JERUSALEM

The office of Moslem priest which is partly inherited (intrafamily) and partly elected by local leaders. During the Ottoman period, the Mufti of Jerusalem was subordinate to the center in Istanbul (Sheikh Al-Islam) like all the other local priests. However, when the relations between the Moslems in Palestine and the center in Turkey were severed, the Mufti of Jerusalem was granted the special position of Head of the Islam (Rais Al-Ulama) in Palestine. In 1921 Haj Amin El Husseini was nominated as the Mufti, a title he held until his death. By then the office of the Mufti was combined with that of the head of the *Supreme Moslem Council* so that the Mufti of Jerusalem became the most influential figure in the Arab community in Palestine.

NAHAL

A military unit combining military service with agricultural training and the establishment of frontier settlements. Founded in 1948 following the dissolution of the *Palmah*, the Nahal was a compromise between the desire of *kibbutzim* members (especially those affiliated with *Hakibbutz Hameuchad*) to have separate army units and the desire to have a national army representative of all social and political groups. As a voluntary unit, it attracted the elite of urban youth. The Nahal has set up scores of frontier settlements in areas where Israel's presence and the establishment of territorial facts were at stake, and has thus served as an important instrument in the management of the Jewish-Arab conflict.

NASHASHIBIS

A family of Palestinian notables and leaders, the best known of whom was Regeb Nashashibi, a member of the Ottoman parliament and a Mayor of Jerusalem (1920-1934). In December 1934 the Nashashibis set up a political party— the National Defense Party (Hizb Al-Defa Al-Watani)—whose chief rival was the *Hussaini* family.

PALESTINE OFFICE

The representative of the World Zionist Organization in Palestine assigned to carry out the Jewish settlement. Founded in Jaffa in 1908, it assisted in the first settlements of the left, setting up the Palestine Land Development Company and purchasing lands. When Palestine came under the British Mandate, the responsibilities of the Palestine Office were transferred to *Vaad Hatzirim* and the executive of the *Jewish Agency*.

PALESTINIAN CONVENTIONS

Initially the Syrian and the Syrian-Palestinian conventions, convened in Damascus in June-July 1919 and February-March 1920 on the initiative of the Moslem-Christian Associations. Participating in these early conventions were delegations from Palestine and Syria; the discussions focused on Syria's claim for independence, with Palestine under its control. The first Palestinian Convention (sometimes referred to as the third) took place in Haifa in 1920. It appealed to the British government to grant autonomy to Palestinian Arabs, expressed its rejection of Zionism, and stressed Moslem-Christian unity. The idea of annexing Palestine to Syria was abandoned, and the process of establishing the independent political identity of the Palestinians was initiated. Later conventions took place in 1922 (in Nablus), in 1923 (in Jaffa), and in 1928 (in Jerusalem).

PALMAH

An elite military unit of the *Hagana* founded in 1941 with the consent of the British government to fight the German Afrika Corps that was advancing in the Western Desert. At the outset it was trained by British military staff and equipped with weapons from British supply depots. When the threat of Nazi invasion was over, the British ended their support of the Palmah; however, it continued its military training and activities in the *kibbutzim* and settlements. A unit of semi-professional soldiers, its main recruiting source was the kibbutz movements (*Hakibbutz Hameuchad* in particular), which made the political center suspicious of its political orientation. In 1948 the government of Israel dissolved the separate headquarters of the Palmah, subordinating it to the General Staff of the Israeli Army.

POALEI AGUDAT ISRAEL

An orthodox movement with a socialist orientation founded in Poland in 1922. Since 1925 it has been a political party in the *Yishuv* and later in Israel. Unlike its parent body (*Agudat Israel*), it cooperated with the organized Yishuv and participated in the Zionist settlement process with eleven settlements of its own.

POALEI ZION

A Zionist socialist party founded at the end of the nineteenth century with an eye to integrating the national Jewish revival with socialism. However, disapproving of the policy of the *Palestine Office*, it withdrew from the World Zionist Organization, and in 1919 its majority merged with *Hapoel Hatzair* and founded *Ahdut Haavoda*. During the Vienna Convention of 1920, the party split into left and right factions on the grounds of its relations with the Comintern. The leftist group regarded the class struggle as first priority, with emigration to Palestine as a peripheral issue, while the rightist group (which included Ahdut Haavoda members in Western Europe and America) emphasized emigration to and settlement in Palestine. The leftist group, which was thereafter known as *Poalei Zion-Smol*, rejoined the World Zionist Organization in 1937.

POALEI ZION-SMOL

A socialist Jewish party founded after the 1920 split in *Poalei Zion*. In Palestine, the party was established in 1924 by several Poalei Zion members who had not joined *Adhut Haavoda* in 1919. In 1946 Poalei Zion-Smol merged with Adhut Haavoda following the latter's separation from *Mapai*, and in 1948 the two united with *Hashomer Hatzair* to found *Mapam*. After 1948 Poalei Zion-Smol ceased to exist as an independent political party, and its members were absorbed into various leftist groups. During the 1920s the party sought an affiliation with the Comintern, but this attempt was thwarted by the Comintern's demand that the party abandon its Zionist identity. Poalei Zion-Smol rejected the ideal of exclusive Jewish labor in Palestine, and was torn by bitter controversies pertaining to its Zionist orientation and its attitude toward the Hebrew language and culture (with many members favoring the adoption of Yiddish as the official language).

PROVISIONAL COUNCIL

Israel's provisional legislative body set up in January 1948 consisting of the executives of the *Vaad Leumi* and the *Jewish Agency*, as well as of representatives of various organizations making up the organized *Yishuv*. Prior to the establishment of the *Knesset*, the council was the ultimate authority; it established the procedures of administration and law, supervised the work of the government, and prepared for the first elections to the Knesset.

RAKAH. See COMMUNIST PARTIES.

REVISIONIST PARTY

Established by Vladimir Jabotinsky in 1925, it called for a more activist Zionist policy. In 1935 it withdrew from the World Zionist Organization, proclaiming the establishment of a Jewish state as Zionism's primary goal. Its aim was to become the "New Zionist Organization" as an alternative to the World Zionist Organization; however, after World War II it rejoined the WZO. Its underground military branch was the *Etzel*, and its political successor in Israel is considered to be the *Herut* party.

SOCHNUT. See JEWISH AGENCY.

SUPREME MOSLEM COUNCIL

Established in 1922 by the former electors (from Palestine) of the Ottoman parliament for the purpose of supervising the religious affairs of the Moslem community in Palestine—e.g., the nomination and dismissal of judges to the sharia courts, the local wakf committees, and the management of Moslem endowments. The council was to be elected every four years. Initially, it was headed by the *Mufti of Jerusalem*, whose personality added weight to the council's authority.

THIYA [Hebrew for Revival]

An extreme right-wing political party which split from the *Likud* in 1979. It opposed the implementation of the Egyptian-Israeli peace treaty and the Israeli withdrawal from Sinai and evacuation of the settlements there. It has attempted to organize elements in Israeli society to resist what it sees as a soft-line policy of the Likud government toward the Arabs. In elections in 1981 the Thiya won three of the 120 seats in the *Knesset*.

VAAD HATZIRIM

A delegation of the Zionist movement and world Jewry that came to Palestine in 1918 to advise the British in carrying out its mandate commission, and to assist in rehabilitating the Jewish community in Palestine after the devastation of World War I.

VAAD LEUMI

The highest institution of the organized Jewish community in Palestine. Recognized by the British government as the representative of the Jewish community, it had limited powers in areas such as taxation, religious affairs, education, social welfare, health, and the supervising of local municipalities. It also handled security matters and recruited volunteers for the British forces during World War II. Its roles and powers were later assumed by the State of Israel.

YISHUV [Hebrew for Community]

The Jewish community in Palestine as a social and political entity. The "organized Yishuv" refers to all the political groups and factions which abided by the authority of the "national institutions" (i.e., the *Vaad Leumi* and the *Jewish Agency*). It did not include the non-Zionist groups—namely the ultra-orthodox *Agudat Israel*, the *Communists*, and the *Revisionist* dissenters. (The term "Old Yishuv" refers to the Jewish inhabitants of Palestine who preceded the Zionist immigrations and were antagonistic toward the secular newcomers.)

SOURCES AND REFERENCES

Abramovitz, Z., and Gelfat, Y.
  1944   *The Arab Economy in Palestine and in the Middle East.* Tel Aviv:
          Hakibbutz Hameuchad.   [Hebrew]

Abu-Lughod, Z.
  1971   "The Demographic Transformation of Palestine." In *The Transforma-*
          tion of Palestine, ed. Ibrahim Abu-Lughod. Evanston: Northwestern
          University Press.

Adam, H.
  1971   *Modernizing Racial Domination: The Dynamics of South African*
          Politics. Berkeley: University of California Press.

"Ahad Haam" (pseud. for Asher Ginsberg)
  1902   "Truth from Palestine." *At the Crossroads,* pt. 1. Berlin.   [Hebrew]
  1912   *Selected Essays.* Philadelphia: Jewish Publication Society of America.

Alexander, Fred
  1947   *Moving Frontiers: An American Theme and Its Application to Aus-*
          tralian History. Melbourne: Melbourne University Press.

Allen, H.C.
  1959   *Bush and Backwoods: A Comparison of the Frontier in Australia*
          and the United States. East Lansing: Michigan State University Press.

Allon, Y.
  1968   *A Sand Curtain. Israel and the Arabs Between War and Peace.* Tel
          Aviv: Hakibbutz Hameuchad.   [Hebrew]

Arikha, Y.A.
  1937   *The Redeeming of Names.* Jerusalem: Jewish National Fund.
                                                                   [Hebrew]

Arlosoroff, C.
  1934   *Writings,* vol. 4. Stiebel.   [Hebrew]
  1945   *Jerusalem Diary.* Tel Aviv: Mapai Publications.   [Hebrew]

Arnon-Ohanna, Yuval
  1981a   *The Internal Struggle within the Palestinian Movement, 1929-1939.*
          Tel Aviv: Yeriv-Hadar.   [Hebrew]
  1981b   "Social and Political Aspects of the Arab Revolt (1936-39)." In *Doc-*
          uments and Portraits from the Arab Gangs Archives in the Arab
          Revolt in Palestine (1936-1939), eds. E. Danin and Y. Shimoni.
          Jerusalem: Magnes.   [Hebrew]

Aron, R.
  1968   *Peace and War: A Theory of International Relations.* New York: Praeger.

Ashbel, A., ed.
  1970   *Sixty Years of the Israel Land Development Corporation.* Jerusalem: Haksharat Hayishuv Society.   [Hebrew]

Assaf, M.
  1967   *The History of the Arabs' Awakening in Palestine and Their Flight.* Culture and Education in cooperation with Davar Publications.
                                                                            [Hebrew]
  1970   *Arab-Jewish Relations in Palestine, 1860-1948.* Tel-Aviv: Educational and Cultural Projects.   [Hebrew]

Aubert, V.
  1963   "Competition and Dissensus: Two Types of Conflict Resolution." *Journal of Conflict Resolution* 7, 1:26-42.

Avidar, Y.
  1970   *En Route to the Israeli Army: Memoirs.* Tel-Aviv: Maarchot.
                                                                            [Hebrew]

Avineri, Shlomo
  1981   *The Making of Modern Zionism: The Intellectual Origins of the Jewish State.* London: Weidenfeld and Nicolson.

Avneri, Uri
  1968   *Israel Without Zionists.* New York: Macmillan.

Avniel, B.
  1936   *The Problem of the Arabs in Israel.* Tel-Aviv.   [Hebrew]

Azaryahu, Y.
  1929   "The Jewish Education in Palestine: History and Evaluation." In *The Jubilee of the Teacher's Association*, ed. D. Kimchi. Jerusalem: Teacher's Association.   [Hebrew]

Baer, Gabriel
  1971   *Introduction to the History of Agrarian Relations in the Middle East.* Tel-Aviv: Hakibbutz Hameuchad.   [Hebrew]

Bannon, John F.
  1974   *The Spanish Borderlands Frontier, 1513-1821.* Albuquerque: University of New Mexico Press.

Bar-Haim, A.
  1972   "Labor Relations in the Jewish Yishuv in Palestine in the Mandatory Period until the End of World War II." Master's thesis, Sociology, Hebrew University of Jerusalem.   [Hebrew]

Bastide, R.
  1972   *African Civilization in a New World.* London.

Bauer, Yehuda
 1973   *From Diplomacy to Resistance: A History of Jewish Palestine, 1939-1945*. New York: Atheneum.

Begin, M.
 1951   *The Revolt*. New York: Henry Schuman.

Bein, A.
 1970   *The History of Zionist Settlement—From Herzl's Time until Today*. 4th ed. Ramat-Gan: Massada.   [Hebrew]

Benbenisti, M.
 1973   *Opposite the Closed Wall*. Jerusalem: Weidenfeld and Nicolson.
                                                        [Hebrew]

Benedict, R.
 1973   *Patterns of Culture*. London: Routledge and Kegan Paul.

Ben-Gurion, D.
 1931   *We and Our Neighbors*. Tel-Aviv: Davar.   [Hebrew]
 1933   *From Class to Nation*. Tel-Aviv: Davar.   [Hebrew]
 1935   *On Guard [Mishmaroth]*. Tel-Aviv: Davar.   [Hebrew]
 1950   *Israel at Battle*. Tel-Aviv: Mapai Publishers.   [Hebrew]
 1967   *Talks with Arab Leaders*. Tel-Aviv: Am Oved.   [Hebrew]
 1968   *Letters to Paula and the Children*. Tel-Aviv: Am Oved. [Hebrew]
 1971   *Memoirs*, vol. 1. Tel-Aviv: Am Oved.   [Hebrew]
 1972   *Memoirs*, vol. 2, Tel-Aviv: Am Oved.   [Hebrew]

Ben-Zvi, Rachel Yanait
 1964   *Anu Olim*. Tel-Aviv: Am-Oved.   [Hebrew]

Bernard, J.
 1950   "Where is the Modern Sociology of Conflict?" *American Journal of Sociology* 55: 11-16.

Bialik, Chaim N.
 1940   "The Chalutz." In *The Chalutz Book*, ed. M. Bassok. Jerusalem: Jewish Agency.   [Hebrew]

Bohannan, P., ed.
 1967   *Law and Warfare*. Garden City: Natural History Press.

Bolton, H.E.
 1917   "The Mission as a Frontier Institution in the Spanish American Colonies." *American Historical Review* 23 (October).

Bone, A.
 1938   *Palestine: The Land and the Economy*. Tel-Aviv: Dvir.   [Hebrew]

Boulding, K.E.
 1959   "National Images and International Systems." *Journal of Conflict Resolution* 3, 2:120-31.

Sources and References

Bowden, T.
1975 "The Politics of the Arab Rebellion in Palestine 1936-39." *Middle Eastern Studies* 11, 2:147-74.

Braslavsky, M.
1956 *The Israeli Labor Movement: History and Sources*, vol. 2. Tel-Aviv: Hakkibutz Hameuchad. [Hebrew]
1959 *The Israeli Labor Movement: History and Sources*, vol. 3. Tel-Aviv: Hakibbutz Hameuchad. [Hebrew]
1961 *Workers and Their Organizations in the First Aliya: History and Sources*. Tel-Aviv: Hakibbutz Hameuchad. [Hebrew]
1962 *The Israeli Labor Movement*, vol. 4. Tel-Aviv: Hakibbutz Hameuchad. [Hebrew]
1966 *The Israeli Labor Movement: History and Sources*, vol. 1. 2nd ed. Tel-Aviv: Hakibbutz Hameuchad. [Hebrew]

Brecher, N.
1972 *The Foreign Policy System of Israel*. London: Oxford University Press.

Brenner, Y.C.
1956 *Complete Works*. Tel-Aviv: Hakibbutz Hameuchad. [Hebrew]

Canaan, H.
1969 *The War of the Press: The Struggle of the Jewish Press in Palestine Against the British Rule*. Jerusalem: Zionist Library. [Hebrew]

Carmi, S., and Rosenfeld, H.
1971 "Immigration, Urbanization, and Crisis—The Process of Jewish Settlement in Palestine in the Twenties." *Mibifnim* 33, 1:49-62. [Hebrew]

Cattan, H.
1969 *Palestine, the Arabs and Israel: The Search for Justice*. London: Longmans.

Central Bureau of Statistics
1981 *Projection of Population up to 2000*. Jerusalem: Government Printer.

Central Bureau of Statistics and Israel Defense Forces
1967 *Census of Population 1967: West Bank of Jordan, Gaza Strip, Northern Sinai and Golan Heights*. Jerusalem.

Central Bureau of Statistics and Jerusalem Municipality
1968 *East Jerusalem: Census of Population and Housing, 1967*. Jerusalem.

Chagnon, N.A.
1968 "'Yanamano' Social Organization and Warfare." In *War*, eds. M. Fried et al. Garden City: Natural History Press.

Clark, S.D.
1962 *The Canadian Community*. Toronto: University of Toronto Press.

Cleeman, M.
1945 *The General Zionists.* Jerusalem: Institute for Zionist Education.

Cohen, Aharon
1970 *Israel and the Arab World.* London: W.H. Allen.

Cohen, E.
1970 *The City in the Zionist Ideology.* Jerusalem: Institute of Urban and Regional Studies, Hebrew University.
1976 "Environmental Organization: A Multidimensional Approach to Social Ecology." *Current Anthropology* 17, 1:49-70.

Cohen, G.
1973 "The Idea of the Partition of Palestine and the Jewish State, 1933-1953 (in the contacts between Italy, the British Government, the Zionist Movement and Arab Leaders)." *Zionism,* coll. 3. Tel-Aviv: Tel-Aviv University and United Kibbutz, pp. 346-417. [Hebrew]

Cohen, Y.
1972 *The Allon Plan.* Tel Aviv: Hakibbutz Hameuchad. [Hebrew]

Converse, E.
1968 "The War of All Against All: A Review of *Journal of Conflict Resolution,* 1957-1958." *Journal of Conflict Resolution* 12, 4:471-532.

Coser, L.
1956 *The Functions of Social Conflict.* Glencoe: The Free Press.

Darwazah, A.
1966 *A Short Survey of the Palestine Problem.* Beirut: Palestine Liberation Organization.

De-Lima, N.
1942 "On Labor in Palestine: The Jewish National Fund from the Beginnings of Its Activities in Palestine until the Purchase of the Valley." Jerusalem: Jewish National Fund. [Hebrew]

Department of Public Measures
1958/9 *Revision of the Map: 1:100,000 Palestine (Map).* By 514 Fd. Survey Coy, R.E., August 1942; revised 1947. Tel-Aviv: State of Israel.

Doukhan-Landau, Leah
1979 *The Zionist Companies for Land Purchase in Palestine 1897-1914.* Jerusalem: Yad Ben-Zvi. [Hebrew]

Druyanov, A.
1919 *Writings on the History of Hibat Zion and the Settlement of Palestine.* Odessa. [Hebrew]

Durkheim, E.
1912 *Les Forms elementaires de la vie religieuse.* Paris: Alcan.
1951 *Suicide: A Study in Sociology.* New York: The Free Press.

Eilam, Y.
1972   *An Introduction to Another History of Zionism*. Levin-Epstein.

Eisenstadt, S.N.
1966   *Modernization: Protest and Change*. Englewood Cliffs: Prentice-Hall.
1967   *Israeli Society*. New York: Basic Books.
1971   *Social Differentiation and Stratification*. Glenview, Ill.: Scott, Foresman.

Eisenstadt, S.N., et al., eds.
1972   *Israel—A Society in the Making: A Sociological Analysis of Sources*. Jerusalem: Magnes.   [Hebrew]

Eliade, M.
1958   *Patterns in Comparative Religion*. New York: Sheed and Ward.

Eliash, S.
1973   "The Controversy Within the Jewish Community in Palestine as to the Partition Plan (Peel Commission Report, July 1937)." Master's thesis, History, Bar-Ilan University, Ramat-Gan.   [Hebrew]

Eliav, Arie Lova
1972   *Eretz Hatzvi*. Tel-Aviv: Am Oved.   [Hebrew]
1974   *Land of the Hart: Israelis, Arabs, the Territories and a Vision of the Future*. Philadelphia: Jewish Publication Society of America. [Quotations from the 1972 Hebrew edition]

Elmessiri, Abdelwahab M.
1977   *The Land of Promise: A Critique of Political Zionism*. New Brunswick, N.J.: North-American.

Epstein, Y.
1908   "The Hidden Question." *Hashiloach* 17:193-206.   [Hebrew]

ESCO Foundation for Palestine
1947   *A Study of Jewish, Arab and British Policies*. 2 vols. New Haven: Yale University Press.

Esquer, Gabriel
1950   *Histoire de l'Algérie*. Paris: Presses Universitaires de France.

Even-Shoshan, Z.
1946   *The General Federation of Labor: An Anthology*. Tel-Aviv: Pioneer Department.   [Hebrew]
1963   *The History of the Labor Movement in Palestine*, vol. 1. Tel-Aviv: Am Oved.   [Hebrew]
1966   *The History of the Labor Movement in Palestine*, vols. 2-3. Tel-Aviv: Am Oved.   [Hebrew]

Fink, C.F.
1968   "Some Conceptual Difficulties in the Theory of Social Conflict." *Journal of Conflict Resolution* 12, 4:412-60.

Firey, W.
1960   *Man, Mind and Land*. Glencoe: The Free Press.

Fischer, C.S.
1975   "The Myth of 'Territoriality' in van den Berghe's 'Bringing Beasts Back In.'" *American Sociological Review* 40, 5:674-76.

Fitzpatrick, Brian
1947   "The Big Man's Frontier and Australian Farming." *Agricultural History* 21 (January):8-12.

French, L.
1932   *Reports on Agricultural Development and Land Settlement in Palestine*. Jerusalem: Palestine Government.

Friedlander, D., and Goldscheider, C.
1974   "Peace and the Demographic Future of Israel." *Journal of Conflict Resolution* 18, 3:486-501.
1979   *The Population of Israel*. New York: Columbia University Press.

Friedman, Menachem
1971   "The Chief Rabbinat—An Unsolved Dilemma." *State and Government* 1, 3:118-28.   [Hebrew]
1977   *Society and Religion: The Non-Zionist Orthodox in Eretz-Israel— 1918-1936*. Jerusalem: Yad Ben-Zvi.   [Hebrew]

Furlonge, G.
1969   *Palestine Is My Country: The Story of Musa Alami*. London: John Murray.

Gabbay, R.E.
1959   *A Political Study of Jewish-Arab Conflict*. Paris: Libraries E. Drot et Minard.

Gates, Paul W.
1957   "Frontier Estate Builder and Farm Laborers." In *The Frontier in Perspective*, eds. Walker O. Wyman and Clifton B. Kroeber. Madison: University of Wisconsin Press, pp. 144-63.

Gerhard, Dietrich
1959   "The Frontier in Comparative View." *Comparative Studies in History and Society* 1 (March):34-51.

Geries, S.
1969   *Les Arabs en Israel*. Paris: Maspero.

Getter, M.
1973   "The Arab Problem in Lehi's Ideology." *Zionism*, vol. 3. Tel-Aviv: Hakibbutz Hameuchad, pp. 430-38.

Giladi, D.
1965   "Private Initiative, National Capital, and Political Crystallization of the Right." *Avanim* 5. Beit-Berl.   [Hebrew]

Goiten, S.D.
    1955   *Jews and Arabs: Their Contacts Through the Ages*. New York: Schocken.

Golomb, E.
    1953   *Hidden Strength*, vol. 2. Tel-Aviv: Aynot.   [Hebrew]

Gordon, David G.
    1966   *The Passing of French Algeria*. London: Oxford University Press.

Grannot, A. [Changed from Granovsky]
    1956   *Agrarian Reform and the Record of Israel*. London: Eyre and Spottiswoode.

Granovsky, A.
    1940a   *Land Policy in Palestine*. New York: Bloch. Trans. from Hebrew.
    1940b   *The Land Struggle*. Jerusalem: Jewish National Fund.   [Hebrew]
    1941   "Our Path in Land Politics." Tel-Aviv: Jewish National Fund.   [Hebrew]
    1943   *The Political Struggle over the Land*. Jerusalem: Jewish National Fund.   [Hebrew]
    1952   *The Land System in Palestine: History and Structure*. London: Eyre and Spottiswoode. Trans. from Hebrew.

Great Britain
    1922   *Report on Palestine Administration*. London: Colonial No. 5.
    1929   *Report of the Commission on the Palestine Disturbance of August, 1929*. London (Cmd. 3530).
    1939   *Palestine: Statement of Policy*. London: Colonial Office. (Cmd. 6019).

Griffin, R.M.
    1969   "Ethological Concepts for Planning." *Journal of American Institute of Planners* 35, 1:54-60.

Gurevich, D.
    1929   *Statistics for Palestine, 1929*.

Gurevich, D., Gertz, A., and Bachi, R.
    1945   *The Jewish Population in Palestine: Immigration, Demographic Structure and Natural Growth*. Pt. 1: *Twenty-Five Years of Immigration: 1919-1944*. Jerusalem: Department of Statistics, Jewish Agency for Palestine.   [Hebrew]

Gurevich, D., Gertz, A., and Zenker, A.
    1947   *Statistical Handbook of Jewish Palestine*. Jerusalem: Department of Statistics, Jewish Agency.   [Hebrew]

Hagana, History of the
    1954   Vol. 1: *From Defensiveness to Defense*. Written by J. Slotzky, J. Herschlag, I. Maor, H.H. Ben-Sasson, and S. Avigor. Tel-Aviv: Maarchot.   [Hebrew]

1964   Vol. 2: *From Defense to Struggle.* Written by J. Slotzky. Tel-Aviv: Am Oved.   [Hebrew]
1972   Vol. 3: *From Struggle to War.* Written by J. Slotzky. Tel-Aviv: Am Oved.   [Hebrew]

Hakibbutz Haartzi—Hashomer Hatzair
1942   *The Sixth General Council: Decisions.* Merhavia: Hakibbutz Hameuchad.   [Hebrew]

Haksharat Hayishuv Society (PLDC)
1925   *The History of One of the Land Purchases in Palestine During the Speculation Period of 1925.* Jerusalem.   [Hebrew]

Hall, E.T.
1959   *The Silent Language.* Garden City: Doubleday.
1969   *The Hidden Dimension.* Garden City: Anchor.

Hansen, M.L., and Brebner, J.B.
1940   *The Mingling of the Canadian and American Peoples.* New Haven: Yale University Press.

Harkabi, Y.
1969   *The Arabs' Lesson from their Defeat: A Collection of Translations from Arabic.* Tel-Aviv: Am Oved.   [Hebrew]
1972   *Arab Attitudes to Israel.* London: Vallentine, Mitchell.

Harpaz, Y.
1940   "The Question of Jewish Labor." In *Anniversary Book of the Hebrew Teachers' Association.* Tel Aviv.   [Hebrew]

Hartz, Louis, ed.
1964   *The Founding of New Societies: Studies in the History of the United States, Latin America, South Africa, Canada and Australia.* New York: Harcourt, Brace and World.

Hattis, S.L.
1970   *The Bi-National Idea in Palestine during Mandatory Times.* Haifa.

Hennessy, Alistair
1978   *The Frontier in Latin American History.* Albuquerque: University of New Mexico Press.

Herzl, Theodor
1960   *Alteneuland.* New York: Bloch.
1961   *Writings,* vol. 9: *Letters.* Jerusalem: Zionist Library.

Hope-Simpson, John
1930   *Palestine: Report on Immigration, Land Settlement and Development.* London: Colonial Office (Cmd. 3686).

Horowitz, Dan
1971   "Belligerency Without Hostilities." *Molad* 27, 19-20:36-55. [Hebrew]
1973   *The Israeli Conception of National Security: The Constant and the Variable in Israeli Strategic Thinking.* Jerusalem: Eshkol Institute, Hebrew University.   [Hebrew]

1982   "Dual Authority Polities." *Comparative Politics* 14, 3:329-49.

_____, and Kimmerling, B.
1974   "Some Social Implications of Military Service and the Reserves System in Israel." *Archives Européenes de Sociologie* 15, 2:262-76.

_____, and Lissak, M.
1973   "Authority Without Sovereignty: The Case of the National Center of the Jewish Community in Palestine." *Government and Opposition* 8: 48-71.
1978   *Origins of the Israeli Polity*. Chicago: University of Chicago Press.

Horowitz, David
1948   *The Development of the Palestine Economy*. Rev. ed. Tel-Aviv: Mossad Bialik and Dvir.   [Hebrew]

_____, and Hinden, R.
1938   *Economic Survey of Palestine*. Tel-Aviv: Jewish Agency.

Horowitz, David
1978   *The First Frontier: The Indian Wars and America's Origins, 1607-1776*. New York: Simon and Schuster.

Huntington, Samuel P.
1981   *American Politics: The Promise of Disharmony*. Cambridge, Mass.: Harvard University Press.

Hurewitz, J.C.
1950   *The Struggle for Palestine*. New York: Norton.

Hushi, A.
1943   *The Covenant of Palestine's Workers*. Tel-Aviv: Am Oved. [Hebrew]

Hyamson, A.M.
1950   *Palestine under the Mandate, 1920-1948*. London: Methuen.

Isaac, R.J.
1976   *Israel Divided: Ideological Politics in Israel*. Baltimore: Johns Hopkins University Press.

Israel Land Authority   [Jerusalem: Government Printer—Hebrew]
1963   *Report for 1961/62*.
1972   *Report Submitted to the Israel Land Council, 1970/1971*.
1974   *Report on Activities of 1972/73*.

Israel, State of   [Jerusalem: Government Printer—Hebrew]
1948   *Official Newspaper, No. 7*.
1949   *Regulations, No. 11*.
1950   *Book of Laws 37*.
1951a   *Book of Laws 63*.
1951b   *Government Yearbook*.
1951c   *Protocol of the Knesset*.
1953   *Book of Laws 122*.

266

1953/4 *Publications Collection, 517-555* (10/29/53-6/13/54).

1955a *Book of Laws 149.*

1955b *Government Yearbook.*

1959 *Government Yearbook.*

1961 *Government Yearbook.*

1964 *Government Yearbook.*

1965 *Book of Laws 445.*

"Israeli," G.Z. (pseud.)
  1953 *MPS-PCP-Maki: The History of the Communist Party in Israel.* Tel-Aviv: Am Oved.   [Hebrew]

Jabotinsky, Vladimir
  1933 *Labor Questions, Essays 1925-1932.* Jerusalem: Revisionist and Beitar Workers' Union in Israel.   [Hebrew]
  1947 *Writings,* vol. 4: *Addresses 1905-1926.* Jerusalem: A. Jabotinsky.   [Hebrew]
  1953 *Writings en Route to the State.* Jerusalem: A. Jabotinsky. [Hebrew]
  1972 *The World of . . . : A Selection of Speeches and the Essentials of His Doctrine.* Compiled and annotated by M. Sela. Tel-Aviv: Defusim.   [Hebrew]

Jennings, R.Y.
  1963 *The Acquisition of Territory in International Law.* Manchester: Manchester University Press.

Jewish Agency for Palestine
  1947 *The Jewish Case before the Anglo-American Committee of Inquiry on Palestine as Presented by Jewish Agency for Palestine. Statements and Memoranda.* Jerusalem: Jewish Agency.

Jewish National Fund
  1924-39 *Report of the Central Office.* Jerusalem.   [Hebrew]
  1939-40 *Bulletin of the Jewish National Fund Local Committee.* Jerusalem.   [Hebrew]
  1942 Anthology A: *Land Redemption in the History of the Yishuv.*
        Anthology B: *Heralders and Founders*
        Anthology C: *From the Beginning of Activity in Palestine until the Purchase of the Valley, 1907-1922.*
        Jerusalem: Jewish National Fund.   [Hebrew]

Johnson, R.N.
  1972 *Aggression in Man and Animals.* Philadelphia: Saunders.

Journal of Conflict Resolution 16, 2.
  1972 "Research Perspectives on the Arab-Israeli Conflict: A Symposium."

Julien, Charles-André
  1952 *L'Afrique du Nord en marche.* Paris: Julliard.

Kalvariski, C.N.
1931 "Jewish-Arab Relations during the First World War," *Sheifoteinu* [Our aspirations], April-May. [Hebrew]

Kamhawi, W.
1962 *The Holocaust and the Building in the Arab Homeland.* Beirut: Dar Alalem Lilmaaya. [Arabic]

Kaplowitz, N.
1976 "Psychological Dimensions in the Middle East Conflict: Policy Implications." *Journal of Conflict Resolution* 20 (June):279-318.

Katz, E., and Gurevich, M.
1973 *The Culture of Leisure in Israel.* Tel-Aviv: Am Oved. [Hebrew]

Katz, Shaul
1982 "Ideology, Settlement and Agriculture during the First Decade of Petach-Thikva." *Kathedra* 22:74-81.

Katznelson, Berl
1946 *Writings*, vol. 4. Tel-Aviv: Mapai. [Hebrew]

Keydar, A.
1967 "Brit Shalom." Master's thesis, Hebrew University of Jerusalem. [Hebrew]

Khouri, Fred J.
1968 *The Arab-Israeli Dilemma.* Syracuse: Syracuse University Press.

Kimche, John, and Kimche, David
1960 *A Clash of Destinies: The Arab-Jewish War and the Founding of the State of Israel.* New York: Praeger.

Kimmerling, Baruch
1974 "Anomie and Integration in Israeli Society and the Salience of the Arab-Israeli Conflict." *Studies in Comparative International Development* 9 (Fall):64-89.
1977 "Sovereignty, Ownership and Presence in the Jewish-Arab Territorial Conflict: The Case of Birim and Ikrit." *Comparative Political Studies* 10 (July):155-75.
1978 "The Israeli Civil Guard," In *Supplementary Military Forces: Reserves, Militias, Auxiliaries,* eds. Louis A. Zurcher and Gwyn Harries-Jenkins. Beverly Hills: Sage Publications, pp. 107-25.
1979 *The Economic Interrelationships between the Arab and Jewish Communities in Mandatory Palestine.* Cambridge, Mass.: Center for International Studies, MIT.
1979a *Social Interruption and Besieged Society: The Case of Israel.* Amherst: State University of New York at Buffalo, Council on International Studies, Special Studies No. 121.
1979b "Determination of the Frameworks and the Boundaries of Conscription: Two Dimensions of Civil-Military Relations in Israel." *Studies in Comparative International Development* 14 (Spring):22-41.

1982   *Zionism and Economy*. Cambridge, Mass.: Schenkman.

King, E., ed.
1941   *Jehosua Hankin: Reflections and Ideas on Jewish Settlement in Palestine*. Tel-Aviv: Nahlat Yehuda.   [Hebrew]

Kriesberg, L.
1973   *The Sociology of Social Conflicts*. Englewood Cliffs: Prentice-Hall.

Landau, J.M.
1969   *The Arabs in Israel: A Political Study*. London: Oxford University Press.

Laqueur, W.
1972   *A History of Zionism*. London: Weidenfeld and Nicolson.

Lemon, Anthony
1976   *Apartheid: A Geography of Separation*. Westmead: Saxon House.

Lerner, Daniel
1958   *The Passing of Traditional Society*. New York: The Free Press.

Lipset, Seymour M., and Rokkan, Stein
1967   "Cleavage Structures, Party Systems and Voter Alignments: An Introduction." In *Party Systems and Voter Alignments: Cross-National Perspectives*, eds. Lipset and Rokkan. New York: Free Press.

Livne, E.
1969   *Aharon Aharanson: The Man and His Time*. Jerusalem: Bialik Institution.   [Hebrew]

Lorch, N.
1961   *The Edge of the Sword: Israel's War of Independence, 1947-1949*. New York: Putnam's.

Lustick, Ian
1980   *Arabs in the Jewish State: Israel's Control of a Minority*. Austin: University of Texas Press.

Lyman, S.M., and Scott, M.
1967   "Territoriality: A Neglected Sociological Dimension." *Social Problems* 15:236-49.

Mackind, K.A.
1951   "Conflict and Loyalties: The Problem of Assimilating Far West into the Canadian and Australian Federations." *Canadian Historical Review* 32 (November):337-55.

Mandel, N.
1965   "Turks, Arabs, and Jewish Immigration into Palestine, 1882-1914." In *St. Antony's Papers, No. 17—Middle Eastern Affairs*, ed. A. Hourani, vol. 4. London.

Mansegh, Nicolas
1934   *The Irish Free State*. Oxford: Oxford University Press.

Sources and References

Marlow, J.
1951   *Rebellion in Palestine*. London: Crescent Press.

McDonald, J.
1951   *My Mission in Israel, 1948-1951*. New York.

Medzini, M.
1935   *Ten Years of Palestinian Policy*. Tel-Aviv: Haaretz.   [Hebrew]

Meged, C.
1970   "The Nes-Ziona Trial." *En Route: Writings on the Study of the Jewish Labor Movement* 3, 5:79-117.   [Hebrew]

Merhav, P.
1967   *A Short History of the Israeli Labor Movement, 1905-1965*. Merhavia: Sifriyat Poalim.   [Hebrew]

Merton, Robert K.
1957   *Social Theory and Social Structure*. Rev. ed. Glencoe: The Free Press.

Mikesell, Marvin W.
1968   "Comparative Studies in Frontier History." In *Turner and the Sociology of the Frontier*, eds. Richard Hofstadter and Seymour M. Lipset. New York: Basic Books.

Milward, Alan S.
1977   *War, Economy and Society: 1939-1945*. Berkeley: University of California Press.

Morison, Samuel E., and Commager, Henry S.
1955   *The Growth of the American Republic*, vol. 2. New York: Oxford University Press.

Motzkin, A.L.
1939   *The Motzkin Book. Selected Writings and Addresses, Biography, and Tributes*, ed. A. Bein. Jerusalem: Zionist Executive and World Jewish Congress.   [Hebrew]

Nadel, George
1957   *Australia's Colonial Culture*. Melbourne: Cheshire.

Naroll, R.
1969   "Deterrence in History." In *Theory and Research on the Causes of War*, eds. D.G. Pruitt and R.C. Snyder. Englewood Cliffs: Prentice-Hall, pp. 150-64.

Neumark, Daniel S.
1957   *The South African Frontier: Economic Influences, 1652-1836*. Stanford: Stanford University Press.

Nora, Pierre
1961   *Les francais d'Algérie*. Paris: Julliard.

O'Dea, Janet
1977   "Gush Emunim: Roots and Ambiguity." *Betvuzot Hagola* 79-80.   [Hebrew]

1978   "Religious Zionism Today." *Forum* 28-29 (Winter):111-17.

Oliphant, L.
1891   *The Land of Gilead.* New York: Appleton and Company.

Olitzur, A.
1939   *National Capital and the Building of the Land, 1918-1938.* Jerusalem:
         Keren Hayesod.   [Hebrew]

Ophir, Y.
1959   *The Book of the National Worker.* Federation of National Workers.
Oppenheim, Lassa F.L.   [Hebrew]
1957   *International Law.* 8th ed. London: Longmans, Green.

Orren, Elhannan
1978   *Settlement Amid Struggle: The Pre-State Strategy of Settlement,
         1936-1947.* Jerusalem: Yad Izhak Ben-Zvi.   [Hebrew]

Ozarkovsky, Y., Yehiel, Y., and Kriesski, M.
1907   *A Proposal for a Curriculum for the Hebrew Elementary Schools.*
         Hebrew Teacher's Association in Palestine.   [Hebrew]

Pail, M.
1973   "The Expropriation of the Political Sovereignty over Palestine from
         the Palestinians by the Arab Governments during the War of Libera-
         tion (1947-1949), and the Position of the Zionist Movement's
         Political Leadership and of Israel on this Phenomenon." *Zionism*,
         vol. 3. Tel-Aviv. Hakibbutz Hameuchad, pp. 439-89.   [Hebrew]

Palestine, Government of
1921   *Disturbances in May 1921: Report of a Commission of Enquiry with
         Correspondence Relating Thereto.* London: His Majesty's Stationery
         Office.
1930a   *Report of the Committee on the Economic Condition of Agricultur-
         alists in Palestine and the Fiscal Measures of the Government Thereto.*
         Jerusalem: Government Printer.
1930b   *C.F. Strickland Report of the Indian Civil Service on the Possibility
         of Introducing a System of Agricultural Cooperation in Palestine.*
         Jerusalem: Government Printer.
1935   *Report on Administration.* Jerusalem: Government Printer.
1946a   *Survey of Palestine.* Prepared for the Anglo-American Committee of
         Inquiry. Jerusalem: Government Printer.
1946b   *Village Statistics, April 1945.* Jerusalem: Government Printer.
1946c   *1:1,000,000 Palestine* (map). By 514 Fd. Survey Coy, R.E., August
         1942 (revised 1947).
1947   *Supplement to Survey of Palestine.* Notes compiled for the United
         Nations Special Committee on Palestine. Jerusalem.

Palestine Royal Commission (Peel Commission)
1937   *Lecture .. Parliamentary Document 5479.*

Parsons, Talcott
1951   *The Social System*. New York: The Free Press.

Paz, S.
1963   *Memoirs*. Haifa: Private publication.   [Hebrew]

Peel Commission. *See* Palestine Royal Commission.

Peres, Y.
1971   "Ethnic Relations in Israel." *American Journal of Sociology* 76, 6:
        1021-47.

Peretz, M.
1967   *The History of the Labor Movement in Palestine*. Merhavia: Cultural
        Department of the National Kibbutz, Workers' Library.   [Hebrew]

Pickles, Dorothy M.
1963   *Algeria and France: From Colonialism to Cooperation*. New York:
        Praeger.

Pollack, A., ed.
1940   *A. Biham: The Jewish National Fund*. Jerusalem: Jewish National
        Fund.   [Hebrew]

Porath, Yehoshua
1974   *The Emergence of the Palestinian Arab National Movement, 1910-
        1929*. London: Frank Cass.
1977   *The Palestinian National Movement: From Riots to Rebellion*.
        London: Frank Cass.

Prescott, J.R.V.
1965   *The Geography of Frontiers and Boundaries*. Chicago: Aldine.

Raanan, Zvi
1980   *Gush Emunim*. Tel-Aviv: Sifriyat Poalim.   [Hebrew]

Ramos, D.
1976   "Marriage and Family in Colonial Vila Rica." *Latin American Re-
        search Review* 11 (January):3-12.

Rapoport, A.
1969   *Strategy and Conscience*. New York: Schocken.

Ratosh, Yochanan, ed.
1976   *From Victory to Collapse*. Tel-Aviv: Hadar.   [Hebrew]

Rhoodie, N.J., and Venter, H.J.
1960   *Apartheid: A Socio-Historical Exposition of the Origin and Develop-
        ment of the Apartheid Idea*. Amsterdam: De Bussy.

Rivlin, G.
1948   *The Heritage of Tel-Hai*.   [Hebrew]

Robbins, M. Roy
1976   *Our Landed Heritage: The Public Domain, 1776-1970*. 2nd rev. ed.
        Lincoln: University of Nebraska Press.

Roey, J.
  1967   "The Attempts of Zionist Organizations to Influence the Arab Press
          in Palestine Between 1908-1914." *Zion* 3-4.   [Hebrew]
  1969   "The Zionist Position Towards the Arabs, 1908-1914." *Keshet* 42-
          43.   [Hebrew]
  1970   "Rehovot's Relations with Its Arab Neighbors (1890-1914)." *Zionism*,
          coll. 1. Tel-Aviv: Tel-Aviv University and United Kibbutz, pp. 150-
          203.   [Hebrew]

Roy, Jules
  1961   *The War in Algeria.* New York: Grove Press.

Rubinstein, Amnon
  1980   *From Herzl to Gush Emunim.* Tel-Aviv: Schocken.   [Hebrew]

Ruedy, John
  1978   "Israeli Land Acquisition in Occupied Territories, 1967-1977." *Ques-
          tion of West Bank Settlements and the Treatment of Arabs in the
          Israeli-Occupied Territories.* Washington, D.C.: Government Printing
          Office, pp. 124-27.

Ruppin, A.
  1937   *Thirty Years of the Building of Palestine.* Jerusalem: Schocken.
                                                                [Hebrew]
  1945   *The Jewish Problem at the Peace Conference.* Jerusalem: Jewish
          Agency for Palestine.   [Hebrew]
  1968   *Autobiography: Youth in the Diaspora, 1876-1907.* Tel-Aviv. Am
          Oved.   [Hebrew]
  1969   *Autobiography: The Beginnings of My Work in Palestine, 1917-1920.*
          Tel-Aviv: Am Oved.   [Hebrew]
  1971   *Memoirs, Diaries, Letters.* Trans. from the Hebrew. Edited by A. Bein.
          London: Weidenfeld and Nicolson.

Ryerson, Stanley
  1967   *Unequal Union.* Toronto: Progress.

Sachs, E.S.
  1965   *The Anatomy of Apartheid.* London: Collet's.

Salpeter, Eliahu, and Elitzur, Yuval
  1973   *Who Runs Israel.* Tel-Aviv: A. Levin-Epstein.   [Hebrew]

Schama, Simon
  1978   *Two Rothschilds and the Land of Israel.* New York: Knopf.

Schweid, Eliezer
  1970   *The Individual: The World of A.D. Gordon.* Tel-Aviv: Am Oved.
                                                                [Hebrew]

Sela, A.
  1972-73 "Talks and Contacts between Zionist and Palestinian-Arab Leaders,
          1933-1939." *The New East* 22, 4-23, 1.   [Hebrew]

Shapiro, O., ed.
1971 *Rural Settlement of New Immigrants in Israel*. Rehovot: Jewish Agency for Israel.

Sharett, M.
1971 *Making of Policy: The Diaries of M. Sharett, 1937*. Tel-Aviv: Am Oved. [Hebrew]
1972 *Political Diary, 1938*. Tel-Aviv: Am Oved. [Hebrew]

Sharp, P.A.
1955 "Three Frontiers: Some Comparative Studies in Canadian, American and Australian Settlement." *Pacific Historical Review* 24 (December): 346-61.

Shils, E.
1965 "Charisma, Order and Status." *American Sociological Review* 30, 2: 199-213.
1975 *Center and Periphery: Essays in Macrosociology*. Chicago: University of Chicago Press, pp. 3-16.

Shimoni, J.
1947 *Palestine's Arabs*. Tel-Aviv: Am Oved. [Hebrew]
1962 "The Arabs in the Face of the Israel-Arab War." *The New East* 12, 3. [Hebrew]

Smooha, Sammy
1978 *Israel: Pluralism and Conflict*. London: Routledge and Kegan Paul.

Soja, E.W.
1971 *The Political Organization of Space*. Washington, D.C.: Association of American Geographers, Resource Paper No. 8.

Sommer, R.
1969 *Personal Space: The Behavioral Basis of Design*. Englewood Cliffs: Prentice-Hall.

Sorokin, P.A.
1928 "Sociological Interpretation of the 'Struggle for Existence' and Sociology of War." In Sorokin, *Contemporary Sociological Theories*. New York: Harper, pp. 309-56.

Sprinzak, Ehud
1981 "Gush Emunim: The Iceberg Model of Political Extremism." *State, Government and International Relations* 17 (Spring):22-49. [Hebrew]

Stavsky, M.
1946 *The Arab Village: Daily Life*. Tel-Aviv: Am Oved. [Hebrew]

Sussman, Z.
1969 *The Policy of the Histadrut with Regard to Wage Differentials. A Study of the Impact of Egalitarian Ideology and Arab Labor on Jewish Wages in Palestine*. Jerusalem.

Sykes, C.
1965   *Crossroads to Israel: Palestine from Balfour to Bevin.* London: New English Library.

Szereszewski, R.
1968   *Essays on the Structure of the Jewish Economy in Palestine and Israel.* Jerusalem: Falk Institute for Economic Research.

Tabenkin, Y.
1967   *Essays, Vol. 1 (1918-34).* Tel-Aviv: Hakibbutz Hameuchad. [Hebrew]
1972   *Essays, Vol. 2 (1935-39).* Tel-Aviv: Hakibbutz Hameuchad. [Hebrew]

Tamarin, G.R.
1973   *The Israeli Dilemma: Essays on a Warstate.* Rotterdam: Rotterdam University Press.

Tatz, C.M.
1962   *Shadow and Subsistence in South Africa: A Study of Land and Franchise Policies, 1910-1960.* Pietermaritzburg: University of Natal Press.

Thompson, Leonard, and Lamar, Howard
1981   "Comparative Frontier History." In *The Frontier in History: North America and Southern Africa Compared,* eds. H. Lamar and L. Thompson. New Haven: Yale University Press, pp. 3-13.

Tillion, Germain
1958   *Algeria: The Realities.* Trans. by R. Matthews. New York: Knopf.

Töennies, Ferdinand
1955   *Community and Association.* London: Routledge and Kegan Paul.

Treadgold, D.
1957   *The Great Siberian Migration.* Princeton: Princeton University Press.

Turner, Frederick Jackson
1920   *The Frontier in American History.* New York: Henry Holt and Company.

Ussishkin, M.
1929   "The Voice of the Land." Jerusalem: Jewish National Fund.
                                                        [Hebrew]
1933   "Land Redemption in Light of the Economic Boom in Palestine." Jerusalem: Jewish National Fund.   [Hebrew]
1939   *The Ussishkin Book: In Honor of His Seventieth Anniversary.* Jerusalem: The Initiating Committee.   [Hebrew]
1940   "Land Redemption—A Political Factor." Jerusalem: Jewish National Fund.   [Hebrew]

Vilnai, A.
1956   *Geographical Encyclopedia of Israel.* Jerusalem: Yediot Achronot.
                                                        [Hebrew]

Vitkin, J.
1936   "The Conquest of Land and the Conquest of Labor." In *Hapoel Hatzair*, vol. 8. Tel-Aviv: Twersky.   [Hebrew]

Wagner, P.
1960   *The Human Use of the Earth*. New York: Free Press.

Wakefield, Edward Gibson
1929   *A Letter from Sydney and Other Writings*. London: J.N. Dent

Ward, Russell
1958   *The Australian Legend*. Melbourne: Oxford University Press.

Washburn, Wilcomb E.
1974   *Red Man's Land/White Man's Law*. New York: Charles Scribner's Sons.

Webb, Walter P.
1964   *The Great Frontier*. Austin: University of Texas Press.

Weber, M.
1954   *Max Weber on Law in Economy and Society*. Cambridge, Mass.: Harvard University Press.

Weigart, G.
1973   *Arabs and Israelis Life Together*. Jerusalem: Published by author.

Weintraub, D., Lissak, M., and Atzmon, Y.
1969   *Moshav, Kibbutz and Moshav: Patterns of Jewish Settlement and Development in Palestine*. Ithaca: Cornell University Press.

Weintraub, D. et al.
1971   *Immigration and Social Change in Agricultural Settlement of New Immigrants in Israel*. Jerusalem: Israel Universities Press.

Weitz, J.
1939   *The Libel of the Land: Land Problems in Palestine*. Jerusalem: Jewish National Fund.   [Hebrew]
1950   *The Struggle for the Nation*. Tel-Aviv: Twersky.   [Hebrew]
1951   *Struggles of Settlement: A Diary*. Tel-Aviv: Twersky.   [Hebrew]
1965   *My Diary and Letters to My Son*, vols. 1-6. Tel-Aviv: Massada.   [Hebrew]
1970   "The Redemption of the Soil." *Forty Years to the Settlement of Wadi Hawarat: 1930-1970*. Hefer Valley Regional Council, pp. 51-62.   [Hebrew]

Weizmann, C.
1937   "The People and Land of Israel." Testimony before the Palestine Royal Commission. Zionist Federation.
1949   *Trial and Error: The Autobiography of Chaim Weizmann*. London: Hamish Hamilton.
1954   *Words and Deeds: Memoirs of the President of Israel*. 5th ed. Jerusalem: Schocken.

Whittlesey, H.D.
1971   "Havshofer: The Geopoliticus." In *Makers of Modern Strategy*, ed. E.M. Earle. Princeton: Princeton University Press.

Willner, D.
1969   *Nation-Building and Community in Israel*. Princeton: Princeton University Press.

Winks, R.
1971   *The Myth of the American Frontier: Its Relevance to America, Canada and Australia*. Leicester.

Wishart, David J., Warren, Andrew, and Stoddard, Robert H.
1969   "An Attempted Definition of a Frontier Using a Wave Analogy." *Rocky Mountain Social Science Journal* 6:73-81.

Wolf, E., and Mintz, S.
1957   "Haciendas and Plantations in Middle America and Antilles." *Social and Economic Studies* 6 (October):274-81.

Wolman, L.
1938   "The Labor Movement and Cooperation in Palestine." Boston: Joint Palestine Survey Commission.

Wood, F.L.
1958   *This New Zealand*. Hamilton: Paul's Book Arcade.

Yehoshua, A.B.
1970   "Facing the Forests." In *Three Days and a Child*. Trans. by M. Arad. New York: Doubleday.
1980   *Between Right and Left*. Tel-Aviv: Schocken.   [Hebrew]

Yelin-Moore, N.
1974   *Israel Liberty Fighters*. Jerusalem: Shikmona.   [Hebrew]

Yellin, David
1905   *The Hebrew Pronunciation and Spelling*. Jerusalem: Lorentz.
                                                              [Hebrew]

Zureik, Elia T.
1979   *The Palestinians in Israel: A Study in Internal Colonialism*. London: Routledge and Kegan Paul.

The following newspapers and periodicals were systematically analyzed:*

Bustenai, 1929-1934   *Hapoel Hatzair*, 1919-1921

Davar, 1926-1927, 1935-1937   *Maariv*, 1949-1973

Doar Hayom, 1920   *Yediot Achronot*, 1947-1913

Haaretz, 1920-1973

*References from these and other newspapers or periodicals are specifically cited in the body of the text.

INDEX

Aaronovitz, A., 79, 80n
Aaronovitz-Vitkin controversy, 79-80, 101
Abandoned Land Ordinance, 134-35
Abdallah ibn-Hussein, King, 63n
Abdul Haadi, Awni, 112, 113
Abramovitz, Z., 32, 33
Absentee landowners, 47
Absentees, legal definition of, 135
Absentees' Property Law—1950, 135, 136, 137
Absorption capacity of Palestine, 18, 96, 213, 221
Abu Gosh village, 127-28, 128n
Acre: district, 33; town, 33, 58
Afrikaner nationalism, 3n
*Agudat Israel, 54n, 98, 172
Ahad Haam (Asher Ginsberg), 10n, 68, 189
Aharonson, Aharon, 99-100
*Ahdut Haavoda, 82, 187
Akaba, 16, 234; Gulf of, 180
Akraba, 166
Alaama, 117
Alami, Mussa, 115, 125, 128, 198
Alaska, 23
Algeria, 3
*Alignment, 157, 161, 162, 168
*Aliya: First, 99n, 100, 108, 116, 207, 210; Second, 26, 74, 79, 82, 99, 100, 111, 207; Third, 95, 210; Fourth, 69, 72, 95, 105; Fifth, 95, 105; pioneering, 104, 105
Alkali, Rabbi Y., 15n
Alliance School, 69
Allon, Azarya, 208
Allon Plan, 159-60, 163n, 168, 170,
174, 178
Allon, Yigal, 158, 222
Alteneuland, 197
Amana settlement movement, 171. See also Gush Emunim
Amazon river, 23
American society, 2, 7, 30
American Zionist Federation, 72
Anatot, 148
Anglo-American Committee of Inquiry, 139
Anna village, 142
Annexation. See Allon Plan; Territorial expansion; Territorial policy
Anomie, 190-91
Antebi, Albert, 69
Anti-Semitism, 185n, 186
Antonius, George, 199
Apartheid, 6n
Arab: agrarian problem, 34; birth rates, 96; citizenship in Israel, 64; culture, 189; flight, 122-33, 147n; immigration to Palestine, 96, 116; labor, 79, 98, 100-102, 103-4, 110; land tenure system, 17, 31-38; leadership, 61, 128-29, 187; military, 126; minority, 139; national consciousness, 79
*Arab Executive Committee, 92n
Arab-Jewish (Israeli) conflict, 98, 102, 190, 199, 222; definition of, 197-200; dynamics of, 82; as territorial conflict, 13, 15, 17, 25-26, 68, 76, 78, 145-46, 181, 215, 216-21, 230
Arab Legion, 124, 125, 128, 231
Arab Liberation Army, 124, 125
Arab national movement, 15-16, 57, 188-90

NOTE: Asterisks indicate Glossary entries.

278

INSTITUTE OF INTERNATIONAL STUDIES
UNIVERSITY OF CALIFORNIA, BERKELEY

215 Moses Hall   Berkeley, California 94720

CARL G. ROSBERG, *Director*

Monographs published by the Institute include:

RESEARCH SERIES

1. *The Chinese Anarchist Movement*, by Robert A. Scalapino and George T. Yu. ($1.00)
7. *Birth Rates in Latin America: New Estimates of Historical Trends*, by O. Andrew Collver. ($2.50)
15. *Central American Economic Integration: The Politics of Unequal Benefits*, by Stuart I. Fagan. ($2.00)
16. *The International Imperatives of Technology: Technological Development and the International Political System*, by Eugene B. Skolnikoff. ($2.95)
17. *Autonomy or Dependence as Regional Integration Outcomes: Central America*, by Philippe C. Schmitter. ($1.75)
19. *Entry of New Competitors in Yugoslav Market Socialism*, by S.R. Sacks. ($2.50)
20. *Political Integration in French-Speaking Africa*, by Abdul A. Jalloh. ($3.50)
21. *The Desert and the Sown: Nomads in the Wider Society*, ed. by Cynthia Nelson. ($5.50)
22. *U.S.-Japanese Competition in International Markets: A Study of the Trade-Investment Cycle in Modern Capitalism*, by John E. Roemer. ($3.95)
23. *Political Disaffection Among British University Students: Concepts, Measurement, and Causes*, by Jack Citrin and David J. Elkins. ($2.00)
24. *Urban Inequality and Housing Policy in Tanzania: The Problem of Squatting*, by Richard E. Stren. ($2.95)
25. *The Obsolescence of Regional Integration Theory*, by Ernst B. Haas. ($4.95)
26. *The Voluntary Service Agency in Israel*, by Ralph M. Kramer. ($2.00)
27. *The SOCSIM Demographic-Sociological Microsimulation Program: Operating Manual*, by Eugene A. Hammel et al. ($4.50)
28. *Authoritarian Politics in Communist Europe: Uniformity & Diversity in One-Party States*, ed. by Andrew C. Janos. ($3.95)
29. *The Anglo-Icelandic Cod War of 1972-1973: A Case Study of a Fishery Dispute*, by Jeffrey A. Hart. ($2.00)
30. *Plural Societies and New States: A Conceptual Analysis*, by Robert Jackson ($2.00)
31. *The Politics of Crude Oil Pricing in the Middle East, 1970-1975: A Study in International Bargaining*, by Richard Chadbourn Weisberg. ($4.95)
32. *Agricultural Policy and Performance in Zambia: History, Prospects, and Proposals for Change*, by Doris Jansen Dodge. ($4.95)
33. *Five Classy Programs: Computer Procedures for the Classification of Households*, by E.A. Hammel and R.Z. Deuel. ($3.75)
34. *Housing the Urban Poor in Africa: Policy, Politics, and Bureaucracy in Mombasa*, by Richard E. Stren. ($5.95)
35. *The Russian New Right: Right-Wing Ideologies in the Contemporary USSR*, by Alexander Yanov. ($5.95)
36. *Social Change in Romania, 1860-1940: A Debate on Development in a European Nation*, ed. by Kenneth Jowitt. ($4.50)
37. *The Leninist Response to National Dependency*, by Kenneth Jowitt. ($3.25)
38. *Socialism in Sub-Saharan Africa: A New Assessment*, ed. by Carl G. Rosberg and Thomas M. Callaghy. ($12.95)
39. *Tanzania's Ujamaa Villages: The Implementation of a Rural Development Strategy*, by Dean E. McHenry, Jr. ($5.95)
40. *Who Gains from Deep Ocean Mining: Simulating the Impact of Regimes for Regulating Nodule Exploitation*, by I.G. Bulkley. ($3.50)

INSTITUTE OF INTERNATIONAL STUDIES MONOGRAPHS (continued)

41. *Industrialization, Industrialists, and the Nation-State in Peru: A Comparative/Sociological Analysis*, by Frits Wils. ($5.95)
42. *Ideology, Public Opinion, and Welfare Policy: Attitudes toward Taxes and Spending in Industrialized Societies*, by Richard M. Coughlin. ($6.50)
43. *The Apartheid Regime: Political Power and Racial Domination*, ed. by Robert M. Price and Carl G. Rosberg. ($12.50)
44. *The Yugoslav Economic System and Its Performance in the 1970s*, by Laura D'Andrea Tyson. ($5.50)
45. *Conflict in Chad*, by Virginia Thompson and Richard Adloff. ($7.50)
46. *Conflict and Coexistence in Belgium: The Dynamics of a Culturally Divided Society*, ed. by Arend Lijphart. ($7.50)
47. *Changing Realities in Southern Africa: Implications for American Policy*, ed. by Michael Clough. ($12.50)
48. *Nigerian Women Mobilized: Women's Political Activity in Southern Nigeria, 1900-1965*, by Nina Emma Mba. ($12.95)
49. *Institutions of Rural Development for the Poor: Decentralization and Organizational Linkages*, ed. by D. Leonard & D. Marshall. ($11.50)

POLITICS OF MODERNIZATION SERIES

1. *Spanish Bureaucratic-Patrimonialism in America*, by Magali Sarfatti. ($2.00)
2. *Civil-Military Relations in Argentina, Chile, and Peru*, by Liisa North. ($2.00)
3. *Notes on the Process of Industrialization in Argentina, Chile, and Peru*, by Alcira Leiserson. ($1.75)
9. *Modernization and Bureaucratic-Authoritarianism: Studies in South American Politics*, by Guillermo O'Donnell. ($7.95)

POLICY PAPERS IN INTERNATIONAL AFFAIRS

1. *Images of Detente and the Soviet Political Order*, by Kenneth Jowitt. ($1.25)
2. *Detente After Brezhnev: The Domestic Roots of Soviet Foreign Policy*, by Alexander Yanov. ($4.50)
3. *The Mature Neighbor Policy: A New United States Economic Policy for Latin America*, by Albert Fishlow. ($3.95)
4. *Five Images of the Soviet Future: A Critical Review and Synthesis*, by G.W. Breslauer. ($4.50)
5. *Global Evangelism Rides Again: How to Protect Human Rights Without Really Trying*, by Ernst B. Haas. ($2.95)
6. *Israel and Jordan: Implications of an Adversarial Partnership*, by Ian Lustick ($2.00)
7. *Political Syncretism in Italy: Historical Coalition Strategies and the Present Crisis*, by Giuseppe Di Palma. ($3.95)
8. *U.S. Foreign Policy in Sub-Saharan Africa: National Interest and Global Strategy*, by Robert M. Price. ($2.25)
9. *East-West Technology Transfer in Perspective*, by R.J. Carrick. ($2.75)
10. *NATO's Unremarked Demise*, by Earl C. Ravenal. ($2.00)
11. *Toward an Africanized U.S. Policy for Southern Africa: A Strategy for Increasing Political Leverage*, by Ronald T. Libby. ($5.50)
12. *The Taiwan Relations Act and the Defense of the Republic of China*, by Edwin K. Snyder et al. ($7.50)
13. *Cuba's Policy in Africa, 1959-1980*, by William M. LeoGrande. ($4.50)
14. *Norway, NATO, and the Forgotten Soviet Challenge*, by Kirsten Amundsen. ($2.95)
15. *Japanese Industrial Policy*, by Ira C. Magaziner and Thomas M. Hout. ($6.50)
16. *Containment, Soviet Behavior, and Grand Strategy*, by Robert E. Osgood. ($5.50)
17. *U.S.-Japanese Competition in the Semiconductor Industry: A Study in International Trade and Technological Development*, by M. Borrus, J. Millstein, and J. Zysman ($7.50)